AF600576

MENTAL ILLNESS AFFECTING MATRIMONIAL CONSENT

This dissertation was approved by the Reverend John Rogg Schmidt, A.B., J.C.D., LL.B., Professor of Canon Law, as director and by the Reverend Frederick R. McManus, J.C.D., and by the Reverend Romaeus W. O'Brien, O.Carm., J.C.D., as readers.

THE CATHOLIC UNIVERSITY OF AMERICA
CANON LAW STUDIES
No. 415

Mental Illness Affecting Matrimonial Consent

A DISSERTATION

SUBMITTED TO THE FACULTY OF THE SCHOOL OF CANON LAW OF THE CATHOLIC UNIVERSITY OF AMERICA IN PARTIAL FULFILLMENT OF THE REQUIREMENTS FOR THE DEGREE OF DOCTOR OF CANON LAW

BY THE
REVEREND WILLIAM M. VAN OMMEREN, J.C.L.
PRIEST OF THE DIOCESE OF SPOKANE

THE CATHOLIC UNIVERSITY OF AMERICA PRESS
WASHINGTON, D.C.
1961

NIHIL OBSTAT:
John Rogg Schmidt, A.B., J.C.D., LL.B.
Censor Deputatus
Washingtonii, D.C., die 29 maii, 1960

IMPRIMATUR:
✠ Bernard J. Topel, D.D., Ph.D.
Episcopus Spokanensis
Spokane, die 31 maii, 1960

Printed by The Abbey Press, St. Meinrad, Indiana, U.S.A.

TO

MY FATHER AND MOTHER

AND TO

MY FRIENDS IN AMERICA

FOREWORD

The apparent increase in the incidence of mental illness, as well as in scientific knowledge regarding mental illness has already left its mark on the marriage tribunals of the Church. A perusal of the Rota decisions of recent years shows that the number of marriages, the validity of which is being questioned on a basis of insanity has been increasing year by year. However, the question of mental illness continues to present difficult legal problems for the ecclesiastical courts.

The present study endeavors to present a historical and canonical treatment of ecclesiastical jurisprudence regarding mental illness and its effect upon the validity of matrimonial consent. It aims to determine the psychical requirements necessary at canon law for the eliciting of a valid matrimonial consent. To that end it considers separately the knowledge, freedom, and maturity of judgment required for entering into a valid matrimonial contract.

After establishing the psychical requirements for matrimony, the present study purposes to examine the effect of mental illness upon a person's psychical capacity for positing the legal act of giving consent to the contract of marriage.

Finally, the writer intends to consider those laws of juridic procedure and evidence which are of especial importance for the adjudication of marriage causes based on a plea of lack of consent by reason of mental illness or psychic deficiency.

As is indicated in the table of contents, the work is divided into two sections. The first traces briefly through Roman and pre-Code ecclesiastical law the history of juridic thought regarding the effect of mental illness on a person's legal capacity for marriage. The second section is devoted entirely to a canonical commentary regarding the effect of mental illness upon matrimonial consent.

In this second section a philosophical and psychological examination of the nature, operations, and mutual cooperation of the intellect and will in man is unavoidable, although such an examination falls *per se* outside the scope of a legal commentary. In the philosophical and psychological considerations the writer adheres to the principles and tenets of Thomistic philosophy and psychology.

A study of this kind cannot hope to end with too definite a note of finality. In reality it constitutes a beginning rather than an ending. It is intended to furnish a legal basis on which it is hoped that others will be able to build a more complete legal structure.

The writer wishes to express his gratitude to His Excellency, The Most Reverend Bernard J. Topel, D.D., the Bishop of Spokane, for the opportunity to undertake advanced studies in Canon Law at the Catholic University of America.

He also wishes to thank the Faculty of the School of Canon Law for their scholarly guidance, the Reverend Eugene Kennedy, M.M., of the Faculty of the Department of Psychology for his assistance, and all others who in any way have helped to make this work possible. The writer wishes to acknowledge especially his deep indebtedness to the Reverend John Rogg Schmidt for the invaluable assistance provided in the writing of this dissertation.

TABLE OF CONTENTS

PART ONE
HISTORICAL SYNOPSIS

PART TWO
CANONICAL COMMENTARY

PART ONE

HISTORICAL SYNOPSIS

CHAPTER I

MENTAL ILLNESS AND ITS EFFECT ON MARRIAGE IN ROMAN LAW

The early history of the treatment of the insane is far from pleasant. At times the mentally ill were thought to be under the influence of gods or demons who manifested their powers over them by throwing them into trances and transports of ecstasy. During the early centuries of the Christian era this concept was displaced by the belief that God permitted the insane person's mind to become affected in punishment for his sins. As a result of these misconceptions the insane were treated as wicked, dangerous criminals. They were chained to the walls of dungeons where they remained till death set them free. At other times they were exposed as objects of public entertainment. For a small fee they were put on display for the amusement of the onlookers.[1]

Amidst this almost general abuse, misunderstanding and ill treatment of the mentally ill, there is one remarkable exception, the early Roman Law.

ARTICLE 1. THE MENTALLY ILL AT ROMAN LAW

Legal protection was given to the *furiosi*[2] by the most important enactment of early Roman legislation, the Twelve Tables (451-450 B.C.). Though this source of archaic juris-

[1] Vanderveldt-Odenwald, *Psychiatry and Catholicism* (2. ed., New York: McGraw-Hill Book Company, Inc., 1957), pp. 44-47.

[2] The term *furiosi* was the most common one used for the insane both in Roman and the early Church Law. Other terms used in the *Corpus Iuris Civilis* are: *dementia, demens, mente captus, fatuus,* etc. A person was considered *furiosus* when he had completely lost the use of reason, while a person afflicted with a mild form of mental illness was regarded as *demens.* Cf. Sesto, *Guardians of the Mentally Ill in Ecclesiastical Trials,* The Catholic University of America Canon Law Studies, No. 358 (Washington, D.C.: The Catholic University of America Press, 1956), pp. 32-33.

prudence has not been preserved as a document, scholars have been able to reconstruct a probable text from various sources. The *furiosi* were placed under the guardianship of their heirs.[3] This enactment of the early Roman Law appears to have been intended more for the protection of the family of the sick person rather than for the sick person himself. The law of the Twelve Tables regulated the question of guardianship for the insane. The law assigned guardianship to the presumptive male successors on intestacy, those very persons who would benefit, should the insane person die without having been able to make a valid last will and testament.[4] Thus it appears that guardianship was originally designed to safeguard the interests of the heirs, or to look to the advantage of the family rather than to protect the mentally disturbed person from the ill effects of his affliction.[5]

The institution of guardianship matured greatly in the centuries that followed the Twelve Tables. It was under the jurists of the classical age that the most important development took place. The writings and treatises of the great legal masters like Labeo, Julianus, Scaevola, Celsus, Papianus, Ulpianus and Paulus form the major part of the Digest of Justinian, while his Institutes follow closely the Institutes of Gaius. It is in the Institutes of Gaius that the

[3] Table V. 7a. and 7b. of the Twelve tables states:
a. Si Furiosus escit, adgnatum gentiliumque in eo pecuniaque eius potestas esto . . .
b. Ast ei custos nec escit.
Cf. Sesto, *Guardians of the Mentally Ill*, pp. 3-4.

[4] Testamentary capacity was attained by reaching puberty, in the case of a boy or, in the case of a lunatic, by recovering his senses, and in the case of the "spendthrift" by having the interdict against him removed. Cf. Jolowicz, *Historical Introduction to the Study of Roman Law* (2. ed., Cambridge: University Press, 1952), p. 122 note 2.

[5] C. G. Bruns, *Fontes Iuris Romani Antiqui* (Tubingae: Mohr, 1909), p. 23; *Fontes Iuris Romani Ante Justiniani*, editio altera et aucta, ediderunt Johannes Baviera, J. Furlani, S. Riccobono, C. Ferrini, V. Arangio Ruiz (I vol. in 3 parts, Florentiae: S. A. G. Barbers. 1940-1943), I, 39. (Hereafter cited as *Fontes Iuris Ante Justiniani*); cf. also Jolowicz, *op. cit.*, p. 121.

earliest systematic treatment of the subject of guardianship can be found.[6]

The extensive treatment of the subject of guardianship for women, children, and mentally ill, found in the *Corpus Iuris Civilis,* is actually a composite of the above-mentioned authors' expositions on the law of guardianship.[7]

In the developed law, guardianship became an institution designed to protect incapable persons from the consequences of their peculiar disability. The function of the guardian of the insane is clearly described in Justinian's Digest. It reads: "*Consilio et opera curatoris tueri debet non solum patrimonium sed et corpus ac salus furiosi.*"[8]

Mental illness in the law of Justinian was not regarded as a disgrace or a cause of repudiation of the citizen who became subject to it. The text in the Digest attributes to Ulpianus the legal axiom that states: "*Qui furere coepit et statum et dignitatem in qua fuit et magistratum et potestatem videtur retinere sicut et rei suae dominium retinet.*"[9] The insane, therefore, was to retain not only the ownership of his property for the duration of his illness, but also his position, rank, and even his magistracy, if he were a magistrate at the time the illness struck him. However, the law did recognize the juridical incapacity of the insane person. He was likened to a person who was absent,[10] asleep[11] or even dead.[12]

[6] Poste, *Gai Institutiones or Institutes of Roman Law by Gaius* (4. ed., revised and enlarged by E. A. Whittuck, Oxford: Clarendon Press, 1904), p. lii.

[7] *Corpus Iuris Civilis* (3 vols., Vol. 1, *Institutiones,* ed. stereotypa 15, recognovit P. Krueger; *Digesta,* ed. stereotypa 15, recognovit Th. Mommsen, retractavit P. Krueger; Vol. 3, *Novellae Constitutiones,* ed. stereotypa 5, recognovit R. Schoell; opus Schoellii morte interceptum absolvit G. Kroll, Berolini, 1928-1929), (Hereafter cited as Inst., Dig., Codex, Novellae); Inst. (1, 13-26); Dig. (26, 1-10); Dig. (27, 1-10); Codex (5, 28-75).

[8] Dig. (27, 10) 7.

[9] Dig. (1, 5) 20.

[10] Dig. (29, 7) 2; (50, 17) 124.

[11] Dig. (41, 2) 1.

[12] Dig. (39, 5) 2.

Consequently he was considered unable to make a valid will according to the principle of law: "Soundness of mind, not health of body, is required of a testator when he makes his will."[13] Gaius in his Institutes wrote: "An insane person cannot contract any business whatever because he does not understand what he is doing."[14] In the matter of legal responsibility[15] or culpability for wrongdoing, the Roman law followed a principle stated in one of the opinions of Paulus, namely, that an insane person, like an infant, was incapable of malicious intent and the will to insult. Accordingly, he was to be considered immune from any action for damages.[16]

Article 2. Marriage Consent at Roman Law

According to Roman law, or, perhaps more accurately, according to Roman life and thought: *"Nuptiae, sive matrimonium est viri et mulieris conjunctio, individuam vitae consuetudinem continens,"*[17] or again, according to the words of the jurist Modestinus: *"Nuptiae sunt conjunctio maris et feminae, consortium omnis vitae divini et humani iuris*

[13] Dig. (28, 1) 2.

[14] *Institutiones Gaii,* 3. 106.

[15] Pickett in his dissertation *Mental Affliction and Church Law* (Ottawa, Ontario: The University of Ottawa Press, 1952) states on p. 14: "There appears to have been no procedure outlined by the law for the solution of doubts and disputes, that might arise from time to time, as to the presence or absence of that degree of mental capacity necessary for the placing of juridical acts in those persons whose insanity was intermittent or partial." He continues: "We can hardly presume that experts in the sphere of health and sanity were resorted to as they are today, for there is no intimation of such a procedure in the law." However, the Roman Law did realize that at times criminals might feign insanity to escape punishment for their wrongdoing. The law prescribed that such people had to be examined and observed carefully to see whether their insanity was real or feigned.—Cf. Dig. (1, 18) 13.

[16] *Sententiae Pauli,* (5, 4) 2. *Sententiarum Receptarum Libri Quinque Qui Vulgo Iulio Paulo Adhuc Tribuuntur; Fontes Iuris Ante justiniani,* II, p. 389.

[17] Inst. (1, 9) 1.

communicatio."[18] Properly considered, the Romans did not regard marriage as a contract in the juridic sense. For them marriage was a way of life, a domestic union, regulated and protected by the law, of a man and a woman for the purpose of a lifelong mutual companionship.[19] Marriage, to them, was a status realized by the agreement of the parties and regulated by the law.[20] The accord of will effected the marriage but it did not constitute a contract according to law because it had for its immediate end the realization of the *consortium vitae* rather than the creation of mutual obligations and rights. The consequent rights and obligations of the association were determined by the law rather than by the wills of the parties.

The term *consensus* as applied to marriage implied both the consent of the contracting parties and the consent of the respective heads of the families of the man and woman. *Consensus* was absolutely necessary for a valid marriage.[21] The Roman concept of marriage demanded a free and mutual consent on the part of the parties. Marriage depended for its existence on the mutual love and affection of the parties: *Ex affectu omnes introducuntur nuptiae.*[22] The state of marriage existed as long as the *maritalis affectio* endured.

This notion of marriage accounts for the scarcity of texts in the sources of Roman law dealing directly with matrimonial consent. However, some evidence concerning it can be found in a few passages. Thus it is stated: *Nuptias, non concubitus sed consensus facit.*[23] This passage, attributed to Ulpianus, distinguished between the *affectio maritalis* and the *affectio concubinaria.* The intention and consent to live

[18] Dig. (23, 2) 1.

[19] Cf. Sohm, *The Institutes* (Translated by James C. Ledlie, 3. ed., Oxford, 1907), p. 452.

[20] Cf. Desforges, *Étude Historique sur la Formation du Mariage en Droit Romaine et en Droit Français* (Paris, 1887), pp. 54-59.

[21] Roby, *Roman Private Law* (2 vols., Cambridge, 1902), I, 131-132; Bernard, *The First Year of Roman Law* (Translated by Chas. P. Sherman New York, 1906), n. 258.

[22] Codex (5, 4) 26.

[23] Dig. (50, 17) 30.

as husband and wife in the state of marriage demands *maritalis affectio* and makes it altogether different from a mere concubinary union. In another place the law states: *Sufficit nudus consensus ad constituenda sponsalia.*[24] Moreover, during the period of the classical Roman Law not only the consent of the parties but also the consent of the *pater familias* was required.[25] This is shown by a pronouncement of the jurist Paulus which is recorded in the Digest: *"Nuptias consistere non possunt nisi consentiant omnes, id est qui coeunt quorumque in potestate sunt."*[26]

Article 3. The Effect of Mental Illness on Marriage at Roman Law.

The effect of insanity on marriage was clearly and succinctly defined by the great classical jurist Paulus. He coined the phrase: *"Neque furiosus neque furiosa matrimonium contrahere possunt sed contractum matrimonium furore non tollitur."*[27] He summarized the classical Roman Law by stating that the insane could not enter into a valid marriage but that subsequent insanity, arising after marriage had taken place, did not destroy that marriage.[28] There is yet another

[24] Dig. (23, 1) 4; (23, 2) 22; (23, 2) 16; (23, 2) 2.

[25] Corbett, *The Roman Law of Marriage* (Oxford, 1930), p. 55.

[26] Dig. (32, 2) 2. The present writer, to avoid going too far afield, prefers to refrain from entering into the various controversies and opinions both regarding the precise nature of marriage consent at Roman Law and regarding the consent required of the *pater familias.* He has chosen to present what seemed to him the most acceptable explanation of the various texts. He does admit that certain texts might be brought up in opposition to this theory of consent at Roman Law. However, all these texts are capable of an acceptable explanation. Cf. Corbett, *The Roman Law of Marriage,* pp. 53-54.

[27] *Fontes Iuris Ante Justiniani,* II, 345; *Sententiae Pauli* (2, 19) 7.

[28] This principle of Paulus was later incorporated into the Visigothic Law. A further interpretation to the text of Paulus was added. It read: "Si qui matrimonium sani contraxerint et uni ex duobus amentia aut furor accesserit, ob hanc infirmitatem coniugia talium solvi non possunt."—*Lex Romana Visigothorum, Sententiae Pauli,* Lib. II, T. 20, n. 4, *Interpretatio* (ed. Gustavus Haene 1, Lipsiae, 1847-1849).

statement of Paulus quoted in the Digest of Justinian giving the precise reason why the insane could not marry. "Insanity does not allow entrance into marriage," he says, "because for marriage consent is needed, but on the other hand, if a marriage has once been rightly contracted then insanity does not invalidate it."[29]

Marriage could be validly contracted by an insane person during a so-called lucid interval. In the *Corpus Iuris Civilis* no direct mention is made of lucid intervals in connection with marriage. One may infer, however, that marriage could be entered into during a lucid interval because it was stated that during a lucid interval an insane person could do everything a sane person could. "During lucid intervals, which are really such, a curator does nothing and the insane person can, during that time, enter upon an estate and do everything else that sane men are competent to do."[30]

SCHOLION I. INSANITY AND DIVORCE IN ROMAN LAW

The law regarding divorce at Roman Law varied greatly through the centuries.[31] Before the influence of Christianity was felt upon post-classical Roman law, divorce was very easy. The only legal restraints on divorce in the classical law were requirements regarding dowry in case of divorce. Even the *pater familias* of the consorts could, in the early classical days, legally terminate the marriage of his son or daughter by a divorce. It was only in the latter part of the second century that this authority of the *pater familias* was abolished.

In Republican times, an agreement or a formal declaration on the part of one of the consorts was sufficient to end a marriage. No cause was required. As in marriage itself, the mere will of the parties to sever their relationship was

[29] Furor matrimonium contrahi non sinit, quia consensu opus est, sed recte contractum non impedit. Dig. (23, 2) 16.

[30] Codex (5, 70) 6.

[31] There seems to be no reason to distinguish between the terms *divortium* and *repudium* except that the latter was also used to signify the end of an engagement.

sufficient. Divorce was very prevalent during the waning years of the late Republic and the early days of the Empire. The only control upon it was to be sought in the strength or weakness of the mores of the people. Any reason sufficed to break up a marriage and consequently, insanity was clearly a valid cause.[32] With the coming of Christianity, however, certain penalties began to be imposed for seeking a divorce without a serious reason. Yet, a divorce undertaken without a valid cause was still regarded as true and valid, though illegal and punishable. Some jurists, like Paulus, held that insanity no longer was a sufficient cause for divorce.[33] Others, prominent among whom was Ulpianus, felt that under extreme conditions insanity should be regarded as a sufficient cause. "If," he declared, "the insanity is so fierce, ferocious and dangerous that no hope of recovery exists, then, if the other party desires to annul the marriage either on account of the cruelty which accompanies the insanity or in view of the fact that, not having any children of his own, he feels urged on by the desire of having offspring, this party, being of sound mind, will be permitted to notify the other, who is insane, of repudiation so that the marriage may be dissolved without fault."[34]

It seems impossible to establish with certainty the policy of Justinian regarding insanity as a cause for divorce, because in his Digest he included both the strict view of Paulus and the more liberal view of Ulpianus.[35] In the Novellae he

[32] Cf. Sherman, *Roman Law in the Modern World* (3 vols. New York, 1924), Vol. II, 75, n. 486.

[33] Dig. (23, 2) 16.

[34] Dig. (24, 3) 22.

[35] Dig. (23, 2) 16; Dig. (24, 3) 22; Bingham in his *Antiquities of the Christian Church* (2 vols., London, 1856), II, 1229, held the opinion that Justinian acknowledged imbecility on the part of the man as a lawful cause for divorce. He based this opinion on the text in Codex (5, 17) 10, which reads: "In causis iam dudum specialiter definitis, ex quibus recte mittuntur repudia, illam addimus ut, si maritus uxori ab initio matrimonii usque ad duos continuos annos computandos coire minime propter naturalem imbecillitatem valeat, possit mulier vel eius parentes . . . repudium marito mittere." However, Justinian refers here

enumerated the acceptable causes for divorce but made no mention of insanity.[36]

SCHOLION II. THE EFFECT OF INSANITY IN THE *Pater Familias* ON THE MARRIAGES OF HIS CHILDREN

For the sake of completeness one should briefly examine the effect of insanity of the *pater familias* upon the marriages of those in his power. His consent was necessary for the valid marriage of one in his *potestas*. What then were the consequences if he himself became insane and was unable to give or deny his consent?

There was little difficulty in the case of the daughter of an insane father. During the period of the classical law, the requisite consent for the marriage of a daughter was a mere negative consent.[37] As long as the father did not actually oppose the marriage of his daughter, it could be entered into validly and lawfully. An insane father could not offer legal opposition and consequently, the daughter was free to marry without his consent.[38]

Ulpianus states in the Code of Justinian: "The question was discussed by the ancients, whether the children of insane parents, when under their power, could marry. Almost all the legal authorities held that the daughter of an insane person could marry, for they held that it was sufficient if the father did not object."[39]

not to mental but rather to physical imbecility or impotence which is clear from the text in the Novellae (22, 6) which states: "... quando aliquis impotens fuerit coire mulieri et agere quae a natura viris data sunt sed biennium quidem secundum de hoc a nobis pridem scriptam legem transcurrat ex nuptiarum tempore ... non enim biennium numerari solum ex ipso tempore copulationis sed triennium volumus."

[36] Novellae (117, 8) 14.

[37] Much greater difficulty arose in marriages with *Manus*. However, this was already a dying institute at the time of the Twelve Tables, and it was in complete disuse at the time of Gaius. Cf. Leage, *Roman Private Law* (2. ed. by C. H. Ziegler, London: Macmillan and Co., 1930, Reprint 1948) p. 102.

[38] Corbett, *The Roman Law of Marriage*, p. 58.

[39] Codex (5, 4) 25.

A must greater difficulty presented itself when a son *in potestate,* wished to enter marriage. His marriage affected the family much more deeply and permanently because his children became part of that family; moreover, the son himself might become the head of the family on the death of his father.[40] As a result, the early Roman jurists often denied to such a son *in potestate* of an insane father the right to enter upon marriage.[41] Later law, however, allowed for the granting of a dispensation from the consent of the father. To settle the matter once and for all, Marcus Aurelius (161-181) published a constitution to which Justinian alluded in his Code. He ruled that children, male or female, of an insane parent were permitted to marry even without an imperial dispensation.[42]

Finally Justinian stated explicitly that children of the insane were free to marry without parental consent.[43]

[40] Inst. (1, 11) 7.

[41] Codex (5, 4) 25.

[42] Cf. Buckland, *A Manual of Roman Private Law* (Cambridge: Cambridge University Press, 1925), p. 114; Georges Bry, *Principes de Droit Romain* (6. ed., revue et corrigée par Paul Bry, 2 vols., Paris, 1927), I, 71.

[43] Inst. (1, 10).

CHAPTER II

THE EFFECT AT ECCLESIASTICAL LAW OF MENTAL ILLNESS ON MARRIAGE CONSENT PRIOR TO THE COUNCIL OF TRENT

ARTICLE 1. THE IUS ANTIQUUM-PRIOR TO GRATIAN (1140)

The earliest text referring directly to mental illness and its effect on marriage consent is often attributed to Pope Fabian (236-250). The text states: "*Neque furiosus neque furiosa matrimonium contrahere possunt. Sed si contractum fuerit non separentur.*"[1] This text was first ascribed to Pope Fabian by Burchard of Worms (†1025). He cited the text in his *Decretum*, which was composed about the year 1012.

The *Decretum* of Burchard was one of the most important and most interesting collections of law of the early Middle Ages. It was an attempt to produce a comprehensive and synthetic handbook of Canon Law. It was meant to be a practical guide for the young clergy, to whom the work was dedicated.

In view of the conditions of his times, Burchard aimed at showing the subordination of the secular princes to the Bishops of the Church in spiritual matters. He further tried to establish the precedence of the divine law over the civil law.[2] To achieve this latter purpose, Burchard, took undue liberties with the inscriptions of many canons by attributing them to early popes and to church councils when in fact their authors had been emperors, princes and jurists of Roman law.

[1] Burchardus, X, 28-29; Migne, *Patrologiae Cursus Completus. Series Latina* (221 tomes, Parisiis, 1844-1855) (hereafter cited as *MPL*), Tom. OXL, col. 819.

[2] The age of Burchard of Worms was a period of lay domination, simony and corruption in the Church, which were being actively combatted by the reform of the monks of Cluny, and the reform of the saintly king of Germany, King St. Henry II.

The text regarding insanity, which Burchard attributed to Pope Fabian, was in reality taken from the Roman jurist Paulus who was a contemporary of Pope Fabian. (Paulus died in the year 231 while Fabian ruled the Church from 236 till 250.)[3]

The early Church frequently accepted civil law statutes where they were in harmony with the Church's teaching. This policy seemed to Burchard to militate against his thesis concerning the precedence of the divine law over the civil law. Consequently he attributed the *lex* of the civil jurist to Pope Fabian. Actually the Church drew heavily on the law of Rome to develop her own institutes, and canonists often cited Roman law and Roman legal thought to explain ecclesiastical norms.[4]

This was to be expected since the Church developed widely throughout the Roman Empire, which possessed a rich system of law. The technical perfection of the Roman system commanded respect and admiration. Pope John VIII (872-882) voiced a general opinion when he stated in a letter to King Louis: *"Romanae Leges divinitus per ora principum promulgatae."*[5] From Justinian to Gratian one may accept the maxim *"Ecclesia vivit lege Romana,"* as true and applicable in those matters where the civil law was not opposed to the doctrine of the Church.[6] For this reason, therefore,

[3] R. C. Pickett in his dissertation *Mental Affliction and Church Law*, p. 41, apparently overlooked the false inscription of this text because he too attributes it to Pope Fabian without questioning its authenticity.

[4] Pope Gregory I (500-604) ordered that the rules of Roman law procedure should be followed in points which were not contemplated by Church law. *Gregorii I Papae Registrum Epistolarum, Ep. XIII, Monumenta Germaniae Historica, Epistolarum Tomus I et II* (edd. P. Ewald et L. Hartmann, Berolini: apud Weidmannos, 1891-1899), I, 47. Cf. also: A. M. Stickler, *Historia Iuris Canonici Latini, I, Historia Fontium* (Augustae Taurinorum: Apud Custodiam Librariam Pontif. Athenaei Salesiani, 1950), p. 427.

[5] C. 16, q. 3, c. 17; Jaffé, P., *Regesta Pontificum Romanorum ab condita ecclesia ad annum post Christum Natum 1198*, 2. ed. correctam et auctam auspiciis Gulielmi Wattenbach curaverunt, F. Kaltenbrunner, P. Ewald, S. Loewenfeld (2 Vols., Lipsiae, 1885-1888), n. 2970 (2247).

[6] Lex Ripuaria, Tit. 58, 1. Cf. K. A. Eckhardt, *Die Gesetze des*

one has a partial explanation as to the silence in ecclesiastical law regarding the effect of mental illness on marriage during the first nine centuries of the Church's history.

Roman law stated: "Neither an insane man nor an insane woman can contract marriage, but insanity does not destroy a marriage already contracted."[7] This rule of law was perfectly acceptable to the Church.

Roman law, however, permitted divorce. Its jurists held that insanity which occurred after marriage was contracted could, at times, be accepted as a valid cause for divorce. The Church could not accept such teaching. Timothy, Patriarch of Alexandria (381-385) unhesitatingly stated that a marriage contracted after a previous divorce, no matter what the cause of the divorce, was an adulterous union. When asked whether a man whose wife had become violently insane could divorce her and contract a second marriage, he replied that this was a question of adultery and therefore, not permissible.[8] The Second Council of Orleans (533) stated: *"Contracta matrimonia accidente infirmitate nulla voluntatis contrarietate solvantur."*[9] However, because the evil of divorce was so widespread in Roman society, the laws of the Church were directed against divorce in general rather than against divorce for the specific reason of insanity.[10]

Regarding the marriages of the children of the insane, the *Lex Romana Canonice Compta,* published probably in Raven-

Karolingerreiches 714-911, 1. Salische und ribuarische Franken (Weimar, 1934).

[7] *Fontes Iuris Antejustiniani,* II, 345.

[8] Pitra, *Iuris Ecclesiastici Graecorum Historia et Monumenta* (2 Tomes. Romae, 1864), Tom. 1, p. 633, c. 15.

[9] H. Bruns, *Canones Apostolorum et Conciliorum Saeculorum* IV-VII (2 vols., Berolini, 1839) (hereafter cited as Bruns), II, 186; Esmein (1848-1913) held that the sickness referred to definitely was intended to be mental illness. Cf. Esmein, *Le Mariage en Droit Canonique* (2 ed., 2 vols., Vol. I, rev. by R. Génestal, 1929; Vol. II rev. by R. Génestal and J. Dauvillier, 1935, Paris, Librarie de Recueil Sirey, 1929-1935), II, p. 77, n. 1.

[10] *Canones Apostolorum,* c. 47. Bruns, I, 8; Council of Vannes (465), c. 2. Bruns, II, 143.

na sometime after 825, repeated as Church law the text from the Institutes of Justinian, where it was stated that children of the insane were free to marry, even without the consent of the insane parent.[11]

Regino of Prüm (915) in his *Libri Duo de Synodalibus Causis* repeated the Roman law regarding insanity and marriage.[12] He stated: *"Neque furiosus neque furiosa matrimonium contrahere possunt, sed si contractum fuerit, non separentur."*[13] But on the other hand, he declared: *"Hi, qui matrimonium sani contraxerint, et uni ex duobus amentia aut aliqua infirmitas accesserit, ob hanc infirmitatem coniugia talium solvi non possunt."*[14] This latter text appeared in the collection of Burchard who falsely attributed it to Pope Nicholas (858-867). It was alleged to have as its source a letter of the Pope addressed to Bishop Carolus of Mainz.[15] The text was accepted as such by Anselm of Luca (1083) and also by Ivo of Chartres (1093).[16] In fact, Gratian himself seems to have been deceived. The text with its falsifica-

[11] *Lex Romana Canonice Compta* (ed. C. G. Mor, Pavia, 1927), CLXXXVI, p. 125; Inst. (1, 10).

[12] McCloskey in his dissertation, *The Subject of Ecclesiastical Law according to Canon 12*, The Catholic University of America Canon Law Studies No. 165 (Washington, D.C.: The Catholic University of America Press, 1945), p. 66, accepted the authorship of Pope Fabian, relying on the inscription given to the text by Burchard of Worms. Moreover, he held that the Pope forbade such a person (insane) to marry, but that, if a marriage nevertheless took place, the parties should not be separated. McCloskey believes that the Pope had in mind the validity of a marriage contracted during a so-called lucid interval when true marital consent could be given. Gonzalez (†1649) on the other hand, held the more probable view that the text simply meant that an insane person could not validly marry, but if, before he became insane, he had entered into a valid marriage, then his marriage continued to exist also afterwards. Cf. Gonzalez, *Commentaria*, Vol, IV, Lib. IV, Tit. I, Cap. XXIV, n. 7.

[13] Regino, II, 129; *MPL*, Tom. CXXII, Col. 309.

[14] Regino, II, 130; *MPL*, Tom. CXXII, Col. 309.

[15] Pickett, *op. cit.*, p. 42, also accepted the inscription of the text.

[16] *Anselmi Episcopi Lucensis Collectio Canonum una cum collectione minore*, recensuit Fridericus Thaner (Oeniponte, 1906), X, 26, 27; *Decretum*, VIII, 166—*MPL*, Tom. CLXI, Col. 619.

tion, together with the one mentioned above as coming from Pope Fabian, are found in the Decretum with their false inscriptions.[17]

Article 2. The Ius Novum—From Gratian to the Council of Trent

Pope Innocent III (1196-1216) in a solution of a marriage case presented to him, applied the principle of Roman law which stated that insanity, though an impediment to marriage, did not invalidate one already contracted.[18] A certain Richard had permitted his daughter to marry a man who was actually insane at the time of the marriage although he appeared to be sane. Because of the mental condition of the man and the unhappiness of the woman a request was made that the marriage be declared invalid on the grounds that an insane person could not give consent and was, therefore, to be considered incapable of marriage. In his response to the request of the Bishop of Vercelli, Italy, Innocent stated that the bishop should examine the case and that, if the alleged facts were founds to be true, the union should be dissolved.[19] Robert of Flamesbury (after 1215) stated that the reason for the incapacity of the *furiosi* to contract marriage was based on their inability to give true marriage consent.[20] The

[17] *Corpus Iuris Canonici,* ed. Lipsiensis 2. post Aemilii Ludovici Richteri curas ad librorum manu scriptorum et editionis Romanae fidem recognovit et adnotatione critica instruxit Aemilius Friedberg (Lipsiae, 1879-1881) Editio anastatice repetita (Lipsiae 1928). *Neque furiosus,* c. 26, C. XXXII, q. 7; *hi qui* c. 25, C. XXXII q. 7; Jaffé, *Regesta Pontificum Romanorum, neque furiosus,* n. †97; *hi qui* n. †2711.

[18] "Neque furiosus neque furiosa matrimonium contrahere possunt, sed si contractum fuerit non separentur."—*Fontes Iuris Antejustiniani,* II, 345.

[19] Dec. 28, 1205, C. 4, Comp. III, *de sponsalibus et matrimoniis,* IV, I—*Antiquae Collectiones Decretalium cum Antonii Episcopi Ilerdensis notis* (Ilerdae, 1576); *Quinque compilationes Antiquae,* ed. Aem. Freidberg (Lipsiae, 1882); C. 24, X, *de sponsalibus et matrimoniis,* IV, 1; *MPL* Tom. CCXV, col. 751; Potthast, *Regesta Pontificum Romanorum inde ab anno post Christum natum MCXCVIII ad annum MCCIV* (2 vols., Berolini, 1874-1875), n. 2634.

[20] Robertus Flamesburiensis, *Summa de Matrimonio et Usuris,* ed.

gloss of Ioannes Teutonicus (†1245) to the text *Neque Furiosus*, in the *Decretum* of Gratian also gave as the reason for the incapacity of the insane to enter marriage, their inability to give true consent to the contract. He also stated, however, that the insane could validly marry during a so-called lucid interval.[21]

Huguccio (†1210) referred to a distinction made in Roman Law regarding lucid intervals. As had the Roman jurist Celsus before him, so Huguccio distinguished between apparent lucid intervals, termed *inumbrata quies*, and real lucid intervals. During the latter a person was considered in full possession of his mental faculties.[22]

Even at that early date it was realized that individuals might give outward appearances of complete mental health while actually the mental illness continued in a more recessive or hidden form.

Rufinus (†1190) commented upon the same text (*neque furiosus*) and thought that the partners should not be separated if the marriage was contracted and consummated before the party became insane.[23] In speaking of perfecting the union by consummation, Rufinus indicated that he accepted the *copula* theory of marriage prevalent at that time, especially at Bologna.[24]

G. F. Schulte (Gissae, 1868), Tit. 13, as quoted in Freisen, *Geschichte des canonischen Eherechts bis zum Verfal der Glossenliteratur* (2 ed., Paderborn, 1893), p. 356.

[21] *Decretum Gratiani emendatum et notationibus illustratum una cum glossis, Gregorii XIII, Pont. Max. Iussu Editum* (2 vols., Romae, 1582), *glossa* ad c. 26, C. XXXII, q. 7, s.v. *neque furiosus*.

[22] D. (41, 2) 18, 1; Huguccio, *Summa*, ad c. 5, C. 15, q. 1, as quoted in Kuttner, *Kanonistische Schuldlehre von Gratian bis auf die Dekretalen Gregors IX*, Studi e Testi, n. 64 (Città del Vaticano: Biblioteca Apostolica Vaticana, 1935), p. 100.

[23] "Neque . . . contractum, antequam insanirent et carnali commixtione perfectum."—Rufinus, *Summa Decretorum* (ed. H. Singer, Paderborn, 1902), c. 26, C. XXXII, q. 7.

[24] Rolandus Bandinelli, who later was to become Pope Alexander III (1159-1181), was a leading proponent of the *copula* theory. This theory held that it was consummation, rather than consent to the marriage contract, which gave marriage its binding force. Consequently it was

The decision which Innocent III transmitted to the Bishop of Vercelli appeared in the Decretals of Gregory IX.[25] Bernard of Parma (†1263) supplied a gloss to the text, in which he reiterated the accepted doctrine of the time regarding insanity and marriage consent. He stated that a valid marriage contract was impossible during periods of insanity, but that a marriage which was entered into during a truly lucid interval was to be considered as valid and binding.[26] This teaching was accepted by all prominent jurists of the day. The works of such scholars as Hostiensis,[27] Raymond of Pennafort,[28] Gulielmus Durandus,[29] Henricus Boich,[30] and Panormitanus[31] are all in accord on the matter.

Raymond of Pennafort in his *Summa* looked upon insanity as one of twelve impediments to marriage. These impediments excluded a valid marriage consent when they existed prior to the marriage, but if they arose after the marriage had taken place, they did not affect the consent in any manner. Raymond spoke of the impediment of insanity as the most obvious example to show this principle in a practical

held by the followers of this theory that if insanity occurred after the contract but before the consummation of the marriage, such a marriage should be regarded as having no binding force: Cf. *infra*, p. 63; "Sed si conjuncti fuerint antequam insaniant et carnali commixtione copulati fuerint, postea non separentur."—*Die Summa Magistri Rolandi*, ed. Fried. Thaner (Insbruck, 1874), p. 187 as quoted in Freisen, *Geschichte des canonischen Eherechts bis zum Verfall der Glossenliteratur*, p. 228.

25 *Decretales D. Gregorii Papae IX una cum glossis restitutae* (Romae, 1582), C. 24, X, *de sponsalibus et matrimoniis*, IV, 1; Potthast, n. 2634.

26 C. 24, X, de sponsalibus et matrimoniis, IV, I, s.v. *furore*.

27 Hostiensis (Henricus de Segusio), *Commentaria in Quinque Libros Decretalium* (5 vols., in 3, Venetiis, 1581), C. 24, X, IV, 1.

28 Sanctus Raymundus de Pennafort, *Summa* (Venonae, 1744, juxta editionem 1720), Lib. IV, Tit. II, 5; Lib. IV, Tit. III, 9.

29 Durandus, *Speculum Iuris* (4 vols., in 3 Venetiis, 1577), Lib. IV, P. IV, § 4, n. 8

30 Boich, *Commentaria in Quinque Libros Decretalium* (Venetiis, 1576), C. 24, X, IV, 1.

31 Panormitanus (Nicolaus de Tudeschis), *Commentaria in Quinque Libros Decretalium* (5 vols., in 7, Venetiis, 1588), C. 24, X, IV, 1.

case.[32] Finally, the Angelic Doctor, St. Thomas Aquinas (1226-1274) also upheld the incapacity of the insane to enter a valid marriage contract while laboring under their mental infliction.[33] Moreover, to contract a valid marriage, St. Thomas demanded a higher degree of mental capacity than that required for the commission of mortal sin. In considering the subject of betrothal, he wrote:

> Ad peccandum mortaliter sufficit etiam consensus in praesens, sed in sponsalibus est consensus in futurum; major autem discretio requiritur ad providendum in futurum quam ad consentiendum in actum praesentem, et ideo ante potest homo peccare mortaliter quam possit se obligare ad aliquid in futurum.[34]

In view of his requirements for betrothal, it can be assumed that St. Thomas certainly demanded an equal degree of mental capacity for undertaking the more serious and binding obligations of marriage itself.

The doctrine regarding the effects of mental illness on marriage consent remained unchanged through the period of the Protestant upheaval, which preceded the convocation of the Council of Trent in 1545.

[32] "Ultimo videndum, quae, et quot sint impedimenta, quae impediunt matrimonium. Est sciendum, quod 12 tantum sunt impedimenta, quae impediunt matrimonium contrahendum, et dirimunt jam contractum, si tamen ipsa, vel aliqua eorum praecedunt matrimonium, quoniam consensum conjugalem excludunt; si vero sequantur matrimonium, non praestant impedimentum, sicut patet per ista exempla. Furiosus non potest contrahere matrimonium; tamen si contraxit ante furorem, non solvitur matrimonium."—Sanctus Raymundus de Pennafort, *Summa*, Lib. IV, Tit. III, § 9.

[33] St. Thomas Aquinas, *Commentaria Praeclarissima in IV Libros sententiarum Petri Lombardi* (2 vols., Parisiis, 1659), Tom. 2, Lib. IV, d. XXXIV, c. 4.

[34] *Sancti Thomae Aquinatis Commentum in quatuor Libros Sententiarum Magistri Petri Lombardi* (adjectis brevibus adnotationibus), *Volumen Secundum* (complectens tertium et quartum librum), (Parmae, Typis Petri Fiaccadori, MDCCCLVIII), Liber IV, dist. 27, q. 2, art. 2, ad 2, as quoted in S. Thomae Aquinatis, *Opera Omnia*, secundum, impressionem Petri Fiaccadori (Photolithographice reimpressa, Parmae, 1852-1873), Tomus VII (New York, Musurgia, 1948).

CHAPTER III

MEDICAL-LEGAL DEVELOPMENT ON MENTAL ILLNESS AS INVALIDATING MATRIMONIAL CONSENT

ARTICLE 1. DOCTRINE OF THE AUTHORS IN THE PERIOD OF THE IUS NOVISSIMUM

The period between the Council of Trent and the Code of Canon Law was one of progressive clarification regarding the effect of mental illness on marriage consent. This progress was made despite the fact that no new legislation was enacted. It was made in the writings of prominent authors who commented on the basic norms established, as was generally believed, by Popes Fabian[1] and Innocent III.[2]

The theories of the authors were applied to practical causes in the decisions of the various ecclesiastical tribunals and Congregations. This application, in turn, brought further clarification of the basic principles involved.[3]

Post-Tridentine authors unanimously demanded two requisites for a valid marriage contract: knowledge of what they were doing on the part of the contracting parties; and freedom to place their act of giving consent without hindrance.[4] The knowledge and freedom necessary for matrimony led to a consideration of mental illness. Mental in-

[1] C. 26, C. XXXII, q. 7; Jaffé, n. 80.

[2] C. 24, X, *de sponsalibus et matrimoniis,* IV, 1; Potthast, n. 2634.

[3] The only specific legislation in this matter is found in the *Instructio pro judiciis ecclesiasticis quoad causas matrimoniales,* which was issued by the bishops of Austria. This instruction received its approbation by the Holy See in 1855 and came to be known as the Instructio Austriaca; Cf. *Acta et Decreta Sacrorum Conciliorum Recentiorum, Collectio Lacensis* (7 vols., Friburgi Brisgoviae, 1870-1892), V, 1316. Article 13 of this instruction states: "Amentes, furiosi, infantes, et quicumque talem, qualem rei natura exigit, consensum praestando impares habentur, matrimonium contrahere nequeunt."—*Ibidem,* 1287.

[4] *Acta Sanctae Sedis* (41 vols., Romae, 1865-1908), XXI (1885), 149.

ability to give a valid matrimonial consent could arise on the part of the subject from either a physical or mental defect. An insane person labored under a mental defect. Since he was unable to deliberate, an insane person could not posit a truly human act and, consequently, was to be considered incapable of marriage.[5] The presumption was, however, in favor of sanity at the time of marriage. One who wished to attack the validity of a marriage on the basis of insanity had to prove that one of the parties was actually insane at the time that the marriage was contracted.[6]

Thus there was no change in principle regarding the capacity of the insane to contract marriage, yet, tremendous progress was being made in the field of medical science. No longer were the mentally ill considered to be cursed by God or possessed by satan, nor were they regarded as dangerous criminals or objects of entertainment. At least in the field of medicine, insanity came to be accepted as a definite illness with specific causes and symptoms. Pioneer efforts were made at diagnosing and treating the mentally ill.

SECTION A. ADVANCE MADE IN THE FIELD OF MEDICINE WITH REGARD TO MENTAL AFFLICTIONS, THEIR CAUSES AND EFFECTS

A good summary of the medical theories regarding mental illness in the post-Tridentine period may be found in the writings of Paulus Zacchia (1584-1659).[7] In 1664, during the reign of Pope Innocent X, Zacchia, a doctor in Rome, was appointed adviser to the Holy See in the field of medical-legal problems.[8]

[5] Covarrubias, *Opera Omnia* (2 vols., Coloniae Allobrogum, 1679), Pars II, C. II, n. 6.

[6] Smith, *Ignorance Affecting Matromonial Consent*, The Catholic University of America Canon Law Studies, No. 245. (Washington, D.C.: The Catholic University of America Press, 1950), p. 12.

[7] Zacchia, *Quaestiones Medico-Legales* (ed. nova, 3 tomes in 1, Lugduni, 1701.)

[8] "Zacchia, Paolo," Enciclopedia Cattolica, XIII, 1762. In his works Zacchia shows himself to be a true scholar with an inquisitive, courageous and, at times, humorous approach to his difficult subject. It is

Especially after the publication of his work on medical-legal problems (1621) he came to be regarded as an expert in this field.

Title 1 of Book II in his work bears, as a summary of its contents, the following legend: *"De Dementia et Rationis laesione et morbis omnibus qui rationem laedant."*[9] Under this heading he proposes to examine the various influences that were considered harmful to the healthy functioning of the human mind. He begins with a definition of terms.

Before entering into a discussion of the various mental disturbances, he makes a few interesting and even humorous remarks. In paragraph 15 of Question 1 he says: "One thing must be noted in advance; Doctors generally have not been slaves to specific terminology. They have at times failed to keep names apart; yes, they have even been known to use one name for another."[10]

Zacchia then promises that he will try to be specific and explain the terminology as he goes along.[11]

1. *General Definitions*

Zacchia begins his examination of the various harmful influences on man's mind by explaining his understanding of the terms: *dementia, amentia,* and *insanitas.*

a. *Dementia.* This is a colloquial term which comprehends

interesting to note that he appears to have been the first man in medical history to suspect contagion in tuberculosis.

[9] Zacchia, *Quaestiones Medico-Legales,* T. I, Lib. II, T. I.

[10] "Illud tamen ante commonendum est; Medicos non fuisse ita nominum proprietati addictos, ut aliquando ea inter se minime distinxerint: imo unum pro alio ad libitum interdum accepisse: nos in rerum natura explananda, quo accuratius fieri poterit, omnia manifesta faciemus."—*Ibidem,* § 15.

[11] It would seem that Zacchia already was aware of one of the great difficulties in attempting to bring medical and legal minds together, viz., the difficulty of a proper nomenclature which would be acceptable to experts in both fields. The difficulty remains the same today. Zacchia promised, and also attempted, to clarify matters. He appears only to have succeeded, as many have after him, in adding a little to the total confusion. Zachia dedicates all of Title 111 in the Sixth Book of *Quaestiones Medico-Legales* to the relationship between the medical and legal sciences.

all influences that lead the human mind to err or to operate below normal capacity. These influences can affect the mind in three different ways. They can weaken the mind so that it loses, as it were, its energy; they can distort and twist the mind so that it does not operate in the right way; finally, they can completely ruin man's mind, so that it does not function at all.[12] When the mind is weakened, there is *fatuitas;* if distorted, *delirium;* if destroyed, there is *mania.* Each one of these has numerous subdivisions.[13] *Dementia,* therefore, must be taken to mean any malfunctioning of the human mind which results from any cause, whether it be sickness, anger, love or any other harmful influence.[14]

b. *Amentia.* In seeking for a definition of the term *amentia* Zacchia admits to a difficulty. "There is," he states, "some doubt in the use of the term *amentia,* because there are some authors who want to give this name to that disturbance which we would prefer to call *stoliditas.*"[15] Actually, he iden-

[12] "Constituamus ergo nos unum quoddam genericum nomen, comprehendens sub se omnes affectus, in quibus mens vel errat, vel debiliter operatur, quod non aliud esse debet, quam hoc nomen dementiae; quocumque enim modo, ac in quocumque tempore aut morbo, rationalis animae functiones non bene, ac naturaliter celebrantur sed vel nullo modo, vel debiliter, vel depravate, tunc dementia sit; quod tamen multis modis contingere potest, non solum per earundem cerebri, animaeque rationalis facultatum diversitate, sed pro modo, et ratione diversa qua eaedem facultates male et non naturaliter operari possunt: quibus tamen omnibus affectionibus recte aptari dementiae nomen potest magis quam quodvis aliud."—*Ibidem,* §§ 9-12.

[13] "... Si rationalis animae functiones, imminuantur, fatuitatem, eiusque species inde generare solent: si depraventur, dilirium: si deperdantur, maniam suis quamque speciebus concomitatam."—*Ibidem,* § 12.

[14] It is surprising to find that Zacchia looked upon love or *amor,* as one of the forms of dementia. In Lib. II, Tit. 1, Questio X, he attempts to prove just that by referring to the effects and symptoms of love. He states: "Love is blind, it leads to dreams by day and night, it brings on light-headedness; a lover is like a person asleep, he degenerates to the nature of the animal (sic). Love makes the will subject to itself and it overrules prudence. A person in love, finally, is like a prodigal." —Zacchia, *Quaestiones Medico-Legales,* Liber II, Title I, q. 10.

[15] "Circa amentiae tamen nomenclaturam dubium aliquod est, cum

tifies *amentia* with *dementia* and uses the two terms indiscriminately.[16]

c. *Insanitas.* In speaking of the term *insanitas,* Zacchia warns that it should be distinguished from *amentia* and *dementia. Insanitas* is less general, for it is merely one of the many forms of *amentia* or *dementia.*[17] He insists on this distinction in view of the fact that some authors apparently identified the terms. Insanity, according to Zacchia, connotes unruliness, loquaciousness, and bizarre conduct, while, he observes that this is not verified in all mental disturbances.[18]

Having explained the general terminology, Zacchia distinguishes the various mental disturbances for one another.

2. *Division of Mental Disturbances*

Mental disturbances are divided as follows:

a. In view of their origin, they can be called primary or secondary.

b. In view of their effects, there are those that weaken, those that distort, and those that destroy the functions of man's mind.

c. In view of their duration, there are those with lasting and passing disturbances.

Primary disturbances result from an actual affliction of the mind and from damage done to the faculty of reason. Secondary disturbances, on the other hand, result from some bodily illness. They are, as it were, inseparable by-products of that particular illness.[19] Mental disturbances with enduring effects are called perpetual. However, Zacchia is careful to point out that this latter classification does not imply that

non desint ex doctoribus viris, qui proprie amentiam dici velint eum affectum, quem alia voce stoliditatem appellamus."—*op. cit.,* Lib. II, Tit. I, q. I, § 13.

[16] *Ibidem,* § 5; § 15.

[17] "Cum ergo insaniae nomen dementias omnes non comprehendat melius est affirmare hujusmodi passiones dementae nomine . . ."—*Ibidem,* § 8.

[18] ". . . non insani quia non erant inquieti, nec loquaces neque actus absurdos facientes ut insani solent."—*Ibidem* § 8.

[19] *Op. cit.,* Lib. II, Tit. II, Q. 2, § 3.

a person with a perpetual or lasting disturbance cannot return to mental health at all. Rather, it means that the person suffers only one attack of this mental affliction, while in intermittent disturbances there is a cycle of regularly recurring attacks. Between the attacks of an intermittent disturbance a person is sane and responsible for his actions.[20]

In schematic form the various disturbances can be shown in the following manner:[21]

According to Origin	Primary	amentia	phrenesis
		mentis captio	oblivio
		mentis alienatio	fatuitas
		insania	indiscretio
		mania	vecordia
		furor	stultitia
		melancholia	delirium
		lycanthropia	vesania
		insipientia	amor
		despientia	ebrietas
		ignorantia	stoliditas
		rabies	enthusiasmus
		ecstasis	rationis permixtio
	Secondary	paraphrenesis	lethargia
		carus	subeth
		coma	catalepsis
		catoche	cataphora
		apprehensio	congelatio
		apoplexia	epilepsia
		furor uterinus	melancholia
		hypochondriaca	
According to Effect	Weaken	fatuitas	stoliditas
		ignorantia	oblivio
	Distort	phrenitis	delirium
		paraphrenitis	

[20] *Ibidem,* §§ 5-10.

[21] For the sake of accuracy the present writer has chosen to use the Latin terminology of Zacchia.

	Destroy	insania melancholia lycanthropia melancholia-hypochondriaca	mania furor amor
According to Duration	Lasting	rabies phrenesis catalepsis	fatuitas lethargus
	Inter-mittent	melancholia epilepsia	apoplexia paraphrenesis

3. *Degrees of Mental Disturbance*

In treating of the various degrees of mental disturbances Zacchia admits to a basic difficulty. He realized that the gravity of illness varied from case to case, and that it was impossible to establish general rules. Yet he tried to give a chart of the progressive malfunctioning of the mind in the various mental disturbances.[22]

"First," he states, "the intellect is, as it were, shrunk or diminished, and it suffers a comparatively minor injury in what is called *imperitia* or *ignorantia*." The ignorance spoken of is not to be understood as a simple lack of knowledge in the accepted meaning of the word, but it is rather a definite defect, a certain listlessness (*ignavia*) of a sick mind.

The intellect is further injured and weakened in *fatuitas*, and this can vary in degree of gravity in individual cases.

Following upon *fatuitas* from the point of view of gravity is *oblivio*. This is an injury to the mind in respect to its ability to reason and to remember.

Stoliditas or *stultitia* ranks fourth place in gravity of disturbance. The mind becomes distorted. This state occurs in sudden and vehement *passiones*, in simple *delirium*, in slight *ebrietas*, gradually becoming a more and more marked distortion in *syncope* and *suffocatio ex utero non multum pertinaci*.

[22] Zacchia, *Quaestiones Medico-Legales*, Lib. II, Tit. I, Q. 4.

The mental faculties are very seriously warped in *amor, melancholia* and its various species, in *phrenitis, rabiosis,* i.e., those bitten by mad dogs and in *furor uterinus.*

Finally, all reason has totally disappeared in *furor, mania* and *sopor.*[23]

4. *Indications of Presence of Mental Disturbance and Use of Witnesses*

When treating of the signs and symptoms of mental disturbances, Zacchia prefaces his remarks by observing that the signs of mental affliction vary not only in basically different disturbances, but also that different people suffering from the same affliction, may at times, present a totally different clinical picture. "Consequently," he states, "there are practically innumerable signs of a sick mind."[24]

It is interesting and revealing that a scientific work, such as *Quaestiones Medico-Legales* definitely was, would give as the signs of mental illness a series of common, everyday acts of man. It is most of all the speech and behavior of a person which betray the state of health or sickness of his mind.

The external signs of mental disturbances are divided into five groups: a. *facta,* b. *verba,* c. *animi passiones,* d. *signa a medicis tradita,* e. *causae extrinsecae.*

a. *Facta.* Under this heading Zacchia places the physical and social actions of a person, e.g., his manner of walking, the twisting of the mouth and of facial muscles, the uncontrollable shaking of arms, legs and head, the wringing of hands, etc. If the patient greets those whom he should not greet, but refuses to greet those whom he should; if he gives his possessions away without cause; if he wanders without purpose or goal; if any or all of these manifestations are ob-

[23] *Ibidem,* §§ 39-42.

[24] "Pene in infinitum variari signa non sanae mentis contingit."—*Op. cit.,* Bk. II, Tit. II, Q. 3, § 1.

served in a person, then he must be considered as presenting definite signs of mental disturbance.[25]

b. *Verba.* *"Fatuus est qui fatua loquitur."*[26] With this axiom: "He who speaks insanely must be regarded to be insane," Zacchia indicated that the speech of a person can be indicative of his mental health. If one cannot find words to express oneself; if answers to questions are incoherent; if a peaceful person speaks belligerently; if a modest person speaks immodestly; if the right order of words is disturbed; if a person speaks in terms of grandeur about himself; if one speaks about onself as a god or a bird, or without heart or head, then such a person must be suspected of being mentally ill.

However, Zacchia warns his readers that at times those who are actually seriously disturbed may appear to speak very sanely and coherently; yes, even with apparent wisdom.[27]

c. *Animi passiones.* Fear without cause, sorrow when there is reason for joy, excessive laughter or crying, all these must be regarded as definite indications of mental illness. If one hopes for the impossible, loves what should be hated, or if one marvels greatly at ordinary things, again there is good reason to suspect a serious mental disturbance.

c. *Signa a medicis tradita.* By these are meant certain conditions of the body which may be noticed only by the practiced eye of the physician. The coloring of the skin,[28] or the murky appearance of the eye, the swelling of the veins, all of these could be signs of a disturbed mind. But these signs, according to Zacchia, can be interpreted only by an expert in the medical field, because each and all of them could be due to other causes.[29]

e. *Causae extrinsecae.* Finally, if a person appears to be

[25] *Ibidem,* §§ 2-8.

[26] *Ibidem,* § 13.

[27] *Ibidem,* §§ 8-22.

[28] Discoloration of the skin was attributed by Zacchia to an excess of certain fluids in the body of the patient. This fluid was termed "Humor melancholicus."—*Ibidem,* § 25.

[29] *Ibidem,* §§ 24-29.

insane or disturbed, Zacchia suggests that his life be examined for any past serious upheavals which may have caused this condition. Great fear, serious disappointments, great sorrow, happiness or frustrated love, could have brought about his present mental condition.[30]

In conclusion to his treatment of the signs and external manifestations of mental illness, Zacchia states that the legal experts, when called upon to make a judgment regarding the responsibility of a person, should carefully examine the acts, words and previous life-experiences of that person, because all these factors help to show the condition of his mind. It is regarding these every day actions of man that witnesses should be questioned in cases of suspected mental illness.[31]

Zacchia indicated that the judgment concerning the mental health of the person involved in legal matters and, consequently, regarding his legal repsonsibility should be made by the legal experts only, though with the help of witnesses and medical experts.

5. *Presumptions, Exceptions and the Use of Medical Experts*

In Question XXIII of Book II, Title I, Zacchia states two general axioms of presumption. The first rule declares: 'If a person is once insane, he must be presumed to remain insane, and the burden of proof to the contrary is on the person who denies the present insanity.[32]

The second rule asserts: "One who was out of his mind

[30] It would appear that Zacchia, as early as 1621, suggested a primitive form of what today is called psycho-analysis. *Ibidem,* §§ 30-35.

[31] "Jam vero ex his colligunt Jurisperiti, quaenam consideranda sint, ubi de aliquo judicium ferendum, an insaniat necne et quid oporteat testes deponere, per quos dementia sit probanda. Primo enim facta, ac verba, ut illis placet, inspicienda. Secundo, animi passiones; Tertio, signa a Medicis tradita; Quarto, causae praegressae, quas evidentes, procatarcticas, extrinsecas et antecedentes nominamus, haec enim omnia signorum vicem gerent in adminiculanda dementia."—*Ibidem,* § 35.

[32] "Semel furiosus semper furiosus praesumitur et contrarium tenenti incumbit onus probandi."—*Op. cit.,* XXIII, § 1.

in the past, must also be presumed to be out of his mind at present."[33]

However, there are certain exceptions to these rules, viz., if a person goes out of his mind, as it were, in a fever or as a consequence of some illness; or, if the loss of reason is of a very short duration, e.g., less than a month. The disturbance must have lasted from a month to a year before these presumptions can be applied.

Zacchia believes that the two rules of presumption are always valid in cases of *melancholia, mania, apoplexia and epilepsia.*[34] In all other cases a person must be presumed to be of sound mind and the contrary has to be proven.[35]

Regarding lucid intervals, certain other presumptions can be found in *Quaestiones Medico-Legales.*[36] If one were insane because of old age, no lucid intervals could be expected. This same rule held true for those struck by lightning, for *lethargici, comatosi, carotici phrenitici and hydrophobi.* If, however, a person does have a truly lucid interval, then he must during that period be treated and held responsible for his actions just as any other sane person.[37]

Zacchia warns his readers to be careful to distinguish between a remission and an intermission in the mental illness. In case of remission the illness is, as it were, covered up and pushed back, but the patient is still to be regarded as insane and not responsible at law.[38]

In all court cases in which people are involved who are suspected of being mentally disturbed, Zacchia recommends that the court make use of medical experts.[39]

Many things which would not be clear to the layman, can be ascertained from the expert testimony of medical men.

[33] "Demens de praeterito praesumitur demens de praesenti." *Ibidem,* § 1.

[34] *Ibidem,* § 10.

[35] "Cum tamen demens nullus praesumitur sed et potius sanae mentis Rota. . . ."—*Ibidem,* § 2.

[36] *Op. cit.,* Lib. II, Tit., I, Q. 20.

[37] *Ibidem,* § 26.

[38] *Ibidem,* § 29.

[39] *Op. cit.,* Lib. II, Tit. I, Q. 1, § 1.

"It is for that reason," he states, "that the Rota uses experts in the field of medicine."[40] They can testify regarding the signs and degrees, etc., of mental disturbances and in that way be of incalculable help to the court in reaching a conclusion in a particular case.[41]

The present writer chose to give a rather elaborate treatment of the work *Quaestiones Medico-Legales* by Paulus Zacchia for the following reasons: This scholarly and often remarkably prophetic work presents a good survey of the medical understanding of mental disturbances at the period of legal history immediately following the Council of Trent. This work has made a great contribution to the medical-legal field. Many principles and presumptions contained in this work were used extensively by the ecclesiastical courts at Rome and by the legal experts in the period immediately preceding the present Code of Canon Law.

SECTION B. MENTAL ILLNESS INVALIDATING MARRIAGE CONSENT AS SEEN IN THE WRITINGS OF THE PRE-CODE AUTHORS

The authors of the post-Tridentine period were in unanimous agreement with those in the centuries before them regarding the doctrine of the incapacity of the insane to contract a valid marriage. The truly insane person was considered to be unable to perform an act of deliberation and, consequently, such a person could not present a valid consent to a marriage contract.[42]

[40] "Rota, non aliam ob rem Medicos in similibus casibus adjudicandum adhibent. . . ."—*Ibidem,* § 2.

[41] *Ibidem,* §§ 1-4.

[42] Covarrubias (1512-1577), *Opera Omnia* (2 vols., Coloniae Allobrogum, 1679), Pars II, c. II, n. 6; Sanchez (1550-1610), *De Matrimonio,* Lib. I, Disp. VIII, n. 15; Pontius (1559-1629), *De Sacramento Matrimonii Tractatus* (Venetiis, 1766), Lib. IV, Cap. I, n. 7; De Lugo (1583-1660), *Disputationes Scholasticae et Morales* (8 vols., Parisiis, 1868-1869), III, *Tractatus de Sacramentis in Genere,* Disp. VIII, n. 108; Pirhing (1606-1679), *Ius Canonicum in Textus Quinque Librorum Decretalium Gregorii IX* (5 vols. in 4, Dillingae, 1674-1678), Lib. IV, Tit. I, § 1, n. 10; Gonzalez-Tellez (1673), *Commentaria Perpetua in*

The defect of insanity was regarded by the authors as constituting a matrimonial impediment which derived from the natural law itself.[43] Consequently, the impediment was not based on the principle that an injustice was done to an innocent party in the marriage contract. Whether or not the sane party realized the mental disturbance of the other was of no consequence in regard to the question of the validity of that marriage.[44] Didymus Upianus declared:

> By the law of nature we are obliged to do whatever we do in a manner befitting our nature and essence. Thus, we are bound in our acts to use our reason and will, which are the faculties that dignify us as men and make us human. We must inquire how and why a thing is done before we do it. Hence, a truly human act requires deliberation. In marrying, therefore, since we perform a human act, we must use our reason and will. We must deliberate. There cannot be any marriage without the consent and will of the contracting parties. Such a marriage would be contrary to the natural law . . . and whatever is opposed to the natural law is invalid. Since the insane cannot thus deliberate and consent, they cannot validly marry.[45]

Further discussion and clarification developed regarding the problem of the degree of knowledge required for the giving of a valid matrimonial consent. Authors of the time indicated that only those who were capable of that degree of deliberation which was required for the commission of mortal

Singulos Textus Quinque Librorum Decretalium Gregorii IX (5 Tomes, Lugduni, 1673), Lib. IV, Tit. I, Cap. XXIV, n. 3; Schmalzgruber (1663-1735), *Ius Ecclesiasticum Universum* (5 vols. in 12, Romae, 1843-1845), Lib. IV, Pars I, Tit. I, n. 14; De Smet (1868-1927), *De Sponsalibus et Matrimonio* (Brugis, 1909), p. 322; P. Gasparri (1852-1934), *De Matrimonio* (3 ed., 2 vols., Paris, 1904), II, n. 884.

[43] Pontius, *De Sacramento Matrimonii,* Lib. IV, Cap. I, n. 7; Gonzalez-Tellez, *Commentaria,* Lib. IV, Tit. I, Cap. XXIV, n. 3.

[44] Covarrubias, *Opera Omnia,* Pars II, c. II, n. 11; Sanchez, *De Matrimonio,* Lib. I, Disp. VIII, n. 15.

[45] Didymus Upianus, *De Matrimonio Ius tum Naturae tum Canonicum* (Venetiis, 1760), n. 636.

sin could elicit a valid consent for marriage.[46] Accordingly Sanchez (1550-1610) came to be regarded as the spokesman for those authors who upheld this rule in opposition to the Thomistic theory which demanded a greater degree of mental capacity than that required for the commission of mortal sin.[47] Sanchez taught that a man is to be considered sane enough to enter the espousal contract when he has that degree of deliberation which suffices for the committing of mortal sin in a grave matter."[48] Therefore, an insane person was obviously incapable of marriage. Not every mentally disturbed person, however, was to be denied the right of marriage. It was observed that certain people appeared to be normal in their mental approach to most subjects, while at the same time, they seemed to be deranged regarding certain limited matters. As a result of this observation, a distinction began to be made between the *amentes* and the *dementes*. A person who was totally deranged was said to be *amens*, while a person who was disturbed only in some spe-

[46] "Constat a furioso nihil fieri posse, consensum liberum exigens qualem petunt sponsalia et matrimonium. Et idem dicendum est de mente capto, qui omnino usu rationis destituitur; secus est, si non caret omnino intellectu, quem vulgo 'tonto' appellamus; hic enim sponsalia et matrimonium inire potest: Ratio est manifesta, quia deliberationem sufficientem habet ad lethaliter delinquendum."—Sanchez, *De Matrimonio*, Lib. I, Disp. VIII, n. 15; Reiffenstuel (1642-1703), *Ius Canoncum Universum* (7 vols., Parisiis, 1864-1870) Lib. IV, Tit. I, n. 11.

[47] As will be seen in the canonical section of the present study, the writer believes, *salvo meliore iudicio*, that the two theories are not as directly opposed to one another as would at first appear and as is commonly accepted. St. Thomas Aquinas demands a greater degree of mental capacity than that required for the commission of mortal sin. Sanchez, on the other hand, would seem to require a degree of mental capacity necessary for the commission of mortal sin in a proportionately serious matter as that of marriage. His mortal sin norm refers to the deliberation required for entering into a valid matrimonal contract; Cf. *infra*, pp. 105-119.

[48] "Hoc tamen unum adverto, judicari sanae mentis, ut valide contrahat sponsalia quando eam deliberationem habet quae in materia gravi sufficeret ad culpam mortalem."—Sanchez, *De Matrimonio*, Lib. I, Disp. VIII, n. 17.

cific sphere of thought, while remaining sane in other matters, was said to be *demens.*

Sanchez stated that the authors of his time did not agree on whether the latter persons (*dementes*) really existed. The arguments used by those who denied the existence of *dementia,* taken in this restricted sense only, were based principally on the accepted teaching that the intellectual faculty of man, as the root of both the intellect and will, was spiritual and one. They reasoned that if this intellectual faculty had become sick and disturbed, the whole of that faculty was to be considered as affected and disturbed.[49] The more common opinion among the older authors, nevertheless, was that the mind could truly be affected in particular spheres, while remaining undisturbed regarding the majority of subjects.[50] If marriage were the matter regarding which such persons were deranged, they were to be denied the right to marry. But if the disturbance should concern some other matter, they were to be considered as capable of giving a valid matrimonial consent.

Gasparri noted that the question was a matter of dispute. He did not commit himself to either opinion, although he observed that in the civil law of his day no distinction was made between *amentia* and *dementia.*[51]

Authors also discussed the efficacy of a virtual intention in regard to marital consent. They wondered whether a marriage could be contracted in virtue of consent given by a person before he became insane. Sanchez held that the parties act as the ministers of the sacrament in marriage and that, consequently, a previously made and unrevoked intention, should not be considered sufficient for a valid marriage contract. He demanded an actual intention in the minister of the sacrament, and the party, therefore, had to be capable of a

[49] Sanchez, *De Matrimonio,* Lib. I, Disp. VIII, n. 22.

[50] Sanchez, *loc. cit.; Pontius, De Sacramento Matrimonii,* Lib. IV, Cap. I, n. 9; Upianus, *De Matrimonio,* n. 640.

[51] P. Gasparri, *De Matrimonio* (1904), II, 884.

human act.[52] Other authors, like Pontius[53] and De Lugo[54] while accepting the conclusion of Sanchez, presented a different reason for their position. They held that the intention formulated by a person who subsequently became insane no longer existed. Thus according to those authors an insane person literally lost his mind and will. A virtual intention, therefore, was impossible in such a person.[55]

SCHOLION. MENTAL ILLNESS AND MARRIAGES BY PROXY

A difficult problem for the authors was occasioned by the question of marriage by proxy.[56] It was asked whether a marriage entered into by proxy was valid if insanity occurred in the *mandans* after he gave the mandate but before its actual execution. Sanchez felt that such a marriage was to be regarded as valid.[57] Even though the parties themselves, and not their proxies, were the ministers of the sacrament, Sanchez believed that such a marriage was nevertheless valid. It was contracted through the agency of the proxy who presented the consent that had been validly given by the *mandans,* while he was of sound mind. This opinion was upheld by Pirhing[58] and Schmalzgrueber.[59] Pontius, on the other hand, denied the validity of a marriage by proxy. He held that the consent of the *mandans* was completely destroyed by the subsequent insanity, and that the proxy no longer could act for the *mandans.*[60] This opinion of Pontius

[52] Sanchez, *De Matrimonio,* Lib. I, Disp. VIII, n. 20; Smith, *Ignorance Affecting Matrimonial Consent,* p. 15.

[53] *De Sacramento Matrimonii,* Lib. IV, Cap. I, n. 12.

[54] *Disputationes,* III, *Tractatus de Sacramentis in Genere,* Disp. VIII, n. 108.

[55] De Lugo, *loc. cit.*

[56] This problem, because of the comparatively slow travel of the day, was a very realistic one and in practical need of a solution.

[57] Sanchez, *De Matrimonio,* Lib. II, Disp. XI, n. 12.

[58] Pirhing, *Ius Canonicum,* Lib. I, Tit. I, n. 79.

[59] "Mors omnia solvit: etiam ergo consensum ad matrimonium cujus contractum impossibilem reddat; non ita impossibilem eundem reddat amentia."—Schmalzgrueber, *Ius Ecclesiasticum,* Lib. I, Tit. XXXVIII n. 20.

[60] Pontius, *De Sacramento Matrimonii,* Lib. II, Cap. XV, n. 14.

was sustained by De Lugo.[61] Later authors, e.g., Wernz (1842-1914)[62] and Gasparri,[63] also denied the validity of such a marriage.

The point was not definitely settled until the promulgation of the Code of Canon Law. Canon 1089, § 3 stated: "If, before the proxy makes the contract in the name of the principal, the latter has revoked the commission, or has fallen into insanity, the marriage is invalid, even though both the proxy and the other contracting party are unaware of what has occurred."[64]

ARTICLE 2. PRE-CODE JUDICIAL PRACTICE IN MARRIAGE CASES INVOLVING A PLEA OF MENTAL ILLNESS

In the period between the Council of Trent and the Code of Canon Law, marriage cases which were referred to the Holy See were adjudicated principally by the Sacred Roman Rota and the Sacred Congregation of the Council.[65] If the validity of a marriage was attacked on the basis of defective consent due to mental illness, the case was ordinarily examined by the Sacred Roman Rota.[66]

[61] De Lugo, *Disputationes*, III, *Tractatus de Sacramentis in genere*, Disp. VIII, n. 108.

[62] Wernz, *Ius Decretalium*, Vol. IV, *Ius Matrimoniale* (Romae, 1904), n. 45, nota 94.

[63] Gasparri, *De Matrimonio* (1904), II, n. 993.

[64] *Codex Iuris Canonici Pii X Pontificus Maximi iussu digestus, Benedicti Papae XV auctoritate promulgatus, Praefatione, Fontium Annotatione et Indice Analytico-Alphabetico ab Emo Petro Card. Gasparri Auctus* (Romae: Typis Polyglottis Vaticanis, 1917; reimpressio, 1934), canon 1089, § 3 (hereafter reference is made simply to the number of the canon).

[65] Cappello, *De Curia Romana iuxta Reformationem a Pio X Sapientissime Inductam* (2 vols., Romae, Ratisbonae, Neo-Eboraci, Cincinnati, 1911-1912), I, 188; Hilling, *Procedure at the Roman Curia* (New York, 1907), pp. 64, 133.

[66] The Rota was silenced in the eighteenth century, but was restored through the Constitution *Sapienti Consilio* of Pius X on June 29, 1909. Cf. *Acta Apostolicae Sedis, Commentarium Officiale* (Romae, 1909), I (1909, 15, 23, 24; *Codicis Iuris Canonici Fontes, cura emi. Petri Card. Gasparri editi* (9 vols., Romae postea Civitate Vaticana. Typis

SECTION A. THE DOCTRINE OF THE AUTHORS AS APPLIED IN COURT DECISIONS

In 1624 the Rota declared that individuals who were deprived of the use of reason should be considered incapable of entering a valid marriage contract.[67] It made no difference whether this lack of reason was verified in every respect or only in the matter of marriage itself.[68] Moreover, insanity, whether temporray or permanent, precluded a valid consent as long as the lack of reason was verified at the moment of the contract.[69]

The judges of ecclesiastical courts appealed to the natural law itself in presenting reasons for their decisions.[70] In at least one case, they declared that a possible injustice inflicted upon the sane party mattered little in so far as the validity of a marriage which was being attacked on grounds of mental illness was concerned.[71]

A person was considered to have the required intellectual capacity for a valid marriage consent if he had the mental capacity necessary for the commission of mortal sin.[72] This

Polyglottis Vaticanis, 1923-1939) (vols. VII-IX, ed. cura et studio Emi. Iustiniani Card. Serédi), n. 682. (Hereafter cited as *Fontes.*) During the intervening period marriage cases were examined in a judicial manner by the Sacred Congregation of the Council.

[67] "Furiosus, mente captus, ac sensu carens non possunt contrahere matrimonium, si ratione vel sensu omnio destitutus, perpetuo furore, vel defectu sensus laborat."—*Sanctae Romanae Rotae Decisiones coram Buratti* (Romae, 1624), annot. ad decis. 763.

[68] "Neque refert si insania ad omnes vitae moralis actus extendatur (quo in casu vocatur amentia), vel ad unam vel alteram rem restringatur (quo in casu vocatur dementia): dementes enim, in iis circa quae insanirent, amentibus aequiparantur."—*Sacrae Romanae Rotae Decisiones seu Sententiae (ab anno 1909)* (Romae: Typis Vaticanis, 1912-), II (1910), 145. (Hereafter cited as *S.R.R. Decisiones.*)

[69] *S.R.R. Decisiones,* II (1910), 145.

[70] *S.R.R. Decisiones,* I (1909), 87; V (1913), 564; X (1918), 143.

[71] *Thesaurus Resolutionum S. C. Concilii* (167 vols., Urbani, 1718-1741; Romae, 1741-1908), CXII, 112. (Hereafter cited as *Thesaurus.*)

[72] ASS, XL (1907), 741; *S.R.R. Decisiones* V (1913), 149, 563; VII (1915), 217; X (1918) 3.

minimum standard of intellectual capacity for a valid marriage consent was declared as a norm accepted by everyone.[73]

While the courts gave heed to the fact that medical experts disagreed on the existence of a difference between *amentia* (total insanity) and *dementia*,[74] the tribunals themselves accepted such a distinction. They held that a person suffering from *monomania* (*dementia*) could validly marry as long as marriage was not the object of his mental aberration.[75]

The ecclesiastical courts also subscribed to the view that an insane person could validly contract marriage during a lucid interval.[76]

If a doubt arose, however, as to whether the contract was made during a lucid interval or during a period of insanity, the courts normally followed the presumption favoring insanity at the time of the marriage.[77] On the other hand, if lucid intervals were the rule rather than the exception, the presumption favored sanity and consequently, the validity of the contract.[78]

A good summary of the practice and doctrine of the ecclesiastical courts in cases of mental illness in relation to marriage consent can be found in the *In Iure* section of a case

[73] "Ratio est quia, in matrimonio, non alia requiritur voluntatis deliberatio, quam quae requiritur ad peccandum lithaliter, uti dicunt theologi, quae profecto deliberatio adesse potest in iis, qui dicuntur semi-fatui. Et haec est doctrina ab omnibus admissa."—*S.S.R. Decisiones*, V (1913), 563.

[74] *Thesaurus*, CLXIV, 355.

[75] *S.R.R. Decisiones*, I (1909), 87; II (1910), 145.

[76] "Si amens lucida habet intervalla, et in his contrahit, matrimonium validum est."—*S.S.R. Decisiones*, VII (1915), 218; Smith, *Ignorance Affecting Matrimonial Consent*, p. 20.

[77] "Cumque testes deponant de Annae insania ante et post matrimonium . . . insaniam contendit, praesumendam esse pariter de tempore celebrati matrimonii."—*Thesaurus*, XXXII (1763), 39

[78] "Certum esse videtur ex depositione testium examinatorum, Barbaram persaepe habuisse lucida mentis intervalla. Qua cerrente probatione, non licet eidem nullum dicere matrimonium, nisi concludentissime probet, ipsam tempore praeciso celebrati matrimonii a recto mentis sensu fuisse prorsus alienam."—*Thesaurus*, XLVII (1778), 173.

adjudicated by the Rota a few years before the promulgation of the Code.[79] The Court declared:

> As is well known, marriage arises only from a valid matrimonial consent. It is, however, certain that the consent required for a valid marriage, as for each human act and for every contract, must find its origin in the knowledge of the intellect and the deliberation of the will. Consequently, the insane must be denied the right to enter upon a marriage.

The Scared Roman Rota then recalled the decision of Pope Innocent III of December 28, 1205, to the Bishop of Vercelli.[80] The Court continued:

> What was said in the decision of Innocent III concerning the violently insane is also extended by all doctors to those who suffer from quiet and tranquil insanity; *Amentia* is to be regarded as a generic term which embraces at least two species, namely, violent and quiet insanity. Marriage is not to be denied to people who suffer from *dementia,* i.e., who are not insane with respect to all things but only regarding one or other point, as long as their mental aberration does not concern marriage itself. These two things, therefore, must be carefully noted: 1) The preceding does not hold true unless the *amentia* (or, respectivély, the *dementia*) is complete (*plena et perfecta*), . . . therefore, those who are only partially insane can validly enter marriage. The reason is, that in marriage no more deliberation of will is required than that which is required for the committing of mortal sin. This is in accord with the teachings of the theologians. The necessary deliberation can be present in the partially insane. The above is the doctrine which is accepted by all. 2) *Amentia* does not prevent marriage unless it is continuous . . . but, in case there is a doubt whether the period of time in which the marriage was contracted was a lucid period or not, then it must be presumed not to have been a lucid interval if the *amentia* is proven to have been present both before and after the celebration of the marriage.

[79] *S.S.R. Decisiones,* V (1913), 563.

[80] *Supra,* p. 17.

SECTION B. THE USE OF EXPERTS IN CASES OF MENTAL ILLNESS AND MARRIAGE

Zacchia's recommendation that expert witnesses be employed in cases involving mental disturbances was generally adopted by ecclesiastical tribunals.[81] In almost every case there is indication that such expert testimony was called upon.[82] However, it must be noted that it was the tribunal which gave the judicial sentence, and not the medical experts. The experts were in no sense regarded as judges.[83]

In one of the earliest decisions of the restored Rota a warning was given against too careful a choice of experts. It was pointed out that many erroneous theories were proposed at the time, and that some of these were accepted as true by certain men of great fame. The Rota warned that these theories frequently reduced the spiritual faculties of man to negligible quantities. On the other hand, the Rota realized that many illnesses and disturbances were due to psychological causes, and that great progress had been made in this particular field of medicine. "Therefore," it stated, "it would be foolhardy to reject conclusions which are unani-

[81] Zacchia, *Quaestiones Medico-Legales,* Lib. II, Tit. I, Q. 1, § 1; Cf. *supra* p. 31.

[82] *Thesaurus,* XXXII, 39; CXLII, 467; CLVIII, 609; CLXIV, 354; *S.R.R. Decisiones,* I (1909), 87-92; II (1910), 146; V (1913), 570; W. M. Pickard, i n his *Judicial Experts: A Source of Evidence in Ecclesiastical Trials,* (The Catholic University of America Canon Law Studies, n. 389) (Washington, D.C.: The Catholic University of America Press, 1958) states on page 55: "All of the pre-Code teaching which the writer could consult revealed absolutely nothing concerning the importance of experts in matrimonial causes wherein invalidity was claimed on the grounds of insanity at the time of the marriage." Pickard states that it appeared to be the accepted practice that the judge would examine the testimony of acquaintances of the allegedly insane person, and pass sentence on the case without seeking the advice of expert physicians or psychiatrists.

The present writer is of the opinion that it was the accepted practice of the courts to call upon experts in the field of medicine, even though there was no prescription of law which made this obligatory.

[83] *Thesaurus,* CXLII, 452; CLVIII, 615; *S.R.R. Decisiones* X (1918), 5.

mously accepted by medical authorities in this field of medical endeavor."[84]

It remained for the Code of Canon Law to make it obligatory that experts be consulted whenever annulments were sought because of a defective consent flowing from a mental deficiency.[85]

A study of the history of Canon Law in relation to mental illness and marriage shows that many advances were made. The basic legal norms according to which the validity of marriages contracted by the mentally sick were judged remained unchanged. Much progress was made, however, in the field of medicine. Consequently, there was a better understanding of the incapacitating effects of mental illness. This progress has continued since the publication of the Code of Canon Law. It is hoped that a further examination of the influence of mental illness upon marital consent, as well as a commentary upon the pertinent law of the Code will throw additional light upon this difficult problem.

[84] "Conclusiones in hac re scientificas unanimi ore a facultate medica admissas reicere nefas esset."—*S.R.R. Decisiones*, I (1909), 87.

[85] Canon 1982.

PART TWO

CANONICAL COMMENTARY

CHAPTER IV

GENERAL NOTIONS

The study of mental illness belongs properly to the field of medicine. Mental illness, however, becomes an object of study for ecclesiastical and civil lawyers because of its influence on the ability on the part of a person afflicted with mental illness to place legal acts. Mental illness can diminish or even totally destroy a person's capacity for legal acts, and, consequently, it can disqualify him for marriage.

Marriage, at Church law, may be considered as a Sacrament or as a bilateral contract between a man and a woman. In the case of the baptized, these two aspects of marriage are inseparably united because, as Canon 1012, 2 states: "between baptized persons there can be no valid contract of marriage without its being a Sacrament."[1]

Whether marriage be a Sacrament or not, it nevertheless retains its essential elements of a natural contract and, as a consequence, is governed by the natural law of contracts. His Holiness Pope Pius XI declared:

> The Sacred partnership of marriage is constituted both by the will of God and the will of man. From God comes the very institution of marriage, the ends for which it was instituted, the laws that govern it, the blessings that flow from it: while man, through generous surrender of his own person made to another for the whole span of life, becomes, with the help and cooperation of God, the author of each particular marriage, with the duties and blessings annexed thereto from divine institution.[2]

In treating of the effects of mental illness on matrimonial consent, the contractual idea is stressed and one prescinds

[1] Canon 1012, 2: "Quare inter baptizatos nequit matrimonialis contractus validus consistere, quin sit eo ipso sacramentum."

[2] Pius XI, litt. encycl. *"Casti Connubii,"* 31 Dec., 1930 *AAS.* XXII (1930), 541.

from the idea of the Sacrament entirely. Consequently, the contract of marriage, in so far as it is effected by man, will be the subject of examination in this study.

The question placed before the court when a marriage is attacked on the basis of mental illness can be summarized as follows: can it be proven that, in the marriage which is now before the court, one of the parties lacked the necessary mental or pyschical capacity of effecting a consent sufficient to enter a valid matrimonial contract as a result of some mental illness or disturbance?

In view of the fact that every marriage is founded on the basis of a natural contract, Church law has to look upon marriage as a legal matter with juridical consequences. The contractual nature of marriage also answers the objection that the doctrine of the Church regarding marriage shows too great a dependency on juridic thought. Marriage is of necessity treated as a legal matter because it is a legal contract.[3]

Before attempting to examine the effects of mental illness on the juridic capacity of a person to enter marriage it will be necessary to establish precisely the minimum mental or psychical ability demanded to enter a valid marriage contract. Only when that mental capacity has been determined can one attempt to draw a line between the psychical ability for marriage and the psychical inability which results from mental illness. In order to establish the psychical requirements for marriage, it is necessary first of all to consider the nature of marriage, the object of marital consent, and the efficient cause which brings a particular marriage into being.

ARTICLE 1. MARRIAGE AND ITS CONSTITUTIVE ELEMENT OF CONSENT

A definition of marriage is not to be found in the Code of Canon Law. The well-known definition of Justinian: "*Nuptiae autem, sive matrimonium, est viri et mulieris coniunctio individuam vitae consuetudinem continens,*"[4] was adopted by

[3] Kienitz, *Christliche Ehe* (Frankfurt, 1938), p. 17.
[4] Inst. (1, 9) 1.

Gratian[5] and the decretals of Gregory IX,[6] but is not to be found in the Code. However, Canons 1012, § 1,[7] 1081, § 2,[8] and 1082, § 1[9] provide the necessary elements for the formulation of a definition.

Marriage considered in the act of its celebration (*in fieri*) can be defined as a legitimate contract wherein a man and a woman by their mutual consent give and accept the permanent and exclusive right to each other's body for acts which of themselves are suitable for the procreation of children. Marriage considered passively, or as a state (*in facto esse*), may be defined as a society of a man and a woman arising from their mutual marital consent.[10] The state of marriage is, as it were, the result of the act of marriage. The present study of the effect of mental illness on marriage considers marriage from the point of view of a state being entered into, i.e., marriage *in fieri*.

SECTION A. THE NATURE, ENDS AND ESSENTIAL PROPERTIES OF MARRIAGE

a. The Nature of Marriage

When marriage is considered *in fieri*, it exhibits all the elements essential to a bilateral contract. Such a contract is

[5] *Dict. ante* c. 1, C. XXVII, p. 2.

[6] C. 11, X, *De Praesumpt*, II, 23.

[7] "Christus Dominus ad sacramenti dignitatem evexit ipsum contractum matrimonialem inter baptizatos."

[8] "Consensus matrimonialis est actus voluntatis quo utraque pars tradit et acceptat jus in corpus, perpetuum et exclusivum, in ordine ad actus per se aptos ad prolis generationem."

[9] "Ut matrimonialis consensus haberi possit, necesse est ut contrahentes saltem non ignorent matrimonium esse societatem permanentem inter virum et mulierem ad filios procreandos."

[10] St. Thomas Aquinas, *Summa Theologica*, diligenter emendata Nicolai, Sylvii, Billuart et C. J. Drioux notis ornata (6. ed., 8 vols., Barri-Ducis, 1870), Suppl. q. 44, art 1-3, *in corp artt;* Sanchez, *De Sancto Matrimonii Sacramento Tomi Tres* (3 vols., Antwerpiae, 1626), Lib. II, Disp. 1, n. 1-2; Schmalzgruber, *Ius Ecclesiasticum Universum* (5 vols. in 12, Romae, 1843-1845), Lib. IV, Tit. 1, n. 288; Cappello, *Tractatus Canonico-Moralis de Sacramentis, Vol. V, De Matrimonio* (6 ed., Taurini et Romae: Marietti, 1950) n. 2.

an agreement of two parties regarding the same thing. It involves an obligation of commutative justice for both parties to give, do, or omit to do something.[11] A consensual contract is a contract effected by the mutual agreement of the parties involved. No further act is required for the existence of such a contract. A real contract, on the other hand, demands a further action to follow upon the consent in order that it be binding as a contract at law.

The elements of a bilateral contract are: 1) a subject, namely, at least two persons capable of contracting; 2) an object concerning which the contract is made; 3) legitimate consent; 4) a consideration or *causa;* 5) an obligation arising from commutative justice; 6) and finally, an obligation incumbent upon each party to the contract.[12] In every valid marriage there are: 1) two persons, a man and a woman; 2) the offer and acceptance of the rights to each other's body in a common conjugal life; 3) the mutual consent of both parties; 4) the proposed procreation and education of children, an acknowledged mutual aid, and the recognized remedy for concupiscence; 5) the assumed duty of conjugal fidelity regarding the marital obligations inherent in the contract; and 6) the reciprocal nature of this duty or obligation as binding equally upon both parties. Marriage, therefore, can be rightly termed a bilateral contract.[13]

As a contract, marriage is subject to the general norms governing contracts. It must contain the essential contractual elements, namely the matter, or the object, of the contract and the consent by which it is effected. These elements must be such as to constitute marriage in its own specific

[11] Smith, *Ignorance Affecting Matrimonial Consent*, p. 31.

[12] Vermeersch, *Theologiae Moralis Principia, Responsa, Consilia* (edito tertia, 4 vols., Universita Gregorianà, Romae: 1933-1937), Vol. II, nn. 374, 376; Cappello, *De Matrimonio*, n. 23.

[13] Cf. Cappello, *loc. cit.* As will be seen in the treatment of the constitutive element of marriage, the contract of marriage is a consensual rather than a real contract. The mutual consent of the parties suffices to make the contract binding. The actual exercise of marital rights by the act of marital intercourse is not required for the validity of the contract.

being, distinguishing it from all other contracts. The contract of matrimony has some unique characteristics which set it apart from all other contracts. Leo XIII in the encyclical "*Arcanum Divinae Sapientiae*" insists that matrimony is never a mere civil contract, but that it is always and everywhere a matter of religion. He writes:

> Marriage has God for its author, and was from the beginning a kind of foreshadowing of the Incarnation of His Son; and therefore, there abides in it something holy and religious; not extraneous but innate; not derived from man but implanted by nature. Innocent III, therefore, and Honorius III, our predecessors, affirmed not falsely or rashly that the sacramentum of marriage exists both among the faithful and among infidels.[14]

It is not only as a sacred and religious contract that marriage differs from all other contracts. Some of the specific characteristics of the contract of marriage pointed out by the authors[15] are the following: 1) The contract of marriage is a natural contract because it is based in a special way on nature itself, and it is intended for the good of nature and of the entire human race. This cannot be said of any other contract. 2) The contract of marriage, unlike other contracts, can take place only between the two different sexes and, moreover, only between one man and one woman. 3) The matrimonial consent cannot be supplied by any human power except by the contracting parties themselves. 4) The rights which arise from the matrimonial contract cannot be altered or taken away entirely by public authority. Neither can these rights be transferred to others. 6) In other contracts the parties themselves can determine the object, effects and obligations of the contract. However, in the contract of mar-

[14] Leo XIII, litt. encycl. "*Arcanum Divinae Sapientiae*," 10 Feb. 1880—*Leonis XIII Pontificis Maximi Acta* (Romae: ex Typographia Vaticana, 1882), II (1880-1881) p. 22.

[15] Cappello, *De Matrimonio*, n. 24; Petrus Gasparri, *Tractatus de Matrimonio* (ed. nova, 2 vols., Romae: Typis Vaticanis, 1932), I, n. 17; Van Welie, *Canoniek Huwelijksrecht*, (Nijmegen-Utrecht: Dekker en van De Vegt N. V., 1954), p. 28.

riage nature itself has determined the essenials of the contract. The will of the parties cannot change the essential elements of the contract. 7) The contract of matrimony is by nature perpetual which again is not the case in any other contract. 8) Finally, those bound by the contract of marriage are bound irrevocably to it. They cannot agree to dissolve the contract. Such a dissolution is possible in other bilateral contracts if the rights of third parties are safeguarded.

Notwithstanding these important characteristics and the objections of some of the authors, matrimony must be considered as a true bilateral contract. for it meets with the general definition of a contract as stated above.[16]

[16] Vlaming-Bender, *Praelectiones Iuris Matrimonii ad Normam Codicis Iuris Canonici* (4. ed. by L. Bender, Bussum in Hollandia, 1950), p. 3, cites and answers some of the arguments of authors who oppose the use of the term contract with regard to marriage. He states: "Hodie aliqui coeperunt impugnare usum verbi contractus quando agitur de matrimonio. Hoc nomen aiunt est saltem minus idoneum, quia ut nimis iuridicum unum tantum matrimonii aspectum, nempe illud iuridicum, in lucem ponit negligens aspectum moralem. Alii, praecipue iuris civilis periti, insuper perhibent contractui proprium esse ut partes libere determinent obiectum consensus contractualis, extendentes aut restringentes hoc obiectum prout ipsis placet. Hoc autem in matrimonio nullatenus admittitur, quia obiectum matrimonialis consensus a Deo est statutum et quidem sic ut hominibus non competat afferre mutationes. Ad clare discernendum matrimonium a contractibus in sensu proposito, necesse est aut valde commendandum ut matrimonium non dicatur contractus, sed alio designetur nomine. Quidam tunc proponunt "institutum" (Gallice: institution), quo nomine designatur aliquod institutum iuridicum, cuius iura et obligationes ab ipsa lege (divina aut humana) sunt statuta, ita ut hominibus nihil remaneat nisi aut totum institutum cum omnibus iuribus et obligationibus instituto propriis actu voluntatis amplecti aut ab hoc se abstinere ... Fatendum videtur usum nominis contractus aliqua secumferre etiam incommoda, praecipue quando in iure civili contractus potius significat duorum consensum in idem placitum quod in quolibet casu a partibus libere statuitur, extenditur aut restringitur. Haec incommoda tamen non raro exaggerantur. Nomen contractus in iure canonice introductum iam ab antiquo tempore etiam maxima habet commoda. In lucem ponit non ipsam maritalem coniunctionem sed voluntatis actum (consensum), ad ordinem moralem et iuridicum pertinentem, façere matrimonium.

One may object that it was only in the twelfth century that marriage was first called a contract, and that it has been only since then that the rules of contractual law have been applied to matrimony. However, it is also true to say that at all times the very existence of marriage at law was made dependent on a declaration of the will of the parties involved.[17] Even though this is not proof that marriage was actually considered a true contract, neither does it exclude the contractual nature of marriage. Perhaps it may be said with Le Bras that religious and social interests and popular practices and customs were responsible for the fact that the contractual nature of marriage was being overlooked or perhaps even forgotten altogether.[18] Definitely the contractual nature of marriage was explicitly recognized by the Scho-

Sic etiam usu nominis in lucem trahitur virum et mulierem ad vitam coniugalem uniri actu voluntatis et non caeco instinctu aut propensione naturali cui homo resistere non potest aut quadam determinatione divina (in sensu panteistico), ut hodie a pluribus perhibetur et multis placet, quia isti conceptus optime inservire possunt ad iustificandas relationes sexuales legibus divinis et ecclesiasticis contrarias. Docens matrimonium esse contractum, Ecclesia proclamat actum quo homines coniuges fiunt esse actum voluntatis, qui est in potestate hominis et qui ut sit bonus conformis esse debet regulis prudentiae et etiam legibus quas Deus et Ecclesia statuerunt propter bonum publicum et privatum."

It would be outside the scope of this study to enter more deeply into this controversy. See also Coronata, *Institutiones Iuris Canonici, De Sacramentis, Vol. III, De Matrimonio* (2 ed., Taurini-Romae: Marietti, 1947), n. 2; Fässler, *Die Schizophrenie als Ehenichtigkeitsgrund im Kanonischen Recht* (Freiburg in der Schweiz: Paulusdrückerei, 1951), pp. 7-9.

[17] Classical Roman law did not consider marriage a bilateral contract in the juridic sense. This law contemplated marriage as a way of life, a domestic union of a man and a woman, regulated and protected by the law for the purpose of a lifelong mutual companionship. However, this way of life also was made to depend on the consent of the parties. Cf. *supra* p. 7.

[18] Le Bras, "Mariage (La Doctrine du mariage chez les théologiens et les Canonistes)," *Dictionnaire de Théologie Catholique*, IX, 2. part, coll. 2182. (Hereafter cited *D.T.C.*)

lastics in the twelfth century.[19] St. Albertus Magnus,[20] St. Thomas Aquinas,[21] and Scotus[22] all speak of marriage as a true contract.

The Code of Canon Law itself presupposes the contractual nature of matrimony. Canon 1012 states. "Our Lord raised to the dignity of a sacrament the marriage contract itself between baptized persons. Hence between baptized persons there can be no valid contract of marriage without its being also a sacrament.[23]

In any contract there must be a "meeting of the minds" of the parties on the object of the contract. In the contract of marriage both parties must agree on the object of marriage itself. The essential object of matrimony is variously designated by authors as the marriage union, the marital relationship and the conjugal right.[24]

[19] As will be seen later, the Scholastics and Canonists of that time did not agree on the constitutive element of the contract of marriage; Cf. *infra*, p. 63.

[20] St. Albertus Magnus in treating of the necessity of consent even in the sacrament of matrimony stated: "Responsio ad hoc est, quod istud sacramentum, ut prius dictum est, consistit in quadam commutatione sive contractu ipsius personae contrahentis: talis autem commutatio non potest fieri sine consensu commutantis, sive contrahentis: et ideo in isto et non in aliis requiritur consensus."—*In IV Sent.* Dist. XXVII, a. 6.

[21] "In matrimonio, cum sit quidam contractus, est quaedam promissio, per quam talis vir tali mulieri determinatur."—*In IV Sent.* Dist. XXXI, q. 1, a. 2, ad 2.

[22] "Contractus matrimonii est maris et feminae mutua translatio corporum suorum pro usu perpetuo ad procreandam prolem, debite educandam."—*Opus Oxon.*, Dist. XXVI, q. un., n. 7; "Dicitur enim contractus, quasi simul tractus duarum voluntatum."—*Ibidem*, n. 8.

[23] Canon 1012 § 1; "Christus Dominus ad sacramenti dignitatem evexit ipsum contractum matrimonialem inter baptizatos. § 2. Quare inter baptizatos nequit matrimonialis contractus validus consistere, quin sit eo ipso sacramentum."

[24] St. Thomas Aquinas, *Summa Theologica*, Suppl., q. 44, art. 1; q. 49, art. 3; Barbosa, *Collectanea Doctorum tam Veterum quam Recentiorum in Ius Pontificium Universum*, (5 vols., Lugduni, 1637), IV, I, n. 7; Payen, *De Matrimonio in Missionibus* (Zi-Ka-Wei, Typographia T'ou-se-we, 1935-1936), I, n. 75.

The Code, dealing specifically with the knowledge necessary for the contracting of a valid marriage, defines the essential object of the contract as a permanent and exclusive society between a man and woman for the procreation of children.[25] Again, in describing marital consent, the Code states: "Marriage consent is an act of the will by which each party gives and accepts the perpetual and exclusive right over the body for the exercise of acts suitable of themselves for the procreation of children.[26] From these two canons it can be concluded that a man and a woman, when marrying, must intend to form a union, to create a bond between themselves, to effect an intimate mutual relationship by giving and accepting the right to each other's body.[27] The essential object of the matrimonial contract, therefore, can be defined as a conjugal society which has its foundation in the mutual concession and acceptance of corporal rights for procreation. The object of the marriage contract, or the intimate union willed by the parties in marriage, implies the necessity for cohabitation and the need of a community of bed and board. However, such cohabitation and community of life does not belong to the essence of the matrimonial contract. They are required, rather, for the integrity and the perfection of conjugal life. They are not required for the *esse* but for the *melius esse* of the marriage contract.[28] The material object of the contract of matrimony is the parties themselves. The parties in marriage give themselves to each other. The formal object, or the further specification of the material object, can be described as the mutual giving and receiving of the right to one another's body for those acts which of themselves are suitable for the procreation of offspring. The words: of acts which of themselves are suitable for the

[25] Canon 1081 § 1: "Ut matrimonialis consensus haberi possit necesse est ut contrahentes saltem non ignorent matrimonium esse societatem permanentem inter virum et mulierem ad filios procreandos."

[26] Canon 1081, § 2: "Consensus matrimonialis est actus voluntatis quo utraque pars tradit et acceptat jus in corpus, perpetuum et exclusivum, in ordine ad actus per se aptos ad prolis generationem."

[27] Payen, *op. cit.*, I, n. 70.

[28] Cappello, *De Matrimonio*, n. 6.

procreation of offspring denote the *finis operis,* the essential end of marriage, while at the same time providing a practical norm to decide what is and what is not lawful in marital relations.

Though a person does not have the absolute and total right over his body, he does have the right to life, to bodily integrity, and to the legitimate use of his body. It is one aspect of this right to the legitimate use of the body which is mutually given and received in the contract of marriage. The right to use one's body is transferred only in so far as the body can be used for acts which of themselves can generate offspring. Marriage, therefore, does not imply a transferral of all the rights that one has over one's body.

A distinction must likewise be drawn between the right that is granted and received in marriage and the actual exercise of that right. Only the giving and receiving of the right itself is essential to the marriage contract. A valid marriage can exist irrespective of the actual execution of conjugal acts.[29]

It is necessary to mention here a controversy which has arisen regarding the formal object of marriage. There are certain well-known authors[30] who insist that the formal object of marriage must be specified even further. Accepting the mutual right to one another's body for acts suitable for the generation of children as the formal object of marital consent, they observe that this right can be exercised only by the act of marital intercourse. The act which is suitable for the procreation of offspring, they contend, can only be the act of carnal copulation. Consequently, they demand a further specific determination of the formal object of the contract of marriage.

Instead of simply accepting as the formal object of

[29] Cf. *infra*, p. 60.

[30] Vlaming-Bender, *Praelectiones Iuris Matrimonii*, p. 381; Knecht, *Handbuch des Katholischen Eherechts* (Freiburg im Breisgau: Herder, 1928), p. 548; Oesterle, "Nullitas Matrimonii ex Capite Ignorantiae," *Ephemerides Theologicae Lovanienses* (Lovanii, Universitas Catholica Lovaniensis, 1924-), XV (1938), 647.

marital consent the mutual right to each other's body for acts which of themselves are suitable for the generation of offspring, they specify it further by defining and requiring as the formal object of marital consent the right to each other's body for acts of marital intercourse or carnal copulation. They demand knowledge of the manner in which marital intercourse is actually executed. This opinion is opposed to the more common and, *salvo meliore iudicio,* more correct opinion which does not demand this further specification.[31] If one gives and receives in marriage the right to the body for acts suitable for the procreation of offspring, one implicitly gives and receives also the right to marital intercourse and, consequently, no further specification of the formal object of marriage is necessary. This latter opinion has the support of both Thomas Sanchez[32] and St. Thomas Aquinas.[33] The opinion which holds that the formal object of marriage is the right to the body for acts of copulation, must of necessity require that the parties specifically know of the nature and manner of the marital act of copulation. In this conclusion lies precisely the importance of this controversy.[34] The second opinion, on the other hand, holds that the general intention coupled with suf-

[31] Gasparri, *De Matrimonio,* II, n. 805; Wernz-Vidal, *Ius Canonicum,* (7 vols. in 8), *Vol. V, Ius Matrimoniale,* (Romae: Apud Aedes Universitatis Gregorianae, 1927-1928), n. 457; Vermeersch-Creusen, *Epitome Iuris Canonici* (Mechliniae-Romae: H. Dessain, 1940), II, n. 369; Chelodi, *Ius Matrimoniale* (3 ed. Tridenti: Libr. Edit. Tridentum, 1921), n. 110.

[32] "Quare dicendum est, consensum matrimonium constituentem, non esse explicite in carnalem copulam, sed in ius, et potestatem ad talem copulam: implicite autem, et virtute ad copulam. Probatur quia carnalis copulo non est de matrimonii essentia, seu ejus effectus et operatio; perfectio autem essentialis consistit in mutua corporum traditione ad copulam: ergo consensus efficiens matrimonium non fertur explicite in copulam, sed in potestatem, et implicite in copulam."—Sanchez, *De Sancto Matrimonii Sacramento,* Lib. II, disp. 28, n. 3.

[33] *In IV Sent.,* dist. 28, q. un. art. 4; dist. 30, q. 2, art. 1.

[34] Oesterle, "Art. cit.," *Ephemerides Theologicae Lovanienses,* XV (1938), 657 states explicitly: "Ille qui non est instructus in scientia sexuali, est incapax ad consensum matrimonialem praestandum."

ficient knowledge of giving the right to one's body for acts suitable for generation is sufficient for the making of a valid marriage contract.[35]

b. The Ends of Marriage

Canon 1013, § 1 states: "The primary end of marriage is the procreation and education of offspring; the secondary end, mutual support and the relief of concupiscence."[36] Procreation is the natural end of the marital act. It is the very purpose of the institution of marriage.

The Sacred Congregation of the Holy Office in its decree of April 1, 1944, declared:[37]

> In answer to the doubt: whether the proposed opinion of some modern authors can be admitted, which opinion denies that the primary end of marriage is the procreation and education of offspring, or holds that the secondary ends of marriage are not essentially subordinate to the primary end, but are rather equal and independent, the answer must be given as being: Negative.

This decree of the Holy Office rejected the following three propositions: First, that all the ends of marriage are equal to the primary end of matrimony. Secondly, that the secondary ends of marriage are independent of the primary end. Finally, that the secondary ends are not subordinate to the primary end of marriage.[38]

Education, the second element of the primary end of marriage, is a necessary right and obligation arising from the procreation of children itself. Man, being composed of a body and a rational soul, has both a physical and a moral life. His physical life is provided for through generation, his rational life is developed through education.[39] Mutual

[35] Cf. *infra*, p. 92.

[36] "Matrimonii finis primarius est procreatio atque educatio prolis; secundarius mutuum adjutorium et remedium concupiscentiae."

[37] *AAS*, XXXVI (1944), 103.

[38] It would be beyond the scope of this study to enter into a further examination regarding the various theories on the purposes or ends of marriage.

[39] Cappello, *De Matrimonio*, n. 8.

aid, a secondary end of marriage, implies the life partnership in which the spouses spiritually, physically, psychologically and economically complement one another. The remedy for concupiscence is a secondary end of marriage. The marriage contract is ordained as a remedy for concupiscense inasmuch as the matrimonial bond provides a legitimate outlet for and fulfillment of sexual desire, while at the same time imposing the obligation of marital faithfulness.[40] The parties in a marriage may have other purposes or motives in mind when they make the marriage contract. Marriage itself, however, the object of their agreement, and as an institution of God and of nature, exists as objectively ordered to the primary and secondary ends of marriage, namely, the procreation and education of children, the mutual aid and the remedy of concupiscence. Canon 1013, § 1, as previously noted, distinguishes between primary and secondary ends of marriage. This distinction arises from the fact that procreation and education of offspring are fundamental and primary in the institution of matrimony as it actually exists. The secondary ends remain subordinate and dependent on the primary end. This distinction, as will be seen later,[41] is an important one. If the parties upon entering the contract of marriage know and do not willfully reject the primary ends of marriage, they automatically know and do not reject the secondary ends of marriage, for these are necessarily contained in the primary end.[42] Canon 1082, § 1 states that it suffices for a valid marriage contract that the contracting parties know that marriage is a permanent society for the procreation of children.[43]

c. *The Essential Properties of Marriage*

Canon 1013, § 2 declares that the essential properties of

[40] Ford, *The Validity of Virginal Marriage* (Worcester, Mass.: Harrigan Press, 1938), p. 20.

[41] Cf. *infra*, p. 95.

[42] Smith, *Ignorance Affecting Matrimonial Consent*, pp. 36-38.

[43] Ut matrimonialis consensus haberi possit, necesse est ut contrahentes saltem non ignorent matrimonium esse societatem permanentem inter virum et mulierem ad filios procreandos.

marriage are unity and indissolubility. It states: "The essential properties of the marriage contract are unity and indissolubility, to which the sacrament gives a special firmness in Christian marriage.[44] Every marriage contract, if it is to be valid, must have these two essential properties.

Marriage can be contracted only between one man and one woman. A new matrimonial contract cannot be validly entered into as long as the parties are bound by a previous bond.[45] Specifically opposed to the property of unity of marriage are simultaneous polyandry (union of one woman with several men) and simultaneous polygyny (union of one man with several women). Polyandry is opposed to the primary end of marriage inasmuch as, by throwing doubt on the paternity of the offspring, it deprives marriage of one of its resources for the education of the child. Polygyny is directly opposed to the secondary end of marriage inasmuch as it hinders domestic peace and reduces each of the wives to a condition of too great inferiority; indirectly it tends also to prejudice the education of children.[46]

The property of indissolubility makes marriage a perpetual union inviolable by merely human authority. It is directly opposed to divorce. Divorce in the strict sense aims at dissolving the bond of matrimony, giving the parties the freedom to enter a second marriage contract. Divorce by human authority, that is, by the parties themselves or by the civil law, is destructive of the primary end of marriage, and directly opposed to the secondary end.[47] Imperfect divorce relieves the parties of the obligation of conjugal society. It consists in a separation from bed and board. It does not include the separation or dissolution of the marriage bond. The bond remains intact and prevents the parties from entering

[44] Essentiales matrimonii proprietates sunt unitas ac indissolubilitas, quae in matrimonio Christiano peculiarem obtinent firmitatem ratione sacramenti.

[45] Gasparri, *Tractatus Canonicus de Matrimonio*, I, n. 10.

[46] Van Welie, *Canoniek Huwelijksrecht*, pp. 20-21.

[47] Cf. Joyce, *Christian Marriage*, (2. ed., London: Sheed and Ward, 1948), pp. 21-23.

into a new marriage contract.[48] The possibility of a dissolution of marriage by divine authority, as in the Pauline Privilege case, or the possibility of a legal separation, with the bond of marriage remaining intact, does not detract from the essential character of indissolubility of marriage.

If the right granted and received in the contract of marriage is not both permanent and exclusive, the contract itself is invalid.[49]

SECTION B. THE CONSTITUTIVE ELEMENT OF THE CONTRACT OF MARRIAGE

a. The Nature and Object of Marital Consent

After an examination of the nature, the object, the ends and the properties of marriage, it is in order to turn now to a consideration of the efficient cause of the marital contract. In other words, what brings a particular marriage into being?

In the encyclical *"Casti Connubii"* Pope Pius XI states:

> Although matrimony is of its very nature of divine institution, the human will too enters into it and performs a most noble part. For each individual marriage, inasmuch as it is a conjugal union of a particular man and woman, arises only from the free consent of each of the spouses; this free act of the will, by which each party hands over and accepts those rights proper to the state of marriage, is so necessary to constitute true marriage that it cannot be supplied by any human power.[50]

With these words Pius XI repeated what was already stated in the Code of Canon Law. Canon 1081 says: § 1. "Marriage is constituted by the duly manifested consent of persons juridically able to marry; and consent cannot be supplied by any

[48] Prümmer, *Manuale Theologiae*, III (4-5. ed., Friburgi Brisgoviae: Herder and Co., 1928), p. 475.

[49] Cf. Canons 1081, § 2; 1086 § 2; Vermeersch-Creusen, *Epitome Iuris Canonici*, II, n. 275; Smith, *Ignorance Affecting Matrimonial Consent*, p. 60.

[50] Pius XI, litt. encycl., *"Casti Connubii,"* 31 Dec. 1930—*AAS*, XXII (1930), 541.

human power. § 2. Marriage consent is an act of the will by which each party gives and accepts a perpetual and exclusive right over the body for the exercise of acts suitable of themselves for the procreation of children."[51] This declaration of the Code, in turn, is nothing but a restatement of the natural law. Human freedom and dignity require that a man and a woman can bind themselves to a valid marriage contract with its many rights and obligations only by a free and deliberate choice. It is precisely on this choice that man's temporal and eternal happiness often depends. In the marriage contract a person transfers to another his God-given right over his body for acts which of themselves are ordained for the generation of offspring. It is only by a free act of the will that this right can be given or received, and no human power can supply for this free act.[52] Marital consent is not only an intrinsic and essential element of marriage, but it is actually the efficient cause of every marriage contract.

The contract of marriage, moreover, is a consensual contract. In other words, mutual consent alone suffices to effect the contract of marriage. Marriage does not depend for its existence on the actual fulfilling of the contract or on the marital act itself. In the ninth century, Hincmar of Rheims (†882) held that the act of copulation was an essential element in the formation of a marriage.[53] This theory of the famous archbishop of Rheims was taught and defended at the law school of Bologna and, according to De Smet, became popular when it was openly defended by Gratian.[54]

[51] § 1. Matrimonium facit partium consensus inter personas jure habiles legitime manifestatus; qui nulla humana potestate suppleri valet. § 2. Consensus matrimonialis est actus voluntatis quo utraque pars tradit et acceptat jus in corpus, perpetuum et exclusivum, in ordine ad actus per se aptos ad prolis generationem.

[52] Van Welie, *Kanoniek Huwelijksrecht,* n. 146.

[53] *De Nuptiis Stephani et Filiae Regimundi Comitis:* "Nec habent nuptiae in se Christi et Ecclesiae Sacramentum, sicut beatus Augustinus dicit, si se nuptialiter non utuntur, id est, si eas non subsequitur commistio sexuum."—Migne, *Patrologiae Cursus Completus, Series Latina* (221 vols., Parisiis, 1844-1864), CXXVI, col. 137; Joyce, *Christian Marriage,* p. 55.

[54] De Smet in his *De Sponsalibus et Matrimonio* (Editio Quarta,

Brugis, 1927), pp. 78-80, n. 97, states: "Descriptam matrimonii indolem vindicarunt non pauci iique insignes Auctores, quos inter Regino Prumensis (†916) et Algerus Leodiensis (†1130), donec communior evaserit in Schola Bononiensi, praesertim postquam eam palam propugnaverat Gratianus, in *Decreto* (circa a. 1140 confecto), quaestione 2a Causae XXVII; hoc scil. loco, adductis argumentis et auctoritatibus pro et contra, controversiam in dictum sensum solvit, salva tamen aliqua restrictione infra indicanda; dissolvi autem docebat initiatum matrimonium per votum, impotentiam et, quod nota, per superveniens matrimonium consummatum; matrimonium vero consummatum indissolubile proclamabet. Nimirum, a) c. 16 et 17, *provocat ad* auctoritatem S. Augustini (Non dubium est illam mulierem non pertinere ad matrimonium, cum qua docetur non fuisse commixtio sexus), et Leonis I Papae in epistola ad Rusticum Narbonensem, de qua modo supra, cujus rescripti tenorem adulteratum refert: 'Cum societas nuptiarum ita a principio sit instituta ut, praeter commixtionem sexuum, *non* habeant in se nuptiae Christi et Ecclesiae sacramentum, non dubium est illam mulierem non pertinere ad matrimonium in qua docetur non fuisse nuptiale ministerium!' b)c. 19-28, *refert varios casus* in quibus, ob votum religionis, permissum est ante copulam matrimonium solvi, et item ob impotentiam; unde concludit in *Dicto* ad c. 28 et 29, inter sponsos solo consensu conjunctos non esse conjugium, intellige perfectum, quemadmodum veros conjuges fuisse negat B. Mariam Virginem et S. Joseph. c) *explicat testimonia quae* contraria videntur, relata sub c. 1-15; quatenus, si agnoscunt rationem conjugii unioni solo consensu efformatae, loquantur de matrimonio *initiato,* non de perfecto proprie dicto: 'sciendum est, ait, quod conjugium de sponsatione initiatur, commixtione perficitur; unde inter sponsum et sponsam conjugium est, sed initiatum; inter copulatos est conjugium ratum.' Vel etiam ita explicat difficultatem, quatenus sponsos solo consensu devinctos vocaverint conjuges *'spe futurorum, non effectu praesentium.'* Quod autem spectat textum peseudo-Chrysostomi, de quo spura, matrimonium scilicet facere non coitum sed voluntatem, ita dicit intelligendum: 'Coitus sine voluntate contrahendi matrimonium et defloratio virginitatis sine pactione conjugali non facit matrimonium, sed praecedens voluntas contrahendi matrimonium et conjugalis pactio facit ut mulier in defloratione suae virginitatis vel in coitu dicatur nubere viro, vel nuptias celebrare.' *Restrictio* autem, quam monuimus suae theoriae attulisse Gratianum, occurrit in sequentibus capitulis, usque ad c. 50 inclusive; non admittit nempe sponsam solo consensu conjunctam, quamvis fateatur eam non esse sero ac perfecto matrimonio copulatam, non admittit, inquam, eam posse libere alteri nubere, *sed duplicem excipit hypothesim:* primo, quando alterius sponsa *rapta fuerit,* reddenda est sponso, et huic adhaerere debet; secundo, mulier a sponso *in domum deducta* et cum sponso *velata et benedicta,* non potest ad alia vota transire;' talium enim discessione violatur benedictio quam nupturae sacerdos imponit.' Ita in Dicto ad c. 50. Distinctionem inter matrimonium initiatum et perfectum retinuerunt *Gratiani discipuli* eamque magis determinaverunt, ac soli matrimonio per copulam perfecto agnoverunt indissolubilitatem, permittentes matrimonium initiatum solvi, non quidem pro lubito, sed variis ex causis, inter quas occurrunt votum castitatis, captivitas, cognatio spiritualis vel affinitas superveniens, ac etiam, juxta plures, sequens matrimonium consummatum." Plöchl, on the other hand, in his excellent study, *Das Eherecht des Magisters Gratianus* (Leipzig und Wien, 1935), pp. 33-39 is convinced that Gratian upheld the contractual nature of matrimony and he finds it difficult to understand that authors could conclude that Gratian defended the *copula* theory. He states: "Aus den bisherigen Erwägungen geht noch ein weiterer grundsätzlicher Wesenzug der gratianischen Auffassung über Zustandekommen der Ehe hervor: Die entscheidende Bedeutung des Ehevertrages. Gratian leitet aus dem übereinstimmenden Willen der beiden Brautteile den Bestand der Ehe ab. Dasz der Magister für die Vertragsnatur der Ehe eintritt, ist m. E. mit so grosser Sicherheit zu erweisen, dasz es wunder nimmt, wie man aus den c. 16., c. 17, und c. 45. C. 27. qu. 2. allein zu dem Schlusz kommen konnte, dasz der Vollzug erst die Eheschlieszung bedeute und das Verlöbnis sonach erst in diesem Zeitpunkte ende. Auch die Muttergottesehe wurde durch einen Vertrag geschlossen und gründet darauf ihren Bestand. Sie ist zugleich das sicherste Beweismittel des Magisters für seine Behauptung, dasz die Ehe durch den Vertrag und nicht erst durch den Vollzug geschlossen wird." In note 34 on page 39, he continues: "Ebenso kann die Stelle im dict. zu c. 39. C. 27. qu. 2. nicht herangezogen werden "Juxta hanc distictionem intelligenda est auctoritas Augustini: 'Non dubium est, illam mulierem non pertinere ad matrimonium, cum qua docetur non fuisse commixtio sexus. Ad matrimonium perfectum subintelligendum est, tale videlicet, quod habeat in se Christi et ecclesiae sacramentum. Ita et illud Leonis Papae intelligendum est."—Die Stelle, die so zu verstehen ist, betrifft c. 17. ibid. und laudet: 'Cum societas nuptiarum ita a principio sit instituta, ut praeter commixtionem sexuum non habeant in se nuptiae Christi et ecclesiae sacramentum, non dubium est, illam mulierem non pertinere ad matrimonium, in qua docetur non fuisse nuptiale ministerium.' M. E. besagen beiden Stellen nach der Ansicht des Magisters nicht, dasz eine unvollzogene Ehe nicht das Sakrament enthält—wie 'perfectum' zu verstehen ist, erklärt er im gleichen dictum: wir haben es schon vorweggenommen—denn sonst könnte er der Muttergottesche nicht den sakramentalen Charakter zubilligen, ohne in einen unlösbaren Widerspruch zu kommen, sondern zum matrimonium perfectum gehört, dass die drei gefordenten Eigenschaften zumindest in ihre Anlage vorhanden sein müssen ('geistigerweise'=dict. zu c. 39. ibid. § 2). Gratian hütet sich zu sagen, dasz sonach die Ehe mit unbedingter Schärfe spricht er aus, dasz es sich um keine Christenehe handeln kann."

The followers of the *copula* theory asserted that in addition to the marital consent, which gave rise only to a *matrimonium initiatum,* the act of copulation (*mutua praestatio corporis*) was absolutely necessary to constitute a valid marriage and to effect a true and lasting marriage bond.

The *copula* theory was opposed by Hugo of St. Victor (1141), who held that consent by itself was sufficient to effect a valid marriage. So important was the element of consent in the opinion of Hugo of St. Victor, that he relegated to a secondary and even unimportant position all consideration of impediments, dowry, parental consent, priestly blessing, and canonical form of marriage.[55] The principal opposition to the *copula* theory came from Peter Lombard (†ca. 1160)[56] and his followers of the School of Paris. Peter and the School of Paris held to the doctrine that the mere consent of the parties, without actual marital intercourse, effected a true and perfect marriage. Alexander III (1159-1181), who, before becoming Pope, had been one of the famous masters at the school of Bologna, abandoned the *copula* theory which he had accepted and taught there. He attempted to settle the question by decreeing that the consent of the contracting parties alone was the efficient cause of marriage.[57] However, Alexander III denied the absolute indissolubility of a non-consummated marriage.[58]

The doctrine of Alexander III on the necessity of consent

[55] *De Beatae Mariae Virginitate,* Cap. I,—MPL, Tome 176 col. 859; Le Bras, "Mariage," *Dictionnaire de Théologie Catholique* (15 vols. Paris: Letouzey et Ané, 1903-), IX, 2. part, col. 2144-2147.

[56] *Petrus Lombardus Libri IV Sententiarum* (2. ed., 2 vols., ad claras aquas ex typographis Collegii S. Bonaventurae, 1916), II, 917, 918, 921; *MPL* Tome 192, col. 910, 911, 912.

[57] C. 4, X, *de sponsa duorum,* IV, 4. This treatment, admittedly a very cursory one of the famous controversy, suffices for the purpose of this study. For a more complete treatment, especially of the teaching of Alexander III, cf. Harrington, "The Impediment of Impotency and the Notion of Male Impotency, (Part I, From Gratian to the Council of Trent)," *The Jurist,* XIX (1959), 31-42; Le Bras, "Marriage, *D.T.C.* IX, 2. part, col. 2144-2162.

[58] C. 4, X, *de sponsa duorum,* IV, 4; c. 2, X, *de conversione coniugatorum,* III, 32.

as the efficient cause of marriage is the teaching found in the Code of Canon Law today.[59] The fact that the contract of marriage in Church Law is bound to a certain definite form, i.e., that the law laid down precisely how the will or consent to the marriage contract is to be expressed if it is to have legal force, changes in no way the fact that it is the consent of the parties, which is the efficient cause of marriage. If there would be no consent, no agreement of wills of the parties, then the Church itself would have no power to supply for the lack of it or to effect in any other way a valid matrimonial contract.

It may be objected that in the *sanatio in radice* the Church validates an invalid marriage even without the knowledge of one or both of the parties involved. One may wonder how this can be done if consent is the one and only cause of a valid marriage.[60] In the *sanatio,* however, the Church does not supply for the consent of the patries. A *sanatio* can be applied only if, and this is a *conditio sine qua non,* the consent of both parties is naturally efficient for a valid contract, and if this consent still continues at the time when the *sanatio* is granted.

The object of marital consent must of necessity be the same as the object of the marital contract itself. When people marry, they must agree, therefore, to give and accept the perpetual and exclusive right over one another's body for the exercise of acts suitable of themselves for the procreation of offspring.[61] If the parties do not consent to this object of the contract, they are not consenting to marriage itself and, consequently, they are not entering a valid matrimonial contract.

The essence of marriage and, therefore, the essential ob-

[59] C. 1081.

[60] C. 1139, § 1: "Quodlibet matrimonium initum cum utriusque partis consensu naturaliter sufficiente, sed iuridice inefficaci ob dirimens impedimentum iuris ecclesiastici, vel ob defectum legitimae formae, potest in radice sanari, dummodo consensus perseveret. Canon 1138, § 3: "Dispensatio a lege de renovando consensu concedi etiam potest vel una tantum vel utraque parte inscia."

[61] 1081, § 2.

ject of marital consent can also be drawn from what are called the "three goods of marriage."[62] The "three goods of marriage" are: 1) the *bonum prolis,* i.e., the right to the body, given and received by both parties, for the purpose of acts suitable for the procreating of offspring. 2) the *bonum fidei,* i.e., the faithfulness by which the parties are bound to each other and which excludes any third parties. 3) The *bonum sacramenti,* i.e., the indissoluble bond, by which the parties are permanently joined to each other, and which terminates only with the death of one of the parties.[63] None of these essential elements of the object of marital consent may be excluded by a positive act of the will of either of the parties. if the consent is to effect a valid matrimonial contract.[64]

b. *The Necessary Qualities of Marital Consent*

Matrimonial consent must be endowed with those qualities that are generally required for the institution of any valid bilateral contract. It must be true, deliberate, mutual, externally manifested and given by legally competent persons.[65]

The knowledge, deliberation and freedom required for the validity of the contract of marriage will be treated in the following chapter of this study. The other qualities of marital consent need only to be mentioned here.

The consent, to be the effective cause of the contract, must be an internally true and actual consent. A merely external, fictitious consent is really no consent at all. On the other hand, it is not required that the consent be explicit regarding all the essentials of the marital contract. Consent "to marry as other people marry," implying all the essential ele-

[62] C. 10, XXVII, q. 2.

[63] Vlaming-Bender, *Praelectiones Iuris Matrimonii,* p. 22.

[64] Cf. Canon 1086, § 2.

[65] Sanchez, *De Sancto Matrimonii Sacramento,* Lib. IV, disp. 10, n. 2; disp. 28, n. 1; disp. 32, n. 1; Schmalzgrueber, *Jus Ecclesiasticum Universum,* Lib. IV, Tit. 1, n. 246; Pirhing, *Ius Canonicum Nova Methodo Explicatum,* Lib. IV, Tit. 1, n. 82.

ments of marriage without positively excluding any by an act of the will is sufficient for a valid marriage contract.[66]

Marital consent, moreover, must be mutual. It must be given by both parties to the marriage contract. Both parties in marriage obtain rights and serious obligations. Both, therefore, must freely consent to take upon themselves these rights and duties. The consent of the parties must also be morally simultaneous, although it is not required that it be physically simultaneous. A simultaneous act is required inasmuch as it is necessary that the consent of one party endure and be not revoked at the time when the consent of the other party is given. As in any other contract, a "meeting of the minds" is necessary for the contract to take effect.

Marital consent, moreover, must be externally manifested. This feature is required by reason of the contract itself. It is humanly impossible to have agreement of wills without an external manifestation of consent. To have legal consequences, an act must be performed in the external forum, so that it can be legally proven to have taken place. Consent is also the external sign of the sacrament of marriage and, consequently, it must be externally manifested.[67]

The person entering the matrimonial contract must be juridically capable of giving consent.[68] The parties to the marriage must not be legally estopped from marrying by any of the impediments to marriage.[69] Finally, the marriage consent must be directed to a determined person. A generic, undetermined consent to marriage, not directed to a specific person, is no consent at all and cannot result in a valid marriage contract.

After a consideration of these general notions of the na-

[66] Van Welie, *Kanoniek Huwelijksrecht*, pp. 222-224; Vlaming-Bender, *Praelectiones Iuris Matrimonii*, p. 376.

[67] Canon 1088, § 2 states: "Sponsi matrimonialem consensum experimant verbis; nec aequipollentia signa adhibere ipsis licet, si loqui possint."

[68] Cf. C. 1081, § 1.

[69] C. 1035: "Omnes possunt matrimonium contrahere, qui iure non prohibentur."

ture and properties of marriage, its object and purpose, and after determining the efficient cause of the marital contract, it is now in order to pass on to a more specific examination of the knowledge, freedom and mental maturity required for a person to contract validly.

ARTICLE 2. PSYCHICAL REQUIREMENTS FOR LEGAL ACTS AT CHURCH LAW

Acts which are freely exercised by man are commonly called human acts. These free acts are peculiar to man and set him part from other living creatures. It is by his knowledge and freedom that man becomes the master of his actions. Man does not deliberate, on the other hand, about necessary physical acts, such as the act of breathing. No volitional act is posited to command the action of breathing. Such acts are called acts of man, rather than human acts.

A specifically human act is an act that issues from the will acting freely, with antecedent knowledge of the nature and end or purpose of the act and with accompanying advertence. Every human act must have three elements, namely, advertence of the intellect, voluntariness of choice, and freedom of operation. It must be performed with advertence, because man cannot will anything unless he knows the object of his willing, according to the axiom: "Nothing can be willed unless it is first known."[70] It must be voluntary, inasmuch as it must actually proceed from the will. It must be free, as the operative result of deliberate free choice.

It is only insofar as man is master of his acts, by reason of his knowledge and free will, that he is responsible for his acts and undertakes a binding obligation, if any, in consequence of his acts. It is precisely this obligatory responsibility for legal acts which must be examined here. The difficult question of man's responsibility must be explored with

[70] "Nihil volitum nisi praecognitum." Cf. D'Annibale, *Summula Theologiae Moralis* (3 vols., 3 ed., Romae, 1892), I, n. 108; Cf. also Davis, *Moral and Pastoral Theology* (4 fols., 6 ed., London: Sheed and Ward, 1949), I, 12.

the help of accepted philosophical and legal principles. The philosophical principles regarding the knowledge and freedom of man will be drawn mainly from the philosophy of St. Thomas Aquinas.[71]

Obviously, canon law, for that matter all law, must recognize on principle that man is actually an intellectual, free, self-governing being, rather than a sort of robot who is exclusively the creature of his unconscious, or of influences such as those of heredity, environment, etc. Accordingly, the legal mind cannot admit that a normal man is irrevocably led in one direction or another by mere emotional or instinctive forces.[72]

It must be kept in mind that not every free and hence legally imputable act is also a legal act in the strict sense. Fässler, in his remarkable study *Die Schizophrenie Als Ehenichtigkeitsgrund im Kanonischen Recht,* rightly observes: "Not every free and deliberate act of a person is automatically also a legal act. A legal act in the strict sense demands that the agent realize that his act is precisely a legal one. Moreover he must posit this act with the purpose of obtaining a definite effect at law."[73] For a person to be held

[71] Quite clearly it would be impossible in a necessarily limited study such as this to enter deeply into the philosophical notions involved. The writer will attempt merely to present, according to Thomistic philosophy, the basic doctrines of knowledge and free will.

[72] There can be no scientific doubt about the fact that human beings, even when acting deliberately, are influenced, whether knowingly or not, by certain internal and external forces over which they have little or no control. However, it cannot be admitted by a theologian, Scholastic philosopher, or lawyer, whether at canon or at civil law, that these influences force man in all his actions. The distinction between influence and force is a basic and essential one. Cf. Ford-Kelly, *Contemporary Moral Theology, Volume One, Questions in Fundamental Theology.* (Westminister, Maryland: The Newman Press, 1959), p. 194.

[73] "Diese Umschreibung der Rechtshandlung läszt erkennen, dasz nicht jede freie und überlegte Handlung eines Menschen eo ipso auch eine Rechtshandlung ist. Eine Rechtshandlung im eigentlichen Sinne setzt voraus, dasz der handelnde Mensch seine eigene Handlung im Rechtssinne erkennt und sie vollzieht mit der Absicht, eine Rechtswirkung zu erzielen." p. 13.

legally responsible for a legal act, it is necessary, therefore, that he knew what he was doing, that he knew his action to be a legal act, and, finally, that he performed the action freely, having been able to choose not to perform that action.[74]

Before being able to determine whether and to what extent a person is responsible for a particular legal act, it must be shown that a normal man can and does act freely under normal circumstances.[75] The free act of the will, in turn, demands knowledge of the act and knowledge of the purpose of the act.

SECTION A. THE OPERATIONS AND MUTUAL COOPERATION OF THE INTELLECT AND WILL IN HUMAN ACTS

a. The Operation of the Intellect[76]

[74] At American Criminal Law these requirements for legal responsibility have led to the acceptance in 21 jurisdictions of the doctrine of the "irresistible impulse." However, many of the jurisdictions refuse to admit the principle of the "irresistible impulse." They admit only the so-called "right and wrong test" formulated in the McNaughton Case in 1843, because they fear that general admission of the former doctrine will break down the law and permit many criminals to go free. Cf. McGrath, *Comparative Study of Crime and Its Imputability in Ecclesiastical Criminal Law, and in American Law*, The Catholic University of America Canon Law Studies, No. 385 (Washington, D.C.: The Catholic University of America Press, 1957), pp. 77-80. One reason why the "right and wrong test" has been objected to by psychiatrists is that it does not take account of the proven psychological facts. It relies exclusively on an appeal to the intellectual perception of right and wrong without paying sufficient attention to the disordered emotional factors that can influence criminal conduct.

[75] The term "normal" has been objected to by certain authors in the fields of psychology and psychiatry, especially if used to describe a person. They feel that it is impossible to draw a line between normalcy and abnormalcy. Be that as it may, it does not mean that there is no difference between the two. It may also be difficult to draw a line between a person who is prudent and one who is not, but there is nevertheless a real difference. When speaking of a normal man, the writer intends to indicate a person who is responsible, i.e., who has sufficient knowledge, volition, and freedom of operation, who can control himself, and who is able to avoid evil and to do good.

[76] At the outset it should be realized that it is not the intellect,

The human intellect, according to Thomistic philosophy, is an operative power of the soul or spirit of man.[77] The human soul, therefore, operates through its operative power, the intellect. Moreover, the human intellect is also a passive power.[78] It is evident that a person can acquire knowledge which he did not previously possess. The intellect passes, in the acquisition of new knowledge, from potency to act or, less technically, from being able to acquire knowledge to actual possession of knowledge. In order to pass from potency to act, the human intellect must go through a difficult and elaborate process which finds its beginnings in sensory experiences.

The proper object of the human intellect is what has been termed the "material quiddity"[79] or the essence or nature of corporeal things. Man's knowledge of immaterial beings, e.g., God, is non-proper and imperfect. It can be attained only by reflection upon the essences of material things. To obtain knowledge of immaterial things man must use the data received from the corporeal beings about him.[80]

nor the will, but rather man, with an intellect and free will, who is responsible for a particular free act. The separation of the individual and distinct acts and operations of the intellect from those of the will, so as to be able to examine the mental processes in man, should not lead to a separation or division of the legal act of man. In that act the successive and distinct operations of the intellect and will are unified. The act itself remains one, and man, with free will and intelligence, is responsible for that act.

[77] Thomas Aquinas, *Summa Theologica,* I, q. 79, art. 1. *Sancti Thomae Aquinatis Doctoris Angelici Ordinis Praedicatorum Opera Omnia Secundum Impressionem Petri Fiaccadori Parmae, (1852-1873)* (25 vols., Photolithographice Reimpressa, New York: Musurgia Publishers), I, 308. (Hereafter cited *Opera Omnia*).

[78] Thomas Aquinas, *Summa Theologica,* I, q. 79, art. 2—*Opera Omnia,* I, 309—as cited by Renard, *The Philosophy of Man* (2. ed., by Vaske, Milwaukee: Bruce Publishing Company, 1956), p. 151.

[79] Thomas Aquinas, *Summa Theologica,* I, q. 84, art. 7—*Opera Omnia,* I, 333—Renard, *op. cit.,* p. 152; Cf. also Brennan, *Thomistic Psychology* (New York: Macmillan Company, 1957), p. 208.

[80] Thomas Aquinas, *Summa Theologica,* I, q. 84, art. 7—*Opera Omnia,* I, 333—as cited by Renard, *op. cit.,* p. 153. There is no need to enter here into the difficult problem of how a material object can move a

The "agent intellect," produces an intelligible species by abstraction from the matter of the corporeal beings or their phantasms (images of sensible things). The phantasm itself is the product of the imaginative sense of man.[81] The "possible intellect" then receives the species. Even though the possible intellect is primarily a passive faculty, it is actuated by the agent intellect acting in conjunction with phantasm. The possible intellect elicits the act of knowledge. There are then, two distinct operations of two distinct powers. At the same time there is only one action of knowing, namely, the operation of the possible intellect consequent upon its actuation by the agent intellect.[82]

After the possible intellect has been actuated, the action which follows is the act of understanding. According to Thomistic psychology, the act of understanding is a uniting of the spiritual faculty, the intellect, with the object which is understood, Knowledge, therefore, must be understood to be a union or identification of intellect with the object known. However, to obtain this union the mind must produce an intention or form of the object which is known. It must receive or conceive the object in itself. The result of this conception in the mind is the concept (*verbum*).[83] There is only

spiritual operative power, namely, the intellect, form potency to act. Suffice it to say that St. Thomas answers this problem by means of what is called the "agent intellect." He says: "Since forms existing in matter are not actually intelligible, it follows that the natures or forms of the sensible things which we understand are not actually intelligible. Now nothing is reduced from potency to act except by something in act; as the senses are made actual by what is actually sensible. We must, therefore, assign on the part of the intellect some power *(virtus)* to make things actually intelligible, by the abstraction of the species from material conditions. Such is the necessity of an agent intellect."—*Summa Theologica,* I. q. 79, art. 3—*Opera Omnia,* I, 310—as cited by Renard, *op. cit.,* p. 156.

[81] Thomas Aquinas, *Summa Theologica,* I, q. 85, art. 1, *in corp.,* ad secundum—*Opera Omnia,* I, 338—cited by Renard, *op. cit.,* p. 139. Cf. also Brennan, *op. cit.,* p. 187.

[82] Thomas Aquinas, *Contra Gentiles,* II, Cap. 73 + 77—*Opera Omnia,* V, 132 as cited in Renard, *op. cit.,* p. 159.

[83] Thomas Aquinas, *Contra Gentiles,* I, cap. 53—*Opera Omnia,* V, 38—as cited in Renard, *op. cit.,* p. 165.

one specific act of the intellect, namely, the act of understanding. In this operation the human intellect forms an intention or word (object as known) and becomes one with the known object. This mental word, which is formed in the mind through the operation of understanding, can be a concept or definition. In this concept the object is understood according to its essence. It can also be a composition or division in which the intellect understands also the properties and accidents of the essence. This second type of mental word is, therefore, a deeper and more complete understanding of the thing which is known. Finally, in the process of reasoning, which is proper to man alone, the intellect proceeds from one composition to another. This action, in turn, terminates in a more elaborate and complex composition.[84]

A question arises with regard to error in the mind. In other words, under what conditions can the intellect fail in its operation of understanding? St. Thomas answers by stating that the intellect cannot be in error *per se*[85] as regards its proper object, the essence of corporeal things. Regarding knowledge of substance, in the definition of which there is no composition, the intellect can in no way be deceived. The same holds true with regard to self-evident first principles.[86] However, in forming a composition or division and, all the more, in the process of reasoning, the intellect can be in er-

[84] Thomas Aquinas, *Summa Theologica,* I, q. 85, art 5—*Opera Omnia,* I, 341—as cited by Renard, *op. cit.,* p. 168.

[85] The intellect may be in error *per accidens* regarding the essence of a thing whose definition involves a composition of incompatible elements or when the definition is erroneously affirmed of another thing. Cf. Tyrrell, *The Role of Assent in Judgment, A Thomistic Study,* No. 100 (Washington, D.C.: The Catholic University of America Press, 1948), p. 106.

[86] Just as the power or faculty of hearing is directed of itself *(per se)* to its proper object, namely, sound, and sight is directed to color, so the intellect of itself is directed to its proper object, namely, the essence or quiddity of things. If the intellect would fail in this regard, then it would not understand falsely, in fact, it would not understand at all.

ror.[87] Through the act of the intellect knowledge is obtained. The act of knowing may be defined as: "An immanent operation[88] enacted through an operative potency which has been actuated by a representative species of the object, thus enabling the knowing subject by its operation to become intentionally united with the object."[89] The terms "speculative" and "practical" intellect, which are often used, refer to two different functions of the intellect of man. The speculative intellect directs what it apprehends not to action but only to a consideration of truth, while the practical intellect directs what it apprehends to action or operation.[90] Man is able not only to understand, but he is also able to reason. The power or faculty to reason is proper to man alone. To understand is to comprehend intelligible truth absolutely, while to reason is to advance from one thing which is understood to another.[91] Reasoning could be called "mental arithmetic" in so far as it is an adding of one truth to another to arrive at a third. However, the faculty of reason is not a separate faculty from the intellect. Man reasons and understands by the same faculty, the possible intellect.

Finally, a distinction can be made between what is called "conceptual knowledge" and "evaluative knowledge." Conceptual knowledge simply tells man what a certain thing is, while evaluative knowledge appraises the value and importance of the object which is known. Evaluative knowledge makes a judgment regarding what is known. In making every-day judgments in practical matters, man perceives both in the same act of understanding. As will be seen

[87] Thomas Aquinas, *Summa Theologica,* I, q. 85, art. 6—*Opera Omnia,* I, 342—as cited by Brennan, *Thomistic Psychology,* p. 209.

[88] An immanent operation is an operation the principle of which is in the operator and in virtue of this principle the operator moves itself to operation. Cf. Thomas Aquinas, *Summa Theologica,* I, q. 18, art. 2—*Opera Omnia,* I, 81.

[89] Renard, *op. cit.,* p. 108.

[90] Thomas Aquinas, *Summa Theologica,* I, q. 79, art. 11—*Opera Omnia,* I, 316—as cited by Renard, *op. cit.,* p. 198.

[91] Thomas Aquinas, *Summa Theologica,* I, q. 79, art. 8—Renard, *op. cit.,* q. 196.

later,[92] this distinction can be an important one. It allows for the possibility that a person has full conceptual knowledge, but little or no evaluative knowledge regarding a certain object or act.[93] The distinction between conceptual and evaluative knowledge has its principal application in practical judgments, such as the judgments of conscience and decisions in practical affairs.

b. The Operation of the Will

St. Thomas Aquinas stated: "... some things act without judgment, as a stone which falls down; and in like manner all things which lack knowledge. Some act from judgment, but not from a free judgment, as the brute animals.[94] But man acts from free judgment and has the power of being inclined to various things."[95] Thomas Aquinas bases his proof for the existence of the human will, as a spiritual faculty proper to man, on the principle that: "Some inclination is consequent upon every form."[96] Since man through intellectual knowledge acquires the forms of things without matter, there must be present within man's nature an inclination surpassing the inclination of the sense appetites,[97] which

[92] Cf. *infra*, p. 125.

[93] Ford-Kelly, *Contemporary Moral Theology*, p. 222.

[94] By means of their estimative sense animals are able to discern what is friendly to them or not, suitable for them or not, and hence, according to Thomistic thought, they have a limited type of "judgment."

[95] *Summa Theologica*, I, q. 83, art. 1—*Opera Omnia*, I, 326.

[96] *Summa Theologica*, I, q. 80, art. 1—*Opera Omnia*, I, 318—as cited in Renard, *op. cit.*, q. 229.

[97] The senses are divided into external and internal senses. The five distinct external senses are: sight, hearing, smell, taste and touch. The internal senses are four: The unitive or common sense, which integrates external sensations, discriminates between proper sensibles and gives sensory awareness; the imaginative sense, to supply sense memory and phantasy; the instinctive sense, which can be estimative to make sensory judgments as to what is useful or harmful, or cogitative which compares experiences and infers a particular judgment. Finally, the memorative sense, which retains insensate intentions of the estimative sense and which gives the power to reminisce. The external senses need the external object to pass from potency to act. Common or unitive sense depends on the external senses, imaginative on

have for their object the sensible forms. This special inclination in man is called the intellectual appetite or will. The will, being the appetite which follows the intellect, has as its objects the same things which are the objects of the intellect. As objects of the intellect they are knowable: as objects of the will they are desirable. Similarly, the object proportionate and proper to the human will is the good in material things, just as the human intellect is directed to the essence of material things. Finally, what is apprehended by the intellect is really distinct from what is apprehended by the senses and, consequently, the will or the rational appetite is also really distinct from the sensitive appetites.[98]

C. *The Freedom of the Will*

It is absolutely fundamental teaching both in Catholic theology and in Thomistic philosophy that the human will is free. Were it not for free will, all counsels, exhortations, commands, prohibitions, rewards, and punishments would be in vain. Without free will there could be no question of responsibility and, consequently, there would be no necessity or purpose for law, whether divine or human, ecclesiastical or civil. Some philosophers deny the freedom of man in

the unitive sense. The cogitative sense is actuated by the external senses, the common sense and the imaginative sense, while the memorative sense retains the species of the cogitative sense.

Knowledge of sensible good results in a desire for that good. This desire is brought about by the sense appetite. Cf. Thomas Aquinas, *Summa Theologica,* I, 80, 1—*Opera Omnia,* I, 318. The two sense appetites are the concupiscible and the irascible appetites. Cf. Thomas Aquinas, *Summa Theologica,* I, 81, 2—*Opera Omnia,* I, 320. The operations or acts of the sense appetites are called the passions or emotions. The passions or emotions are: love, desire, hate, aversion, hope, daring, anger, despair, fear, joy and sadness. Passions can and do influence reason. They can color the phantasm from which is formed the intelligible species for the judgment of the suitability of the action. Cf. Thomas Aquinas, *Summa Theologica,* I-II, q. 24, art. 3—II, q. 94—Renard, *op. cit.,* pp. 110-145; 205-207.

[98] Thomas Aquinas, *Summa Theologica,* I, q. 80, art. 2—*Opera Omnia,* I, 319.

theory,[99] but even they, in practical life, must and do live as if (in their opinion) they and others actually had free will.[100]

The freedom of the will can be understood as philosophical freedom[101] and as, what has been called, psychological freedom. By philosophical freedom is meant the freedom which is required for a human act. It presupposes advertence and rational deliberation, and it has its basis in the power of the intellect to make objectively indifferent judgments. By acting freely, in this sense, is meant that at the time the choice to act is made, man is able to make an opposite choice, even if with difficulty or with repugnance.[102] Freedom understood in this sense does not admit of degrees. A person either does or does not have the power to make a choice. He either can choose the opposite of what he does or he cannot do so. There cannot be any degrees in between. By psychological freedom, on the other hand, is meant freedom from influ-

[99] Spinoza, with his intellectualist determinism; Leibniz, with his psychological determinism *et alii.*

[100] Cavanagh, in an article entitled: "Criminal Responsibility and Free Will, "*Bulletin of the Guild of Catholic Psychiatrists,* 3, n. 2 (Dec. 1955) 24-33 at 27, presents the following considerations to show that human beings are responsible and therefore free: "This responsibility is easily recognized if one gives a moment of thought to these facts: 1) Every one recognizes his own responsibility. 2) Everyone holds others responsible for various injuries or damage which one has suffered at their hands. 3) Everyone acts upon the belief in the power of his own initiative. These three factors plus one's daily experience in the matter of free choice add up to free will."

[101] It must however, be observed that the will is not free with regard to absolute good. The will has for its proper object the good, in so far as it is good, and hence, that object which is absolutely good cannot be rejected by the will, if the will is to act at all. Similarly the will must desire perfect happiness which is the only object that can satisfy completely this intellectual appetite; Cf. Thomas Aquinas, *Summa Theologica,* I-II, q. 10, art. 2—*Opera Omnia,* II, 44; *De Veritate* q. XXII, art. 5—*Opera Omnia,* IX, 319. as cited in Renard, *op. cit.,* q. 236.

[102] Ford-Kelly, *Contemporary Moral Theology,* p. 212. Ford and Kelly rightly remark: "Freely does not mean easily or without reluctance, although sometimes free choices are easily made."—*Ibidem,* p. 204.

ences, circumstances, pressures, illnesses, etc., which make the exercise of philosophical freedom difficult. Freedom in this sense, by its very definition, allows varying degrees.[103] "It is unfortunate," Ford and Kelly observe, "that the one phrase 'freedom of will' should be used to describe these two widely different things. Philosophical freedom is something positive and active. It is the power or faculty by which the will determines itself to this or that. It is freedom to determine its own choice. Psychological freedom is the facility of choice which results from the absence of obstacles and pressures."[104]

There is no need, at present, to enter into a complete study of the philosophical problem of the freedom of the will. Suffice it to say that according to Thomistic philosophy the will cannot be forced to act.[105] Since the will is an appetite, an inclination of nature, it cannot be forced to act. To force an inclination of nature would be a contradiction.[106] Consequently, according to St. Thomas, not even God could force the will to act.[107] God could not force a natural appetite, for the appetite is the nature itself as inclined to its end. The nature, as long as it remains what it is, cannot be changed as regards its radical tendency or finality to its end. Of course, force can prevent or change the acts which the will commands to be done. To illustrate this proposition, it can be easily seen that the will cannot be forced to love a particular person. The external expression of that love, on the other hand, can be prevented by force. Moreover, the will is

[103] Ford-Kelly, *op. cit.*, p. 212.

[104] Ford-Kelly, *op. cit.*, p. 213.

[105] Thomas Aquinas, *Summa Theologica*, I, q. 19, art. 3; q. 59, art. 3; q. 83, art. 1,—*Opera Omnia*, I, 85; I, 232; I, 326; *De Malo*, q. 6, art. un.—*Opera Omnia*, VIII, 308. Cf. Renard, *op. cit.*, pp. 228-243.

[106] Thomas Aquinas, *Summa Theologica*, I, q. 82, art. 1—*Opera Omnia*, I, 324—as cited by Renard, *op. cit.*, p. 233.

[107] Thomas Aquinas, *De Veritate*, q. XXII, art. 8—*Opera Omnia*, IX, 324—as cited in Renard, *op. cit.*, q. 233.

also free to choose or not to choose particular goods.[108] Thomas Aquinas states:

> Man does not choose of necessity . . . The reason for this is to be found in the very power of the reason. For the will can tend to whatever the reason can apprehend as good . . . In all particular goods, the reason can consider the nature of some good, and the lack of some good, which has the nature of an evil; and in this way, it can apprehend any single one of such goods as to be chosen or to be avoided. The perfect good alone ,which is happiness, cannot be apprehended by the reason as an evil, or as lacking in any way. Consequently, man wills happiness of necessity, nor can he will not to be happy or to be unhappy. Now since choice is not of the end, but of the means . . . it is not perfect good, which is happiness, but of other and particular goods. Therefore, man chooses, not of necessity, but freely.[109]

If and in so far as man is free in his actions, so far he is also responsible for his actions. For, if he is free, he himself can and does choose to act rather than not to act, to act in this way rather than that, to choose these particular means to an end rather than those. However, as was remarked above,[110] man's freedom, his psychological freedom, can be modified by obstacles and pressures of one kind or another. If the obstacles to freedom are great and numerous, the freedom itself lessens. It becomes hard for the will to choose and to direct the execution of bodily activities in the face of the obstacles. As a consequence, the responsibility of man decreases in the same proportion as the obstacles to free choice and free external action increase.[111] Should the obstacles and influences be of such force that they prevent a free choice or action in a particular case, then the person

[108] Only limited or qualified goods are a matter of choice; absolute good is not a matter of choice.

[109] Thomas Aquinas, *Summa Theologica,* I-II, q. 10, art. 6—*Opera Omnia,* II, 45—as cited in Renard, *op. cit.*, p. 239.

[110] *Supra,* p. 76.

[111] Some of the obstacles to, or modifiers of, freedom are force and fear, ignorance, passion, temperament, drugs, acquired habits, education, environment, mental illness and unconscious motivation.

who placed the action would not be responsible for this action, for it would no longer be a human act but, rather, it would be an act of man.

d. The Cooperation of the Intellect and Will

Man can act freely and, consequently, he must be held responsible for his free actions. The only questions remaining to be answered are: How does a free act occur? What is the influence of intellectual knowledge on the free act of the will? The will is the appetite of the intellect, it can love only a known good, and consequently, knowledge is required for the will to act. The intellect moves the will by presenting to it some specific good. The will, in turn, is capable of controlling to a certain degree the intellect. The will can direct the intellect to consider one object rather than another, the good in one object rather than the lack of good in the same object. By doing so, the will influences the judgment of the intellect, which again will specify the act of choice. Thomas Aquinas explains the interaction between the intellect and will as follows:

> A thing is said to move in two ways. First, as an end, as when we say that the end moves the agent. In this way the intellect moves the will, and moves it as an end. Secondly, a thing is said to move as an agent, as what alters moves what is altered, and what impels moves what is impelled. In this way the will moves the intellect and all the powers of the soul. The reason is that, wherever we have an order among a number of active potencies, the potency which is related to the universal end moves the potencies which refer to particular ends... Now the object of the will is the good and the end in general, whereas each power is directed to some suitable good proper to it, as sight is directed to the perception of color, Therefore, the will as an agent moves all the powers of the soul to their respective acts, except the natural powers of the vegetative part, which are not subject to our choice.[112]

[112] Thomas Aquinas, *Summa Theologica,* I, q. 82, art. 4—*Opera Omnia,* I, 324; *Summa Theologica,* I-II, q. 9, art. 1—*Opera Omnia,*

However, it must be remembered that man's free acts are not separate acts of the will or of the intellect. They are rather the acts of man as man, namely of a being with intellect and free will. Even though the act of man is one and comes from man as an individual, yet it is possible to, psychologically, dissect the free human act. This is done, in Thomistic philosophy, in the following twelve steps: 1) The intellect comes to know a good and judges its objective value; 2) the will either is satisfied just to know this good, or it moves the intellect to judge whether the good is obtainable; 3) the intellect then makes the judgment whether the good is obtainable; 4) If so, the will moves to obtain the end or object by bringing the mind to a consideration of the possible means to obtain that end; 5) the intellect considers the various means and 6) the will consents to any of the means considered; 7) the intellect proceeds to make a practical judgment on one particular means proposed by the intellect; 9) the intellect directs the will to move the proper faculties or powers of the body to action; and 10) the will sets them in action to obtain the end; 11) when the end is obtained, the intellect will make a judgment regarding the fact that the end is obtained; 12) the will rests in enjoyment of the good or end which has been reached.[113] According to St. Thomas, the causality of intellect and will is a mutual one. The intellect and will act upon each other simultaneously. It is as the result of this mutual cooperation that the free human act occurs.[114]

The responsibility of man for a given action depends on how well the intellect and will were able to function according to their proper nature at the time when the action was posited. This psychological disposition depends on the influences, if any, which came to bear on the intellect and will,

II, 39—as cited in Brennan, *op. cit.*, p. 235 and Renard *op. cit.*, p. 246.

[113] Renard, *The Philosophy of Man*, p. 253.

[114] The free act is formally an act of the intellect but materially an act of the will; Cf. Thomas Aquinas, *Summa Theologica*, I-II, q. 13, art. 1—*Opera Omnia*, II, 51—as cited by Renard, *op. cit.*, p. 256.

and which may have made it difficult or impossible for the intellect and will to act properly.

In view of this complex psychological texture and climax in mental activity, it was deemed necessary to examine, though admittedly in a very summary fashion, the various elements in the free human act. Mental illness, as will be seen in a later chapter, can influence the operations of the intellect and will in such a manner as to make the free human act difficult and at times even impossible. If the human act in general would become impossible by reason of mental illness, legal acts also would be impossible and, consequently, also the legal act of giving a valid matrimonial consent. However, it is possible for a person to be able to posit a human or free act while at the same time his freedom, knowledge, deliberation and discretion have been limited to such an extent that the person is unable to posit a certain legal act. As will be seen, more is required on the part of the intellect and will for certain legal actions than that which is required merely for a human act.

SECTION B. RELATIVE PSYCHICAL CAPACITY FOR LEGAL ACTS

Not every free human action is necessarily a legal act in the strict sense. For such an action it is required that the agent know the nature of his action precisely in so far as it is a legal act. He must know that his action has a specific effect at law. He must intend, by placing the act, to obtain the same effect which the law has attached to the particular action involved.[115] The placing of a valid legal act requires that the person know what he is doing, namely, what legal act he is placing, and also, that he have the freedom to act or not to act.

The question can be raised regarding the degree of knowledge and freedom required for a legal act. In other words,

[115] "Sensu stricto autem actus juridicus est actus humanus socialis legitime positus et declaratus, cui a lege ideo et eatenus effectus juridicus determinatus agnoscitur, quia et quatenus effectus ille ab agente intenditur."—Michiels, *Principia Generalia De Personis in Ecclesia* (editio altera, Parisiis-Tornaci-Romae: Desclée et Socii, 1955), p. 572.

does a person who has sufficient knowledge and freedom to place a human act necessarily have sufficient knowledge and freedom to place a legal act as well? It may be asked further: are the psychical requirements for one legal act the same as those required for a specifically different legal act? Are specific degrees of psychical capacity required for specific legal acts?

a. Relative Psychical Capacity

It is easy to understand that more is required of the intellect and of the will for a particular legal act, for instance, the legal act of religious profession[116] or of marital consent[117] than for some other act, such as for example, the rearranging of the furniture in a room. It is a much more difficult matter to determine the degree of knowledge and freedom required for a legal act. Actually it is impossible to formulate a definite norm which would establish a specific degree of knowledge and freedom as being necessary and sufficient for all legal acts. Each legal act demands its own specific degree of psychical capacity. The degree of knowledge and freedom required for legal acts is, therefore, a relative one. The psychical capacity must be in direct proportion to the object of the legal act involved.[118] If the object of a legal act is complex, more will be required of the intellect and will than if the object is comparatively simple. Again, if the legal act has grave and enduring consequences at law, more will be demanded of the intellectual and volitional faculties of a person who places that act, than if the effects were neither serious nor permanent. Moreover, the legislator may specify certain minimum standards and conditions for the validity of certain juridical acts; he may determine a minimum age before which a person cannot validly place a particular legal act.[119] The legislator specifies such a minimum standard as a collective norm which by implication deter-

[116] Canon 1307.

[117] Canons 1081-1082.

[118] Cf. Fässler, *Die Schizophrenie als Ehenichtigkeitsgrund im Kanonischen Recht*, p. 14.

[119] Ford-Kelly, *Contemporary Moral Theology*, p. 211.

mines the psychical requirements for a specific type of legal act.

b. Legally Established Norms for Legal Acts

It can easily be understood that the validity of a legal act depends to a great extent on the psychical capacity of the person who places the act. As a consequence, before any legal act may be posited, it would seem necessary to examine the person who is about to place the act to determine whether he knows the nature of the action, its object and purpose, its various qualities and inherent effects at law. Moreover, the person should be examined not only regarding his abstract knowledge (conceptual knowledge)[120] of the action, but also as to whether he fully realizes the objective importance of that action and its inherent implications (evaluative knowledge).[121] Finally, it would be necessary to determine the degree of psychological freedom[122] of the person involved, which determination, in turn, would necessitate an examination of his psychological make-up and of the various influences of environment, heredity, education, etc., which may have modified his psychological freedom.[123] All these considerations, obviously, would be impractical in everyday life. It is for this reason that the legislator has set down norms to determine the necessary mental capacity for certain types of legal acts. In those instances where the legislator has not indicated a minimum norm or standard, the interpreters of the law should attempt to establish such a rule or norm according to which the validity of legal acts may be determined. In establishing such norms, the legislattor or interpreter of law must proceed in the following manner.

First the legislator or interpreter of law must determine the degree of knowledge, freedom, and maturity of judgment that is required for the validity of a particular legal act. Secondly, he must determine the degree of knowledge, freedom

[120] Cf. *supra*, p. 73.

[121] *Ibidem.*

[122] Cf. *supra*, p. 76.

[123] *Ibidem.*

and maturity of judgment that is usually enjoyed by average, normal persons at various age levels.[124] The degree of knowledge, freedom, and maturity of judgment actually possessed by an average person at various age (chronological, psychic, physical) levels is to be measured against that which, in the experience of man, occurs or is usually present at the various age levels. The normal is that which usually occurs as verified by human experience.

Having determined the knowledge, freedom, and maturity of judgment usually found at the various age levels, and also having determined the actual knowledge, freedom, and maturity of judgment required for a specific legal act, the legislator or interpreter of law then is able to establish a norm for determining the psychical capacity for a particular legal act in the following manner: At a certain specified age level, it is generally observed that a person normally has the knowledge, freedom, and maturity of judgment necessary for the placing of this particular legal act. According to such a norm the psychical capacity of individuals for a certain legal act can be tested.[125]

[124] Cavanagh defines the normal person as follows: "The normal person may be defined as one who conforms to the average human being in his methods of thinking, feeling, willing and acting, is reasonably happy, emotionally balanced, and adjusted and oriented toward future goals."—"Criminal Responsibility and Free Will," *Bulletin of the Guild of Catholic Psychiatrists,* III (Dec. 1955), 25; Cf. also *supra,* p. 69.

[125] In psychological testing, e.g., in the I.Q. test, the norms are set in a similar fashion. "The term mental age, as now used in psychology, was first coined by Binet, who offered it as a way of defining different degrees or levels of intelligence. The novel point was that he proposed to define those levels in terms of the measured abilities of children at different ages. This presupposed that intellectual ability could be measured and that it increased progressively with age. Both of these assumptions have proved correct. Binet's great contributions, however, were more specific. (1) He devised a series of graded intellectual tasks whereby intelligence could in fact be effectively measured; (2) he described a mode of evaluating the results in terms of age units, such that the average child of 6 might be said to have a mental age of 6, the average child of 9 a mental age of 9 years, and so on. The technique of scoring tests in terms of age units has come to be known as

An example may clarify these notions. One may inquire about the amount of strength required to lift a heavy load. Obviously, the answer depends first of all upon the actual weight of the object to be lifted. If, for example, the weight were 125 lbs., one could ask: When does the normal, average male have sufficient strength to lift 125 lbs.? After testing a number of average males at various chronological age levels, the answer could be established at a particular age, e.g., eighteen years. Consequently, the norm of strength required of a male to lift 125 lbs. would then have been determined to be the degree of strength normally enjoyed at the chronological age of eighteen years, or in other words, the strength of an eighteen-year-old is needed.

In a similar way the question could be asked: How much knowledge, freedom, and maturity of judgment would a person need in order to place a valid act? The answer would depend on the particular legal act involved.

The legislator frequently demands a measuring up to the norm, as a necessary condition for the validity of a legal act. For instance, Canon 573 makes the completion of the twenty-first year a necessary condition for the validity of the legal act of taking perpetual vows. Thus, were a person with the psychical capacity of a normal individual of twenty-one to enjoy the required knowledge, but possess only the chronological age of nineteen, he would not validly profess his vows, unless he had first received a dispensation. In other cases the lawgiver may choose to be less specific, using for example, such terms as: "deficiency of reason by lack of age"[126] or, "the age of reason." The age of reason is presumed to be reached at the chronological age of seven. This presumption must, of course, yield to the contrary fact in a given case.[127]

the mental age method, and the scores obtained by this method as mental ages (M. A5s)."—David Wechsler, *The Measurement and Appraisal of Adult Intelligence* (4 ed., Baltimore: The Williams, & Wilkins Company, 1958), p. 24.

[126] Canon 854.

[127] Canon 88, § 3.

Where a doubt of fact exists as to the presence of the psychic capacity and necessary knowledge for a specific legal act, the case must be solved according to the legally established norm, standard or presumption. It is precisely such doubtful cases which may be proposed to a court for adjudication. The task of the court will be one to decide as to whether this particular abnormal person[128] either measures up or has measured up to the determined norm. Using again the example of lifting a specific weight,[129] one can make the following observation: experience teaches that a normal, average male of 18 years can lift 125 lbs. If one considers an individual who is not normal, for instance, a person who has been weakened by poliomyelitis, one may reasonably question whether such a handicapped person, who may be twenty-five year old, can lift 125 lbs. In the event that an actual test is impractical or impossible, one can still answer the question regarding the person's ability to lift 125 lbs. by determining whether he has the physical strength normally found in a person of eighteen years. If so, he can be said to be able to lift that specific weight; if not, he cannot be said to have the power.

The court must proceed similarly in doubtful cases regarding a person's psychical capacity (i.e., knowledge, freedom and maturity of judgment) for the valid placing of a specific legal act. It is among these doubtful cases that one finds the marriage causes in which mental illness is alleged as an incapacitating cause which impedes the valid placing of the legal act required for entering into the matrimonial contract. In such an instance the court must determine the knowledge, freedom and maturity of judgment that suffice for the legal act of giving a valid marital consent. Moreover, it must determine at what stage of human development these psychical requirements are usually met by a normal person. From this consideration the norm is drawn. The court will then

[128] A person must be classed as abnormal not only if he falls short of the normal but also if he far exceeds the normal. Every person who is mentally abnormal is not necessarily mentally sick.

[129] Cf. *supra*, p. 85.

investigate and judge whether this particular person qualifies in relation to this standard or norm at the time when the marriage ceremony took place, and consequently, whether this person was able to have given a valid marital consent.

In the next chapter, therefore, it will be necessary to examine the psychical requirements for matrimony and to formulate a norm according to which doubtful cases can be adjudicated.

CHAPTER V

THE PSYCHICAL REQUIREMENTS FOR MATRIMONY

In article 1 of the foregoing chapter the nature, the object, the end, and the essential qualities of matrimony have been considered. Consent was shown to be the constitutive element of marriage, and the necessary qualities of marital consent were enumerated. In article 2 the operations of the intellect and will were analyzed in order to furnish a better understanding of consent as a free human action. A free human action, finally, was proven to be a necessary condition for the validity of all legal acts, while the degree of knowledge and freedom necessary was shown to be dependent on the specific nature of the legal act. In the present chapter the general notions of the previous chapter will be drawn together, so as to obtain a better understanding of the psychical requirements necessary for entrance into a valid matrimonial contract.

ARTICLE 1. THE KNOWLEDGE NECESSARY FOR A VALID MATRIMONIAL CONTRACT

SECTION A. THE KNOWLEDGE NECESSARY REGARDING THE NATURE AND OBJECT OF MATRIMONY

Canon 1082, § 1 defines the minimum knowledge required for a matrimonial contract: It states: "In order that matrimonial consent be had it is necessary that the contracting parties at least be not lacking in the knowledge that marriage is a permanent society of a man and woman for the procreation of children." The second paragraph continues: "Such ignorance is not presumed is those who have attained puberty."[1] Man cannot consent to what he does not comprehend.

[1] § 1: Ut matrimonialis consensus haberi possit, necesse est ut contrahentes saltem non ignorent matrimonium esse societatem permanen-

Marital consent is not possible, therefore, without at least some rudimentary knowledge of what constitutes the essential object of the marriage contract. This essential object as seen above, is the mutual transfer of rights over one another's body for acts which of themselves are suitable for the generation of children.[2] Canon 1082, § 1 states that the parties must at least not be ignorant of the fact that marriage is a permanent society between a man and a woman for the procreation of offspring. It is, however, not necessary that this knowledge be perfect.[3] The words of the canon "*saltem non ignorare*" indicate that an imperfect and rudimentary knowledge suffices. Only that ignorance, therefore, will invalidate a matrimonial contract, which directly affects those elements which are essential to marriage itself. Thus the parties must know that marriage is a permanent union or society between a man and a woman. Moreover they must also know the object of this union, namely, the mutual transference of the right to the body for acts which of themselves are suitable for the generation of children. If the parties to a marriage contract were ignorant of the true object of marriage, if they, for instance believed marriage to be a union between a man and woman for a mere scientific or educational end, such marriage would have to be considered invalid.[4]

The parties must not be ignorant of the fact that children are born *of*, and not merely *in*, the marriage.[5] They must know that there is in marriage a mutual transfer of rights and consequent obligations. They must also realize that

tem inter virum et mulierem ad filios procreandos. § 2: Haec ignorantia post pubertatem non praesumitur.

[2] Cf. *supra*, p. 64.

[3] "Verum haud opus est, ut illud penitus et undequaque noverit, nam etsi noverit in confuso (imperfecte), illud, quale quantumcumque est, velle intelligitur."—D'Annibale, *Summula Theologiae Moralis* (3 vols., 5. ed. Romae, 1908), I, 118.

[4] *Sacrae Romanae Rotae Decisiones Seu Sententiae* (ab anno 1909; Romae: Typis Vaticanis, 1912—), VII (1914), 307. (Hereafter cited *S.R.R. Decisiones.*)

[5] *S.R.R. Decisiones,* XXVI (1934), 613.

these rights and obligations are directed to the object of marriage, namely, the procreation of offspring.[6] The parties, therefore, must know and intend to concede the right to each other's body for the performance of those acts which of themselves are ordained for the procreation of offspring. If correctly understood, one can say that it suffices for the validity of a marriage contract if the contracting parties explicitly will or intend to do what others do when they marry, or to contract marriage as it was instituted by God, and thus only implicitly to will all that pertains to the essence of the marriage contract.[7] The sufficiency of such a general intention does not take away the necessity of knowledge that in marriage a corporal right is given and received. Neither is such an implicit intention of the parties to be taken as a substitute for knowledge of the essential elements of marriage.[8]

The parties must realize that for the procreation of offspring some sort of bodily cooperation between the parties is required. They must at least know that this is a corporal or physical cooperation and not just a mental or psychological one. Canon 1082, § 1, implies that the acts which are the object of the marital right are corporal acts. Consequently the canon implies that these acts must be known as corporal acts. Canon 1082, § 1, states that the parties to a marriage contract must know that marriage is a permanent society. Knowledge of marriage as a society implies by law knowledge that in marriage there is a mutual transfer of rights to acts which involve cooperation as determined by the conjugal right on which the conjugal society is founded.[9] But cooperation in accordance with the conjugal right, which in the contemplation of the law is essentially a corporal right, is equivalent to corporal cooperation, which in practice is

[6] Smith, *Ignorance Affecting Matrimonial Consent,* p. 78.

[7] Gasparri, *Tractatus de Matrimonio,* II, n. 780.

[8] Smith, *op. cit.,* p. 79.

[9] Wernz-Vidal, *Ius Matrimoniale,* n. 547; Payen, *De Matrimonio in Missionibus,* III, nn. 1623-1626.

reduced to corporal acts. Smith in his study adds another consideration. He states:

> A further indication that it is necessary for a person who contracts marriage to know that he is conceding the right to the performance of corporal acts is derived from a consideration of the essential object of the matrimonial consent. The essential object of a matrimonial consent consists in the concession and acceptance of a right to the married partner's body for the purpose of performing acts (*in ordine ad actus*). The object of the consent, therefore, is not simply the concession and acceptance, of the right to the body, but the concession and acceptance of the right to the body for the performance of acts which are the object of the right to the body, and which, inasmuch as they proceed from the right to the body, are specified as corporal acts.[10]

It may reasonably be asked whether the validity of matrimonial consent requires that the parties have specific knowledge of the act of copulation itself. Is it necessary for them to know how the bodily cooperation is executed? Would it be true to say that persons who are not enlightened in sexual matters are *ipso facto* unable to give valid matrimonial consent?[11]

Vlaming, Knecht, Oesterle, and others who hold that the object of marriage (the mutual right to each other's body for acts suitable for the generation of children) needs the further specification "for acts of marital intercourse or copulation,"[12] necessarily demand that the parties specifically know the nature and manner of the marital act of copulation.[13]

It has been shown in article 1 of Chapter IV that the ex-

[10] Smith, *op. cit.*, p. 85.

[11] Schönsteiner, *Grundriss des Kirchlichen Eherechts* (2. ed., Wien, 1937), p. 565-p. 569.

[12] Cf. *supra*, p. 55.

[13] These authors do not agree among themselves as to the precise degree of knowledge regarding copulation required for a valid contract. —Smith, *op. cit.*, pp. 81-82.

ercise of the corporal right is not essential for a valid marriage contract; consequently, the actual act of copulation does not belong to the essence of the contract but is only an effect thereof.[14] If the act of copulation does not belong to the essence of the contract, it is only reasonable to wonder why ignorance of carnal copulation should be considered a basis to invalidate matrimonial consent. Moreover, the Roman Rota has held that knowledge of carnal copulation is not necessary for a valid matrimonial contract. It has upheld the validity of marriages which were brought before it on the grounds of ignorance regarding the act of marital intercourse.[15] This view is also the teaching of Wernz-Vidal, Vermeersch-Cruesen, Chelodi, and Gasparri[16] and it is, *salvo meliore iudicio,* in the opinion of the present writer, the only correct teaching. It is sufficient for the contracting parties to know in general that they are conceding and accepting a corporal right for the performance of acts suitable for the procreation of children. By knowing and consenting to this object, the parties implicitly consent to the act of copulation. They must know, therefore, that to secure the end of matrimony there is to be some corporal union or corporal familiarity, but the precise mode of this union or familiarity need not be known.[17]

At times one of the parties to a marriage contract may state that he was not ignorant of the fact that marriage consisted in the mutual transfer of the right to each other's body for some physical cooperation from which children could be born. He may claim, however, that he did not know the precise nature of this physical cooperation, and that he would not have given consent had he known that in marriage he

[14] Cf. *supra,* p. 56.

[15] *S.R.R. Decisiones,* II (1910), 117; *S.R.R. Decisiones,* XVIII (1926), 4-11; *S.R.R. Decisiones,* XVIII (1926), 68-75.

[16] Cf. *supra,* p. 55.

[17] "Ius ad ipsam (copulam carnalem) tradi et accipi satis implicite cognosci et in consensu comprehendi potest ab eo qui non ignorat, ex cooperatione utriusque coniugis filios procreari et ad hoc matrimonium ordinari."—Wernz-Vidal, *Ius Matrimoniale,* n. 457 ad annot. 13.

was giving his partner the right to have carnal intercourse. Such a plea has no effect at law.[18]

At first sight it may appear that the party's claim, if it could be proven, should be honored at law. The statement of the party is, however, merely an indication of an interpretative intention. As such it was non-existent at the time when the contract was entered into, and consequently, it had no influence upon the consent when it was given. If the law were to allow that such an interpretative intention could affect the validity of a marriage contract, the results at law would be chaotic. Every disillusioned partner to a marriage contract could claim to have had such an intention and demand to be freed from his marital bond by simply declaring: "If I had only known. . . ."

The knowledge necessary to enter into a valid marital contract can, therefore, be summarized as follows: The parties must know that marriage is a permanent society of a man and a woman for the procreation of offspring. This knowledge must embrace the concept that for the procreation of children a physical cooperation of the partners is necessary, and that in view of this physical cooperation, the right to one another's body is transferred in the matrimonial contract. It is not required that the parties have specific knowledge of the act of copulation itself. Neither does a misconception or error regarding the nature or manner of the act of copulation affect the validity of marriage.

SECTION B. THE KNOWLEDGE NECESSARY REGARDING THE ENDS OF MATRIMONY

Matrimony, the union of a man and a woman founded on the mutual giving and receiving of the corporal right, is ordained by nature for the procreation of children. The natural

[18] "Intentio interpretativa est de illa quam homo numquam habuit, est tamen ita comparatus animo, ut eam haberet, si de ea cogitaret."—Ferraris, *Prompta Bibliotheca, Canonica, Iuridica, Moralis, Theologica, necnon Ascetica, Polemica, Rubricistica, Historica* (9 vols., Romae, 1885-1899), IV, *s.v.* Intentio.

effect of the corporal cooperation (the object of the conjugal right) is the generation of children.

Canon 1082, § 1, declares that the validity of matrimonial consent requires that the contracting parties know that procreation of offspring is the end or purpose of matrimony, even though the contracting parties may validly and licitly marry for any other honorable motive, as long as they know that marriage, as instituted by God and by nature, has for its purpose the procreation of children.[19] If a man or a woman does not associate the procreation of offspring with the marriage contract as its end or purpose, he or she does not have the requisite knowledge to elicit a valid matrimonial consent. One cannot consent to something that is not known. A person does not know matrimony as such (*opus*), and consequently he cannot consent to it, if he or she does not know the purpose or end (*finis operis*) of matrimony.

The required knowledge, however, need not be perfect knowledge. Neither does the fact that actual generation is known to be impossible in this particular case invalidate the marital contract. A person may know what the purpose of marriage is and consent to it and at the same time be perfectly aware that this purpose or end will not be attained in a particular case. Thus it may be known that one partner is sterile, or both parties may mutually agree to forego the exercise of their marital rights. In the first instance the parties transfer the right to the body for acts which of themselves are suitable for the procreation of children, even though these acts, when exercised are incapable of producing offspring. Here one must attend closely to the essential difference between sterility and impotency at canon law. A sterile person can give his partner the right over his body for acts which of themselves (i.e., as such) are suitable for the generation of children. The fact that these acts do not produce the actual effect of procreation is irrelevant. In the

[19] Canon 1082 § 1: Ut matrimonialis consensus haberi possit, necesse est ut contrahentes saltem non ignorent matrimonium esse societatem permanentem inter virum et mulierem ad filios procreandos.

case of impotency,[20] on the other hand, the party cannot transfer the right to his body for such acts. One cannot give to another what one does not actually possess.[21] When the parties agree not to exercise the marital right, they actually confer the right but enter upon an agreement not to exercise their right. The agreement to by-pass the exercise of the right indicates the transfer of right as well as a knowledge of the intrinsic purpose of that right.[22]

The secondary ends of matrimony are included in the primary end.[23] As a result, the secondary ends of marriage need not be known explicitly when the marital consent is given. It is true that all the ends of marriage belong to the essence of marriage as an institution, but the secondary ends are subordinate and dependent on the primary end.[24]

In conclusion it may be said that the parties have sufficient knowledge regarding the ends of marriage if their concept of marriage is that marriage is a state instituted for the procreation and education of children. If correctly understood this general concept includes both the primary and secondary ends of matrimony. Smith in his study states:

> The Code makes no specific reference to the education of the children or to the secondary ends of marriage, namely, the mutual aid and remedy for concupiscence, in its declaration concerning the requisite knowledge for the eliciting of a valid matri-

[20] Impotency is defined as: "Incapacitas viri aut mulieris ad copulam coniugalem."—Cappello, *De Matrimonio*, nn. 344-347; Gasparri, *De Matrimonio*, I, n. 511; Chelodi, *Ius Matrimoniale*, n. 69.

[21] "Ad effectum matrimonii irritandi, sola coeundi impotentia in nostro foro attenditur; nam impotentia generandi, ex quocunque defectu proveniat, validitati nuptiorum non nocet, siquidem obiectum immediatum contractus matrimonialis non est ius ad actionem naturae a qua pendet foecundatio et conceptio, cum non sit in coniugum potestate illud tradere atque promittere, sed est ius ponendi coniugalem actionem, seu copulam carnalem in ordine ad prolis generationem, quod ius dumtaxat in contractu matrimoniali promittere coniuges valent."—*S.R.R. Decisiones*, XXII (1930), 107.

[22] Gasparri, *Tractatus De Matrimonio*, II, n. 901.

[23] Cf. *supra*, p. 56.

[24] *Ibidem*, p. 56.

monial consent. However, if a person has knowledge of all the elements contained in canon 1082, § 1, he cannot but know that marriage is further ordained for the education of children, for the exchange of mutual aid, and as a remedy for concupiscence. Because of the necessary connection between the procreation and education of children, a person could not know that marriage is ordained for the procreation of children without realizing at the same time that the obligation of educating children pertained to the marriage state. Then, too, one who is familiar with the concept of society, comprehending at it does the note of cooperation, necessarily knows that the purpose of marriage is to provide mutual aid for the spouses. Finally, when a person knows that the marriage contract involves the giving and accepting of a right to the married partner's body for the performance of corporal acts, he must realize that marriage offers a legitimate way to obtain relief from carnal concupiscence.[25]

SECTION C. THE KNOWLEDGE NECESSARY REGARDING THE PROPERTIES OF MATRIMONY

Canon 1082, § 1, indicates the knowledge regarding the essential properties of marriage which is necessary for entrance into marriage. The parties must know that marriage is a society between one man and one woman. They are also to know that this society is a permanent one. Consequently,

> ...if a person ignorant of the unity and permanence of matrimony contracts marriage with the idea that he may concede the corporal right to another, so that the right to his body may be shared simultaneously by two or more persons, he does not give a valid consent to marry; or if a person enters into a marriage contract thinking that the duration of the marriage is determined by the will of the parties themselves to be husband and wife, so that when the will to be married ceases the marriage bond likewise ceases to exist, neither his con-

[25] Smith, *Ignorance Affecting Matrimonial Consent*, pp. 89-90.

sent nor the consequent state can be termed matrimonial.[26]

Fässler does not accept this teaching. He compares canon 1081, § 1, with canon 1082, § 1. He takes canon 1082, § 1 to be a further limitation of canon 1081, § 2. The latter canon gives, according to Fässler, the perfect definition of marital consent, while canon 1082, § 1, provides the minimum knowledge required of the parties to a marriage contract. Consequently, he holds that all elements which are not enumerated in this canon, as far as the necessity of their being known is concerned, remain irrelevant for the validity of the consent. This irrelevancy refers also to the essential properties of marriage, as in his opinion, is proven from canon 1084 which states: "a simple error concerning the unity, indissolubility or sacramental character of marriage, even if it be the motive of the contract, does not vitiate the consent."[27] Fässler does agree, however, that these properties of marriage may not be excluded by a positive act of the will at the time when the parties give their consent to the marriage.[28]

[26] *Ibidem*, p. 90.

[27] "Simplex error circa matrimonii unitatem vel indissolubilitatem aut sacramentalem dignitatem, etsi det causam contractui, non vitiat consensum matrimonialem."

[28] "Das Kirchliche Rechtsbuch gibt Beispiele genug dafür, dass gewissen Anforderungen, welche die Kirche stellt, der Charakter des blossen Wunsches zukommt, dass andere Anforderungen Zur Erlaubtheit einer Rechtshandlung notwendig sind, und dass es schliesslich Anforderungen gibt, deren Mangel das Rechtsgeschäft ungültig machen, das Rechtsgeschäft überhaubt nicht erstehen lassen. Diese letzteren stellen das Minimum rechtlicher Anforderungen dar, da es Erfordernisse sind, welche auf die von der Natur der Sache verlangte Notwendigkeit reduziert sind. Solche, auf die naturgeforderte Notwendigkeit reduzierte Anforderungen bezüglich des Ehevertrags-objektes finden diesem Kanon aufgezählt sind, bleiden bezüglich der Erkenntnis für wir umschrieben im can. 1082 § 1. Alle andere Elemente, die nicht in die Gültigkeit des Konsenses irrelevant. Dies betrifft somit auch wesentliche Eigenschaften der Ehe, wie es klar und deutlich hervorgeht aus can. 1084. Dank dessen darf und muss man die Eher der Heiden, Häretiker und Schismatiker als gültig annehmen, die kein oder ein

The opinion of Fässler, however, must be rejected. Ignorance of the essential properties must not be confused with simple error regarding them. Ignorance of itself pertains to ideas and to knowledge, while error refers to judgments.[29] When a person is ignorant of the essential properties of marriage he has no idea of the lasting and exclusive nature of the marriage bond. If, on the other hand, a person is in error regarding these essential properties, he has made a judgment regarding them. He has associated the ideas of permanence and exclusiveness with marriage even though he has made a mistake in judging about them. When a person believes, for instance, that a marriage contract can be broken by the power of the State, he admits to knowledge about the permanence of marriage. Such a person is in error regarding the power of the State, since he believes that the State can break an otherwise permanent bond. Thus, simple error regarding the essential properties of marriage, even if it be the cause of the contract, does not invalidate marital consent, unless the error has resulted in a positive act of the will by which the person excludes one of the essential properties of marriage at the time of giving matrimonial consent. Ignorance is the absence of knowledge and it connotes the absence of an explicit or even implicit act of the will to form an exclusive and permanent marriage bond. Consequently, marriage entered into by a person who is ignorant of the essential properties of marriage is no marriage at all.

Finally, it is not necessary that the parties be fully aware at the moment of entering into the contract of all that marriage entails, or that they know all the consequences of marriage. Much less is it required that the parties know the full import of marriage in its ethical, historical, cultural aspects. As will be seen in the next article, however, it is neces-

irreges Wissen haben z. b. bezüglich der Einheit oder Unauflöslichkeit der Ehe, vorausgesetzt, dass diese wesentliche Eigenschaften nicht durch positiven Willensakt ausgeschlossen wurden."—Fässler, *Die Schizophrenie als Ehenichtigkeitsgrund im Kanonischen Recht*, pp. 34-35.

[29]Cerato, *Matrimonium a Codice Iuris Canonici Integre Desumptum* (4. ed., Pativii, 1929), nn. 78-79.

sary for entrance into a valid marriage, that a person be able to make a mature judgment about marriage as a good to be obtained by himself.

Article 2. The Requisite Mental Maturity for Matrimonial Consent

It has been shown in the previous section that the parties to a valid marriage must not be ignorant at least of the fact that marriage is a permanent society of a man and a woman for the procreation of children. To enter a valid marriage contract the parties must consent freely to what they know marriage to be. This conclusion gives rise to several questions. Is mere conceptual knowledge[30] of the nature, object, and properties of marriage sufficient for a valid consent? Or again, is some degree of evaluative knowledge also required?[31] Further, it can be asked whether philosophical freedom alone is sufficient, i.e., a freedom to consent or not to consent,[32] or whether a minimum degree of psychological freedom[33] is also required for validity? If so, then it is of vital importance to determine the precise degree of psychological freedom that is necessary for a person to be able to bind himself to the permanent bond of matrimony with its serious rights and obligation.[34] In attempting to answer these questions exactly, the canon and civil lawyer as well as the moral theologian encounter the most serious obstacles in determining human responsibility. The legal mind has to determine the juridic responsibility of the person, while the moral theologian is concerned with the individual's moral responsibility in placing a human act.[35] Before attempting

[30] Cf. *supra*, p. 73.

[31] Cf. *supra*, p. 74.

[32] Cf. *supra*, p. 76.

[33] Cf. *supra*, p. 77.

[34] Castañeda Delgado, *La Enajenación mental y el consentimiento Matrimonial a la luz de la Psiquiatria y de Jurisprudencia de la Sagrada Rota Romana*, Tesis Doctoral en la Facultad de Derecho Canónico, Universitas Pontificia Salmanticensis (Valodolid: Editorial Sever-Cuesta, 1955), p. 47.

[35] Ford-Kelly, *Contemporary Moral Theology*, p. 209.

to face these questions for a solution, or at least, for some indication as to where the solution is to be found, the following observations must be made.

If the psychical requirements of intellect and will for a valid matrimonial consent are very great, the result will be that even minor mental defects will invalidate marital consent. On the other hand, only graver and more serious mental defects or disturbances will make marital consent impossible if the psychical requirements for marriage are ascertained as being established on a lower psychological level.

Some indication of the extent of these requirements for marriage may be gleaned from the fact that marriage is not meant to be an exclusive state attainable by the few. The right to marry is a primary, innate, and inalienable right of man which cannot be antecedently and completely denied except to those who are certainly incapable of marriage. In case of doubt this right to marriage may not be denied to a person, as is clear, for instance, in cases of doubtful impotency.[36] Canon 1068 states: "Impotency anterior to the marriage and perpetual whether in the man or in the woman, whether known to the other party or not, whether absolute or relative, annuls marriage by the very law of nature." "However," the law continues in paragraph two, "if the impediment of impotency is doubtful, whether the doubt be one of fact or of law, the marriage is not to be hindered."[37]

Leo XIII in his encyclical "*Rerum Novarum*" of May 15, 1891, declared: "In choosing a state of life, it is indisputable that all are at full liberty to follow the counsel of Jesus Christ as to observing virginity, or to bind themselves by the marriage tie. No human law can abolish the natural and original

[36] Frattin, *The Matrimonial Impediment of Impotence: Occlusion of Spermatic Ducts and Vaginismus*, The Catholic University of America Canon Law Studies, n. 381 (Washington, D.C.: The Catholic University of America Press, 1958), p. 45.

[37] § 1. Impotentia antecedens et perpetua, sive ex parte viri sive ex parte mulieris, sive alteri cognita sive non, sive absoluta sive relativa, matrimonium ipso naturae iure dirimit. § 2. Si impedimentum impotentiae dubium sit, sive dubio iuris sive dubio facti, matrimonium non est impediendum.

right of marriage, nor in any way limit the chief and principal purpose of marriage, ordained by God's authority from the beginning."[38]

The Sacred Roman Rota, in one of its decisions observed: "we are prevented from demanding too much in this matter by our common doctrine which declares that even *semifatui* must be admitted to marriage."[39]

The objection that the civil law often demands more for the validity of other contracts is not a valid one. Marriage is no ordinary contract, but is one to which man has a primary natural right. It can be a source of grace, and, in many cases, a necessary means to reach one's eternal destiny. Moreover, marriage is for most people a morally necessary means for a right and reasonable life. O'Brien states:

> The strong inclination given to each individual for sexual gratification is lawfully satisfied in marriage and the contract, considered from this viewpoint, has as its secondary end, the fomenting of mutual love and the remedy for concupiscence. Consequently, the marital union is a morally necessary means of reasonable life and self-development in the majority of persons. The only other conceivable and lawful substitute is celibacy, which is possible only for the minority. If the right of individuals to marry was abolished they would be deprived of a morally necessary means of right and reasonable life. Even the minority who do not wish or need to marry have a natural right to embrace or reject the conjugal state. This constitutes the juridic origin of marriage, the ordination of nature and the revelation of God.[40]

[38] "In diligendo genere vitae non est dubium, quin in potestate sit arbitrioque singulorum alterutrum malle, aut Jesu Christi sectari de virginitate consilium, aut maritali se vinculo obligare. Ius coniugii naturale ac primigenum homini adimere, caussamve nuptiarum praecipuam, Dei auctoritate initio constitutam, quoquo modo circumscribere lex hominum nulla potest."—*Codicis Iuris Canonici Fontes,* III, n. 611, p. 359, n. 9.

[39] *S.R.R. Decisiones,* XXXIII (1941), 168.

[40] O'Brien, *The Right of the State to Make Disease an Impediment to Marriage,* The Catholic University of America Studies in Sacred

The Code of Canon Law, finally, reiterates the principle that man has a natural right to enter matrimony when it asserts that all can contract marriage, unless they are prohibited by law.[41]

In view of these facts, one must agree that the psychical capacity for marriage must be placed within the grasp of the vast majority of people; marriage may not be, as it were, placed beyond the psychological range of the average person, or even beyond many whose psychological range is below average. Moreover, the fact that a certain person should not have married does not imply that that person was not able to marry. Quite often people seek after an annulment of a marriage which has turned out to be unfortunate. At times they assert that they were too young to know what marriage entailed, or, that their marriage partner was unbalanced, immature, or, even insane. The majority of these marriages should perhaps not have been contracted but, *de facto,* they were entered into and are to be recognized as valid marriages. It is not the question whether it was prudent to have entered a marriage which is examined by law, but only whether the marriage is valid. In all marriage cases the prevailing basic assumption is laid down by canon 1014 which states: "Marriage enjoys the favor of the law; therefore, in case of doubt, its validity must be maintained until the contrary be proved, taking into account the rule of canon 1127."[42]

The second presumption is a basic assumption of the natural law, which holds that all men must be considered sane until the contrary is proved.[43] The fact, therefore, that a

Theology, second series, No. 73 (Washington, D.C.: The Catholic University of America Press, 1952), p. 88.

[41] Omnes possunt matrimonium contrahere, qui iure non prohibentur —c. 1035.

[42] Matrimonium gaudet favore iuris; quare in dubio standum est pro valore matrimonii, donec contrarium probetur, salve praescripto can. 1127.—An investigation of canon 1127 must be considered to fall outside the scope of the present study.

[43] Hayes, "Mental Disease and the Ecclesiastical Courts," *The Jurist,* XVI (1956), 278.

person may not appear to be perfectly normal or adjusted, does not imply immediately that such a person may not contract marriage validly. Actually, a psychically perfect human being is but a theoretical fiction. If a perfect standard of human personality is imagined, everyone will be abnormal to some degree.[44]

It is important to realize that the vast majority of marriages, whether they be attacked or not, are valid marriages. In a study, such as the present one, it is easy to succumb to the temptation of trying to enlarge the field of possibilities for declaring unhappy marriages to be invalid marriages. This inclination may be prompted by the avowed purpose of saving the souls of those involved in such unhappy marriages. However, if one were to succeed in covering a greater number of marriage cases under the heading of "Invalid by reason of psychical incapacity," one would thereby at the same time prevent a greater number of people from entering into the marriage state. The salvation of those who would be disqualified may often depend on their ability to enter a valid marriage. Moreover, the primary purpose of the law in examining the validity of marriages is to establish the objective truth, in order to determine the juridic status of the parties involved. Every marriage case, no matter how sad or deserving, has to overcome the basic assumption of law which states that marriage, once entered into, must be regarded as valid until proven invalid.

Oesterle enumerates four presumptions which militate against a declaration of nullity by reason of psychical incapacity. The four presumptions in favor of the validity of marriage, as given by Oesterle, are: (1) every person must be presumed to be mentally normal. *"Natura ipsa parit homines sanae mentis."* (2) any act which has been posited is presumed to be a valid act. (3) the preparation for the marriage, and the actual marriage ceremony point to a presumption of the validity of that marriage. (4) nature itself inclines man to marriage. Consequently, marriage does not

[44] Terruwe, *Wat is Psychisch Gezond Leven?* (3 e. druk, Roermond-Maaseik; J. J. Romen & Zoonen, 1957), p. 31.

require such protracted reflection and consideration as other serious matters.[45]

A second important observation which has to be made before examining further the psychical capacity for marriage is that consent given in marriage is an act which is one and individual. It is difficult to express the exact notion of what this act implies. The connotation, however, is that various factors enter upon and influence the act of consent. The consent itself remains as one act though it results from the various operations and mutual cooperation of the intellect and will. It should not be dissected with an attribution of one part of the act to the intellect and another part to the will. To divide the act is to falsify it. Even though the operations of the intellect and will are successive and distinct before the actual expression of consent, they result in one act.[46] It is, therefore, neither the intellect nor the will, but the subject man who acts or consents.

When one attempts to determine the validity or invalidity of marital consent from the point of view of sufficiency or insufficiency of psychical capacity, it is the one act of consent which must be examined. Accordingly, it is not necessary to

[45] Die Praesumptionen zu Gunsten der Gültigkeit der Ehe: a) Die erste Praesumption ist diese: Jeder Mensch ist geistig normal. "Natura ipsa parit homines sanae mentis." Diesen Gedanken hob der Kanonist in seinem Gutachten in der berühmten C. Herbipolen. vom 7. Juli, 1883 (*Thesaurus* S.C.C., vol. 142, pag. 466 sq.) hervor; ebenso die S.R.R. in verschiedenen Sentenzen. "Qui asserit aliquem esse insanum, repugnat ipsi naturae, atque ei adversatur praesumptio, quae a natura ipsa descendit." b) Die erste aller Praesumptionen ist diese: der gesetzte Akt ist gültig (S.C.C. in C. *Nespolitana-Florentina*, 22 Dez. 1906, *Thesaurus* S.C.C., v. 165, pag. 1328) c) Die Vorbereitung auf die Ehe und die Trauung selbst sprechen zu Gunsten der Gültigkeit des Aktes. Soll der Pfarrer nichts gemerkt haben? Vorausgesetzt, dass Brautunterricht gegeben wurde. d) Die Natur selbst drängt den Menschen zur Ehe. Daher erfordert der Abschluss der Ehe night einen so langwierigen Gedankengang wie andere schwierige Rechtsgeschäfte."—Oesterle, "Amentia"—*Ephemerides Iuris Canonici*, Annus XI, Num. 3. (Officium Libri Catholici, Romae : Catholic Book Agency, 1955), p. 292-293.

[46] Cf. *supra*, p. 80.

make a complete psychological study of man; neither is it necessary to appraise the mental health or sickness of a person as such, or to determine the precise nature of his mental problems. What is necessary is to determine the requirements for the special act of marital consent, so that it be the act of a sufficiently sane person. The only reason why one may be obliged to evaluate the health status of the intellect and will separately would be to determine the binding effect of the resulting act of consent. It is the act of giving marital consent, a totality made up of several integral factors, which needs to be examined in the present article. The examination of this consent demands consideration of two positions. In the first place, whether the mere knowledge of what marriage is and what it entails is sufficient for marital consent, or whether there is also required a more or less mature judgment regarding the nature and implications of marriage, so that one would demand a considered or deliberated and mature consent for a valid marriage contract. It is this totality of many factors in the marital consent which needs to be examined. It is only secondary that the individual and separate operations of the intellect and will must be investigated.

SECTION A. THE NORMS DETERMINING PSYCHICAL CAPACITY FOR MATRIMONY DERIVED FROM THOMAS SANCHEZ AND ST. THOMAS AQUINAS

Sanchez (1550-1610) held that knowledge of the nature, object and properties of marriage alone was to be considered insufficient to enter a valid marital contract. He required a definite degree of deliberation and maturity of judgment on the part of the partners. The opinion commonly attributed to him compares the degree of knowledge and freedom required for marriage with the degree of knowledge and freedom required for the commission of a mortal sin. In treating of the maturity of judgment necessary for the contract of betrothal, or the solemn engagement before marriage, he states that the same deliberation is sufficient and necessary for betrothal, which is sufficient and necessary for guilt in a lethal matter.[47]

A person's good judgment, according to Sanchez, can be clouded by passion or some disturbing influence to such an extent that a serious wrong done by a person in such a state may not be considered a mortal sin. Neither could a person in such a state of confusion validly bind himself, according to this opinion to a betrothal or marriage contract. The contracts of betrothal and marriage are serious matters on a par with the seriousness of mortal sin and, consequently, the same degree of deliberation should be necessary for betrothal as is required for mortal sin.[48]

On the other hand, Sanchez decided in favor of the validity of a betrothal and subsequent marriage contract of a person who was not completely without the power of deliberation. He did so by appealing to this same norm for determining the mental capacity of the person. He declared: "this person has sufficient power of deliberation to be able to sin seriously."[49]

Although Sanchez is commonly regarded as the author of this opinion, he really inherited it as a measure for deter-

[47]Nihilominus dicendum est, eam deliberationem sufficere et exigi quae in materia lethalis culpae sufficeret, ut consensus esset culpa mortalis, unde si quis ira, aut alio passionis motu subito percitus sponsalia contrahat, si tanta fit passio, ut rationis iudicium obtenebrarit et deliberationem ad peccatum mortale requisitam impedierit, ut si illo subito motu hominem interimeret, non esset mortale: tunc sponsalia non erunt valida defectu deliberationis; si autem non ita impedit deliberationem, quin homicidium illud tunc admissium esset culpa let halis, sponsalia erunt valida. Probatur id requiri, quia sponsalia suapte natura obligant ad mortale, ergo petunt deliberationem ad mortale requisitam: et confirmatur quia minor deliberatio non est sufficiens ad violandam fidem sponsalium nect ut actus sit simpliciter voluntarius.—Sanchez, *De Matrimonio*, Lib. I, Disp. VIII, n. 5.

[48] *Loc. cit.*

[49] Secus est si non caret omnino intellectu, quem vulgo *tonto, o atondado* appellamus, vel dicimus *no tiene tanta sabiduria como Salomono,* ironice. Hic enim sponsalia et matrimonium inire potest... et ratio est manifesta, quia deliberationem sufficientem habet ad lethaliter delinquendum."—*Ibidem*, Disp. VIII, n. 15.

mining the psychical capacity for marriage and betrothal from his predecessors. Amanieu, in an article in the *Dictionnaire de Droit Canonique,* remarks that one could actually speak of this theory as the traditional view.[50] For the commission of a mortal sin Sanchez required that a person compare the thing which he is planning to do with its very opposite.[51]

The opinion, attributed to Sanchez, has had to endure some serious and, at times, vehement attacks. Triebs felt that it had done untold harm. "In how many cases," he asked, "has the acceptance of the erroneous teaching of Thomas Sanchez led to a declaration of validity of a marriage where a declaration of nullity would have been in order?"[52] Oesterle also expresses gratification at the fact

[50] "Elle est antérieure a lui (Sanchez) et comme il le dit, d'ailleurs, ce théologien l'a empruntée a ces prédécesseurs. Elle est donc traditionelle dans la théologie Catholique"—Amanieu, "Aliénation mentale en matière de nullite de mariage," D. D. C., I, 436.

[51] Ut autem adsit deliberatio sufficiens ad mortale et sic ad votum, et sponsalia, debet praemeditari is, qui vovet, aut contrahit, causam nempe iram, angustiam morbi, belli, vel aliam passionem et amorem impellentem et finem quem intendit . . . requiri, ut aliquis conferat id de quo deliberat cum eius opposito, alias non esse simpliciter liberum et huius ratio est, quia discursus, quo intellectus rem aliquam cum eius opposito confert, aperit viam ut voluntas possit rem illam amplecti, vel repudiare, illi ostendens in utroque aliquam boni rationem, quam eligat: quare ubi non est talis collatio non est simpliciter et perfecte libertas—Sanchez, *De Matrimonio,* Lib. I, Disp. VIII, n. 7.

[52] "In dieser Beziehung hat die Lehre des Klassikers des Eherechts, des Thomas Sanchez, wonach zum Abschluss der Ehe jene geistige Überlegung genüge , welche zur Begehung einer Todsünde erforderlich sei, viel Unheil angestiftet. Daraus wurde gefolgert, dass der blosse Vernunftgebrauch zum Eheschlusse genüge . . . Es ist dankbar zu begrüssen, dass die Rota mit dieser Lehre aufgeräumt hat . . . Der geistliche Richter wird sich in Zukunft diese Norm zur Richtsnur machen müssen. In wiefiel Fällen mag die Befolgung der irrigen Lehre von Thomas Sanchez zur Gültigkeitserklärung einer Ehe geführt haben, wo die Nichtigkeitsverklärung notwendig gewesen wäre.—*Praktisches Handbuch des geltenden kanonischen Eherechts in Vergleichung mit dem deutschen staatlichen Eherecht für Theologen und Juristen* (3 vols., Breslau, 1929), III, 443.

that the opinion of Sanchez seems to be more and more abandoned.[53]

Opponents of the theory attributed to Sanchez appeal to the teaching of St. Thomas Aquinas (1225-1274). The latter demanded a higher degree of psychical capacity for a solemn betrothal than for the commission of a mortal sin. For the contract of marriage itself he demanded an even greater maturity of judgment and discretion.[54]

The teaching of St. Thomas may be summarized as follows: Examining the required age for entering into the betrothal contract, he divides the use of reason into three stages corresponding to three definite age levels. During the first period a person cannot comprehend things by his own mental processes nor is he able to learn from others. In the second stage he is able to learn from others but he is still unable to think matters out by himself. In the third period he can learn from others, and he can also reason and deliberate without the assistance of others. The first period lasts till the age of seven and, consequently, before that time a person cannot enter a contract of any kind. In the second period, also a duration of seven years, a person can come to know things with the help of others, especially those matters to which human nature is naturally inclined. As a result, a person in this age group can bind himself to a contract of betrothal. When this period closes at the age of fourteen, he can even bind himself to a contract which concerns himself alone, for instance, to enter religious life or to marry. Only at the end of the third seven-year period can he bind himself to contracts which affect the rights of others. Thus, for example, it is only then that a person can dispose freely of his belongings.[55] For a valid betrothal St. Thomas re-

[53] Oesterle, "Amentia"—*Ephemerides Iuris Canonici,* Annus XI, Num. 3, 292.

[54] Thomas Aquinas, *Commentaria Praeclarissima in IV Libros Sententiarum Petri Lombardi,* IV, Dist. XXVII, q. 2, art. 2—*Opera Omnia,* VII, 952

[55] Utrum tempus septennii sit competenter assignatum sponsalibus contrahendis? Solutio: Respondeo dicendum quod septennium est tempus determinatum a jure sponsalibus contrahendis satis rationabi-

quired more deliberation and judgment on the part of the parties involved than he required for the commission of a mortal sin. For mortal sin all that is needed, according to St. Thomas, is to consent knowingly and willingly to a present act. Bethrotal, on the other hand, looks to the future and, consequently, more is required on the part of the intellect and will for betrothal than for mortal sin. He concludes: "a person can sin mortally before he can bind himself to something in the future."[56]

Sanchez realized that his opinion was opposed to the teach-

liter quia cum sponsalia sint quaedam promissio futurorum, ut dictum est, oportet quod illorum sint qui aliquo modo promittere possunt, quod non est nisi illorum qui habent aliquam prudentiam de futuris quae usum rationis requirit, respectu cujus triplex gradus notatur secundum Philosophum in I Ethic. Primus est, cum quis neque intelligit per se neque ab alio capere potest. Secundus status est, cum homo ab alio capere potest, sed ipse per se non sufficit ad intelligendum. Tertius est, cum homo ab alio jam capere potest et per seipsum considerare. Et quia ratio paulatim in homine convalescit, secundum quod quietantur motus, et fluxibilitas humorum; ideo primum statum rationis obtinet homo ante primum septennium; et propter hoc illo tempore nulli contractui aptus est, et ita nec sponsalibus. Sed ad secundum statum incipit homo pervenire in fine primi septennii; unde etiam tunc temporis pueri ad scholas ponuntur; sed ad tertium statum incipit homo pervenire in fine secundi septennii quantum ad ea quae ad personam ipsius pertinent in qua ratio naturalis citius convalescit; sed quantum ad ea quae extra ipsum sunt in fine tertii septenni. Et ideo ante primum septennium nulli contractui homo aptus est; sed in fine primi septennii incipit esse aptus ad aliqua promittendum in futurum, praecipue de his ad quae ratio naturalis inclinat magis; non autem ad obligandum se perpetuo vinculo, quia adhuc non habet firmam voluntatem; et ideo possunt tali tempore contrahi sponsalia. Sed in fine secundi septennii jam potest obligare se de his quae ad personam ipsius pertinent, vel ad religionem, vel ad coniugium. Sed post tertium septennium etiam potest de aliis se obligare, et secundum leges constituitur ei potestas, disponendi de rebus suis post vigintiquinque annos. —*loc. cit.*

[56] Et ideo dicendum, quod ad peccatum mortale sufficit etiam consensus praesens; sed in sponsalibus est consensus in futurum. Major autem rationis discretio requiritur ad providendum in futurum quam ad consentiendum in unum praesentem actum et ideo ante potest homo peccare mortaliter quam possit se obligare ad aliquid in futurum.—*loc. cit.*

ing of St. Thomas Aquinas. He cites St. Thomas as one of the adversaries to his opinion that a person able to commit mortal sin is also able to bind himself to a solemn engagement contract. However, he defends his theory by explaining that the same degree of knowledge and freedom is considered sufficient to bind oneself to the solemn vow of sacred orders and to the simple vow of religion. Both of these entail perpetual obligations and bind more stringently than the contract of betrothal.[57]

Even though Sanchez definitely disagreed with St. Thomas Aquinas as far as the betrothal contract is concerned, it is not quite so certain that he was in disagreement also regarding the marriage contract itself. It must be admitted that authors who consider the subject of the discretion required for a valid marriage contract[58] seem to take it for granted that Sanchez was opposed to Aquinas, not only with regard

[57] In n. 15 of Disputation XVI of Book I, Sanchez asks whether that use of reason which is commonly had at the age of seven and which is sufficient for mortal sin is also to be considered sufficient for a bethrothal contract. "An sufficit is usus rationis ante septennium ad sponsalia contrahenda, qui satis est ut puer ille possit lethaliter delinquere?" He then cites St. Thomas as being opposed to his teaching, but he defends his opinion by saying: "His non obstantibus probabilius credo sufficere eum usum rationis, qui ad culpam lethalem satis est. Probatur quia is usus rationis satis est ad obligandum se per votum solemne ordinis sacri, quod tamen est perpetuum et per votum simplex religionis quae est obligatio status perpetui, et maior quam sponsalium, quia votum annexum ordini sacro, nullo modo solvi potest nisi per dispensationem Pontificiam: Votum etiam illud religionis indiget eadem dispensatione, vel paterna irritatione nec potest propria pueri voluntate dissolvi: at sponsalia sola pueri voluntate puberis facti, dirimi possunt. Probatur quia si ea futurorum providentia, quam postulat prior sententia, desideraretur: incaute praescriptum esset septennii tempus, ea enim tenerrima aetate praesentium non habet puer providentiam, nedum futurorum: et vix eo rationis usu gaudet, ut capax sit lethalis culpae. Pro hac sententia sunt caeteri D. D. allegati n. 9. absolute docentes usu rationis praeveniente, posse sponsalia contrahi ante septennium.—*op. cit.*, I, Disp. XVI, n. 16.

[58] Cf. Triebs, *Praktisches Handbuch des geltenden Eherechts*, III, 443; Oesterle, "Amentia"—*Ephemerides Iuris Canonici*, Annus XI, Num. 3, 292; Doheny, *Canonical Procedure in Matrimonial Cases*, Vol. I, *Formal Procedure*, 785.

to the betrothal contract, but also with regard to the marital contract itself. Perhaps, however, *debita cum reverentia,* this view is doing an injustice to Sanchez. Without doubt Sanchez required more for a person to marry validly than he considered necessary for him to become validly engaged. Thus he refused to admit that a seven-year-old child, who was presumed to have the use of reason and, consequently, had to be considered capable of mortal sin and of entering the betrothal contract, could also enter a valid matrimonial contract. "For," he said, "at such a tender age there is not sufficient discretion to bind oneself to the perpetual bond of marriage."[59] He held that betrothal could be terminated when a child reached puberty and that, consequently, not as much discretion was required for engagement as for marriage itself which was a perpetual contract that could not be broken by the wills of the parties involved.[60] Under the caption "*De malitia supplente aetatem,*" Sanchez considered the maturity required for marriage to be more than physical maturity. He included in the notion of maturity the idea of prudence and discretion to understand the import and effects of matrimony. "Marriage," he said, "because it is such a serious and perpetual matter, demands more discretion than that which is found at such an early age," that is, at an age before puberty.[61] Again, when he compares physical maturity with psychical maturity, he states: "One sometimes finds a child who at an early age is physically capable of marital

[59] Sanchez, *De Matrimonio,* VII, disp. 104, n. 22.

[60] Nec obstat sponsalia ante septennium valere, modo tunc rationis usus adsit. Quia cum sponsalia adveniente pubertate solo puberis consensu cessari valeant, non tantam discretionem ad sui valorem desiderant, quantam matrimonium, quod est vinculum perpetuum.—Sanchez, *De Matrimonio,* VII, disp. 104, n. 23.

[61] At multo probabilius est nomine malitiae supplentis aetatem ad matrimonium petitam, comprehendi potentiam ad copulam, ac prudentiam et discretionem ad intelligendam consensus conjugalis vim. Quae cum sit res gravissima et perpetua exigit majorem discretionem ea, quae in tenera aetate reperitur; quare non sufficit ad matrimonii impuberis valorem sola generandi potentia aetatem praeveniens, nisi ea quoque prudentia adsit.—*Ibidem,* n. 21.

intercourse but at that same early age there is not likely to be present that degree of discretion which is required for the most grave and perpetual bond of matrimony."[62]

SECTION B. A POSSIBLE CONCORDANCE OF THE VIEWS OF ST. THOMAS AQUINAS AND OF THOMAS SANCHEZ

It is the opinion of this writer that Amanieu succeeds in harmonizing the views of Sanchez and St. Thomas Aquinas.[63] He also explains the opinions expressed by the Rota, which may at first sight appear contradictory in so far as some decisions seem to follow Sanchez,[64] while others seem to adhere to the opinion of St. Thomas Aquinas and to demand more than a mere capacity for mortal sin,[65] and others still in which both opinions regarding the psychical capacity for marriage seem to find acceptance.[66] Amanieu summarizes the jurisprudence regarding the psychical capacity for marriage as follows:

> In what then does the degree of intelligence and freedom necessary for the validity of marriage consist? According to the jurisprudence this is characterized by two things: (1) the intelligence and freedom sufficient for committing mortal sin, and at the same time, (2) the knowledge, more or less general, of the nature and significance of the matrimonial contract. Even though the first of these conditions is realized at approximately the age of seven, the second does not appear until the age of puberty. The first of these requisite condi-

[62] . . . quia in tenera aetate invenitur aliquando robur ad copulam cum tamen in ea non soleat tanta discretio adesse quanta ad vinculum matrimonii desideretur.—*Ibidem*, n. 27.

[63] Amanieu, "Aliénation mentale en matière de nullité de mariage." —*D.D.C.*, I, 436.

[64] *S.R.R. Decisiones*, V (1913), 564; V (1913), 149; XIV (1922), 210; XIV (1922), 223; XVI (1924), 372.

[65] *S.R.R. Decisiones*, XI (1919), 172; XIV (1922), 314; XV (1923), 128; XVI (1924), 217; XVIII (1926), 183, 216; XXIII (1931), 152; XXV (1933), 407; XXVIII (1936), 770; XXXII (1940), 86; XXXIII (1941), 653.

[66] *S.R.R. Decisiones*, XXII (1930), 128; XX (1928), 66.

tions is generally quoted as being derived from Sanchez. However, it originated before his time and, as he himself stated, he had borrowed it from his predecessors. It is, therefore, the traditional teaching in Catholic Theology. However, this test, by itself, is not sufficient. It determines only the state of intelligence and free will. Without a doubt, it was precisely this limitation which was pointed out in the sentence of November 14, 1919 (A.A.S. XIII [1921] 57) by the same judiciary of the Sared Roman Rota, *coram Prior,* which appears to reject this rule after first accepting it. (*S.R.R. Decisiones,* VII [1915], dec. XX, *coram Prior, loc. cit.*) It is not sufficient to consider the intelligence only in so far as its capacity is concerned; that would, moreover, not even be sufficient to determine whether in a particular instance a mortal sin had been committed or not. It it also necessary that the intelligence has actually exercised its power, and that it has actually acquired the knowledge necessary for the act about which one is concerned in a given case. It is precisely this distinction which the judges and authors refer to in the second part of the rule, which we have just given, namely, by requiring knowledge of the nature of marriage and the obligations which marriage entails. It is not necessary, however, that the parties have the knowledge of theologians or jurists. It is sufficient if they know in general, *saltem in confuso,* that the union of marriage is a lasting one with a view to leading a common life and to procreating children. These matters, as one can see, become quite easily known in the life of a person, and it is on these matters that the mind, which is sufficiently developed to have knowledge of good and evil, must fix itself with the power of reflection which it possesses... The precise point which one cannot cover with a general rule concerns the manner of recognizing and of proving that this state of intelligence and of knowing did actually exist at the moment of giving marital consent.[67]

Notwithstanding the explanations by Amanieu, the ma-

[67] Amanieu, "Aliénation mentale en matière de nullité de mariage." -*D.D.C.*, I, 436.

turity of judgment or discretion and the degree of deliberation necessary for the giving of a valid matrimonial consent continue to present serious difficulties to many jurists. It would seem that many of these difficulties arise from a vagueness in terminology or from a misunderstanding of the terminology employed by other authors rather than from a legal difficulty.

The present writer intends to describe the problem by quoting rather extensively from four dissertations which were written recently at the universities of Ottawa, Lublin, Salamanca and Washington. After presenting the views expressed by the authors, and the sources on which they based their opinions, the writer will attempt to show that the authors do not actually differ in their opinions as much as may at first appear, but that the apparent differences between them are differences in terminology rather than in legal thought.

Curran, in a historical study of the effects of mental illness on matrimonial consent,[68] made the following observations regarding the opinions of Sanchez and St. Thomas Aquinas. He stated:[69]

> "According to Sanchez, a person had a sufficient intellectual capacity to marry if he was capable of that deliberation which was verified in the committing of a mortal sin.[70] Although Sanchez' statement was presented without any argumentation to support it, it was accepted and repeated almost without comment by many subsequent authors.[71] The opinion which in respect of marriage exacted

[68] *Mental Diseases and Disorders as Invalidating Matrimonial Consent, A Historical Synopsis,* Typewritten licentiate dissertation, School of Canon Law, (archives unique copy No. 8147), The Catholic University of America, Washington, D.C., 1952.

[69] Curran, *op. cit.*, pp. 46-48.

[70] Curran cities: Sanchez, *De Matrimonio,* Lib. I, disp. III, nn. 15, 17.

[71] The following references are given: Pontius, *De Sacramento Matrimonii,* Lib. IV, Cap. I, n. 7; Reiffenstuel (1642-1703), *Ius Canonicum Universum* (7 vols., Parisiis, 1864-1870), Lib. IV, Tit. I, n. 11; Leurenius, *Ius Canonicum,* IV, I, 47; Vecchiotti, *Institutiones,* III, Cap. XI, 47; D'Annibale, *Summula,* I, n. 30; Wernz, *Ius Matrimoniale,* n. 93.

> a higher degree of deliberation than the degree or measure involved in the committing of a mortal sin was not without its defenders. Pontius singled out Peter Ledesma (†1616) as an outstanding proponent of this theory. Unfortunately, Ledesma's work *De Magno Matrimonio Sacramento,* is not available for direct inspection and verification.[72]

Curran continues:

> De Smet, writing shortly before the promulgation of the Code, took a somewhat different approach to this question. He felt that an insane person was prohibited from marrying if he did not have sufficient use of his reasoning faculties to understand the substance of the marriage contract. He did not attempt to determine whether a person with the bare use of reason was to be regarded as possessed of this capacity or deprived of it.[73] Gasparri, likewise, felt that in order to be an apt subject for the contracting of marriage, one must be endowed with a mental capacity that enables one substantially to appreciate what is implied in the marriage contract. He went further, however, than did De Smet, in determining the persons who enjoy this capacity. He stated that it was commonly admitted that those under the age of puberty and near the state of infancy were not bound either by the civil law or by the natural law, to any contract. This same rule could also, in his opinion, be applied to marriage. Implicitly, at least, he was supporting the theory of St. Thomas and rejecting that of Sanchez, since even a person just beyond infancy might well be capable of committing a mortal sin.[74]

Pickett in his study made at the University of Ottawa in 1952 described the problem of the discretion and deliberation necessary for a valid matrimonial contract as follows:[75]

[72] Reference is made to Pontius, *De Sacramento Matrimonii,* Lib. IV, Cap. I, n. 7.

[73] Curran refers to De Smet, *De Sponsalibus et Matrimonio* (Burgis, 1909), p. 322.

[74] Curan cites the 1904 edition of Gasparri, *De Matrimonio,* II, n. 881.

[75] *Mental Affliction and Church Law* (The Catholic University of Ottawa Canon Law Studies, n. 25, Ottawa: The University of Ottawa Press, 1952), pp. 144-147.

The great difficulty in the matter of insanity and marriage is to determine just what degree of discretion in a person is sufficient for the making of a valid matrimonial contract. Any human act necessitates the use of intellect and will. The making of a contract obviously implies the placing of a human act and, therefore, demands the use of intellect and will. Since marriage is an extremely important, far-reaching, irrevocable and sacred contract, it follows that the use of a comparable degree of intelligence and freedom of will is necessary on the part of one who would validly marry.[76] Admittedly, no concrete or definite rule can be set forth in such an intangible matter.[77] The Code itself, in Canon 1082, § 1, declares that those who would give the required consent in marriage must, at least, not be ignorant of the fact that marriage is a permanent union between a man and a woman for the procreation of offspring. § 2 of the same Canon states that this ignorance is not presumed in parties after the age of puberty. It is sometimes inferred from the declaration of Canon 1082, § 2, that such ignorance is to be presumed before the age of puberty.[78] It is very doubtful whether this is a valid inference. However, we must conclude that the Code itself sets the minimum of knowledge regarding marriage, for a valid contracting of the same, as that normally existent in one at the age

[76] Pickett refers to the 1932 edition of Gasparri, *De Matrimonio*, vol. II, n. 783: "Proinde ut matrimonium ipso naturae jure valeat, utraque pars usus rationis ita pollere debet, ut quid sit matrimonium eiusdemque essentiales proprietates satis intelligere valeat, idest matrimonium consistere in jure perpetuo et exclusivo in corpus in ordine ad actus per se aptos ad prolis generationem (Can. 1081, § 2), secus patet neque explicitum neque implicitum consensum habere posse."

[77] A reference is made to: Louis Cangardel, *Le Consentement des epoux au mariage* (Paris: Librairie du Recueil Sirey, 1932), p. 107; Wm. J. Doheny, *Canonical Procedure in Matrimonial Cases*, vol. I, p. 784; *S.R. Rotae Decisiones*, 20 (1928), dec. 6, n. 18, p. 70.

[78] Pickett refers to: J. Chelodi, *Jus Canonicum de Matrimonio* (editio quinta, Vicenza: Soc. Anonima Tipografica, 1947), n. 110, p. 133; *S.R. Rotae Decisiones*, 20 (1928), dec. 6, 4, p. 59; Cf. also Francis Wanenmacher, *Canonical Evidence in Marriage Cases* (Philadelphia: Dolphin Press, 1935), n. 466, p. 298; Gasparri, *De Matrimonio*, vol. II, n. 784, p. 13.

of puberty. Such a norm seems to canonize the opinion of St. Thomas that greater discretion is necessary for entering upon the betrothal or marriage contract than that required for the commission of a mortal sin. For the law supposes that a normal child of seven years is capable of sinning grievously.[79]

On the other hand, the opinion usually referred to as that of Sanchez, namely, that the power of discretion which suffices for the commission of a mortal sin is sufficient in a party to valid marriage, has long been a generally accepted opinion. It can hardly be said to be abandoned today as Cangardel declares it to be,[80] for the Rota in one of its *In Jure* disquisitions as recent as 1928 declares the rule of Sanchez to be accepted by all authorities, quotes with approval the *dictum* of Pontius that it is a certain and general rule, and, finally, notes that, according to Gasparri, is it the common opinion.[81] The Rota also emphasized the rule of Cardinal D'Annibale to the effect that insanity usually appears gradually and imperceptibly (*sensim sine sensu*), and in the period of latent incubation, as it is called, as long as there is in the subject that degree of intelligence which is enjoyed by those who have just emerged from infancy, such a one is not to be considered insane.[82] It is true, however, that the Rota elsewhere repudiates the rule of Sanchez[83]

[79] Reference is made to Canons 88, § 3, and 906.

[80] Cangardel, *op. cit.*, p. 107.

[81] The following footnote is given: *S.R. Rotae Decisiones,* 20 (1928), dec. 6, n. 13, p. 66. The *In Jure* section of this decision of the Rota is an extraordinarily thorough exposition of the law on the matter of insanity relative to marriage. In its 4000 words, many intricacies of the problem are elucidated. With reference to the point at issue at the moment, in n. 4 a satisfactory reconciliation of the opinion of St. Thomas and that of Sanchez is set forth. Cf. also *S.R. Rotae Decisiones,* 7 (1915), dec. 20, n. 4, pp. 217-218.

[82] The following footnote is given: *S.R. Rotae Decisiones,* 20, (1928), dec. 6, n. 16, p. 67, n. 20, p. 71: " 'Regulariter ad amentiam pervenitur *sensim sine sensu;* in periodo autem *incubationis* uti aiunt latentis, quamdiu tanta in eo superest vis intelligentiae, quanta pollent hi, qui infantiam vix egressi sunt, non amentibus sunt accensendi'(I, 31, n. 15.)"

[83] Reference is made to: *S.R. Rotae Decisiones,* 21 (1919), dec. 19,

> on the discretion requisite for a valid marriage. It would seem to be necessary, therefore, to make a subtle distinction between *intelligence* and *knowledge* in the matter at hand. The power of intelligence which is peculiar to a normal child at seven years of age is sufficient for the validity of a marriage contract. The law of nature, however, and that of the Code (Canon 1082) demand the knowledge (*in materia matrimoniali*) normally present only at the age of puberty for the validity of the same."[84]

Pickett cites Bensch from the University of Lublin as an author who entirely rejects the rule of Sanchez. Bensch in a summary to his dissertation on the effect of mental illness on the validity of matrimonial consent states: "The maturity of judgment of a person can be said to be proportionate to matrimony when it obtains and employs those psychical faculties which are generally found to be present at the time that natural puberty is reached. This assertion is proven both by natural and positive law, ancient as well as recent."[85]

Bensch continues: "This principle being established, it is necessary to reject the opinion of all those authors who assert that for a valid entering into a marriage contract only that mental discretion is required which is required also for mortal sin, and which, according to that opinion, can be found in children at the completion of the seventh year of age."[86]

n. 6, p. 174: "Regula simplex, ad omnes casus diiudicandos dari nequit, nec certe approbari potest regula a Sanchesio indicata (Lib. I, disp. 9, n. 5), quod nempe satis est ut contrahens deliberationem sufficientem habeat ad lethaliter delinquendum..."

[84] Pickett, *op. cit.*, p. 146.

[85] "Proportionata autem ad matrimonium dici potest maturitas judicii hominis, qui illas facultates psychicas assecutus est iisque fruitur, quae in omnibus generatim reperiuntur tempore naturalis pubertatis advenientis. Id quod probatur tum ex jure naturae, tum ex jure positivo, antiquo simul et recenti."—Bensch, *Wplyw Chorob Umyslowych na Waznosc Umowy Malvenskiej (Influxus Amentiae in Validitatem Consensus Matrimonialis)*, (Lublin: Catholic University, 1936), p. 294.

[86] "Quo principio statuto, refutatur opinio plurimorum, qui in matrimonium valide ineundum eam sufficere mentis discretionem dicunt, quae

Castañeda, finally, in a doctoral dissertation on mental illness and marriage written at the University of Salamanca,[87] upholds the view that the two opinions of St. Thomas Aquinas and of Sanchez do not contradict each other, but rather that they complement each other. He states: "The problem of the requisite degree of the maturity of judgment necessary for marriage branches out into two separate questions totally distinct from each other. One involves the intellectual capacity or the maturity of reason necessary to contract marriage validly, while the other question refers to the will, viz., to determine the degree of deliberation or the maturity of the will required for matrimony."[88]

Castañeda then observes that the opinions of Sanchez and of St. Thomas Aquinas each refer to only one part of the problem. He states that the two opinions must be taken together to supply the entire answer to the problem of the psychical capacity for matrimony. He accepts the opinion of Sanchez as giving an adequate norm to determine the necessary deliberation required for matrimony. At the same time he accepts the opinion of St. Thomas Aquinas as giving the answer to the question of the requisite intellectual maturity.[89]

requiritur ad lethaliter peccandum, quaeque, saltem ex sententia eorum, in infantibus septennio expleto invenitur." *loc. cit.*

[87] Castañeda Delgado, *La Enajenación mental y el Consentimiento Matrimonial a la Luz de la Psiquiatría y de la Jurisprudencia, de la Sagrada Rota Romana,* pp. 53-54.

[88] De aquí que el problema del grado de madure del juicio necesario en orden a la capacidad para contraer matrimonio, se excinde [sic] en dos cuestiones netamente distintas, saber: en una cuestión de *entendimiento,* dirigida a determinar cuál sea el grado de capacidad intelectiva o de madurez de razón para poder contraer y en una cuestión de *voluntad* en orden a determinar el grado de deliberación volitiva o de madurez de voluntad relativo al mismo vínculo matrimonial.—Delgado, *op. cit.,* p. 53.

[89] Y a cada una de estas dos cuestiones responden y se acomodan las dos sentencias que antes hemos examinado y que no sólo no se contradicen entre sí, sino que se completan en una solución total, ya que cada una del ellas aisladamente sólo contiene la solución de uno de los dos diversos aspectos del problema; es decir, cuando se trata de deter-

Castañeda concludes:

> When Sanchez compares matrimony with mortal sin, he does so with regard to deliberation or volitional capacity only, demanding one and the same degree for both. At the same time he agrees perfectly with St. Thomas, when, to be able to validly contract marriage, he requires a greater degree of discretion and of mental development than that which would be sufficient for the commission of a mortal sin; thus, when explaining the impediment of age, Sanchez states that the Church, in establishing the impediment, took into consideration, besides the actual generative power of the contracting parties, the discretion of judgment, *ex jure naturae* necessary for marriage. Sanchez adds that such a discretion may be presumed only after puberty.[90]

Castañeda finally cites Schmalzgruber as making the very same distinction between deliberation and discretion. He states: "Schmalzgruber, likewise, distinguishes perfectly well between the discretion and the deliberation necessary for matrimony. Regarding the latter, he does not require more than the deliberation necessary for the commission of

minar el grado de capacidad intelectiva requerida para el matrimonio (problema de la demencia natural) hace bien la doctrina actual en exigir con Santo Tomas una madurez de juicio superior a la que bastería para cometer un pecado mortal, capez de adquirir aquel conocimiento que del matrimonio exige en [sic] canon 1082; por el contrario, cuando se trata de determinar el grado de capacidad volitiva requerida para el mismo, tendrá exacta aplicación la regla de Sanchez al considerar necessaria y suficiente aquella deliberación de la voluntad que se requiere para el pecado mortal.—Castañeda Delgado, *op. cit.*, p. 53.

[90] En efecto, cuando Sánchez equipara el matrimonio con el pecado mortal lo hace en cuanto a la capacidad *deliberativa* y *volitiva*, exigiendo un mismo grado para ambos; pero está perfectamente de acuerdo con Santo Tomás en exigir para poder contraer matrimonio una mayor discreción y desarrollo mental que el que sería suficiente para el pecado mortal; así, explicando el impedimento de edad, dice que la Iglesia, al establecerlo, ha tenido en cuenta, además de la potencia actual generativa de los contrayentes, *la discreción de juicio ex jure naturae,* discreción, añada, que sólo se presume *después de la pubertad.*—Castañeda Delgado, *op. cit.*, p. 54.

a mortal sin. As to the former, he exacts with Saint Thomas a discretion of reason sufficient to know the conjugal state and the perpetual and indissoluble bond that results from the marriage contract."[91]

Before attempting to correlate the opinions expressed in the quotations given from the dissertations of Curran, Pickett, Bensch and Castañeda Delgado, one final lengthy quotation regarding the deliberation and discretion necessary for matrimony will be taken from the very excellent study by Smith on the subject of ignorance in regard to marriage.[92] It is with the opinion expressed by Smith that the present writer wants to take his stand, even though the writer would like to add one further consideration. The additional consideration will be treated in the scholion to the present chapter. Smith states:

> Where is the line of demarcation to be drawn? As a general principle, it may be stated that one who is capable of the degree of deliberation postulated for the commission of mortal sin is likewise endowed with the requisite mental capacity for the contracting of marriage.[93]
>
> In the light of the applied principle, it is not implied that anyone who is capable of committing any mortal sin must be judged to be capable also of eliciting a valid matrimonial consent. The ability of a person to perform an act is dependent upon the discretion of the person, which in itself must be proportionate to the act performed.[94] The eliciting

[91] También Schmalzgrueber distingue perfectamente bein entre la discreción y la deliberación exigidas para el matrimonio. En cuanto a la segunda, non exige más que la que se requiere para el pecado mortal. Por lo que toca a la primera, pide con Santo Tomás una discreción de razón suficiente para conocer el estado conyugal ye el vínculo perpetuo e indisoluble que lleva consigo (*Sponsalia et matrimonium;* tit. 2, n. 23,—*loc. cit.*

[92] Smith, *Ignorance Affecting Matrimonial Consent,* pp. 50-52

[93] Smith refers to: *De Santo Matrimonii Sacramento,* lib. I, disp. VIII, n. 15; Reiffenstuel, *Ius Canonicum Universum,* lib. IV, tit. I, n. II; *S.R.R. Decisiones, XXII* (1930), 131, n. 8.

[94] Reference is made to: S.R.R., Nullitas Matrimonii, 28 aug. 1911, coram R. P. D. Aloysio Sincero, dec. XXXIX, n. 42—*S.R.R. Decisiones,* III (1911), 450.

of a matrimonial consent, having as its object the complex concept of marriage, requires a greater maturity of judgment and discretion than does the commission of a simple mortal sin.[95]

Thus anyone who has reached the age of reason may be deemed capable of committing a mortal sin, whereas the possession of the use of reason alone is hardly an indication that a person has the requisite mental capacity to give consent for marriage. For this reason the principle here proposed cannot simply be concerned with the discretion which involves a maturity of judgment and of knowledge pertinent to marriage, but must furthermore be concerned with the fuller deliberation which implies a sufficiently mature judgment and knowledge pertinent to the act whereby the matrimonial consent is given. In the application of this principle it is presupposed that the parties had, while of sound mind, a degree of discretion which sufficed for the valid contracting of marriage. The gradual deterioration of the mind wrought by progressive insanity then has its effect on the discretion that is proportionate to the consideration of the concept of marriage, and not simply in relation to the possible commission of a mortal sin. Therefore, according to the norm given, if the state of the mind allows of a deliberation which is founded on a discretion proportionate to the concept of marriage, in the same degree that is required for the commission of a mortal sin, when the deliberation is founded on a discretion proportionate to the possible commission of the sin, then the mentally afflicted person must be deemed capable of eliciting a valid matrimonial consent.[96]

[95] Reference is made to: St. Thomas, *In 4 Libros Sententiarum*, lib. IV, dist. 27, q. 2, art. 2, ad 2um: "Ad peccandum mortaliter sufficit etiam consensus praesens, sed in sponsalibus est consensus in futurum; major autem rationis discretio requiritur ad providendum in futurum, quam ad consentiendum in unum praesentem actum; et ideo ante potest homo peccare mortaliter, quam possit se obligare ad aliquid futurum."—*Opera Omnia*, studio ac labore Stanislai Frette et Pauli Mare (34 vols., Parisiis: Apud L. Vives, 1871-1880).

[96] Smith, *op. cit.*, pp. 51-52.

Smith notes that Cappello[97] and Doheny[98] deny the efficacy of the principle as proposed by him. These authors argue that a greater amount of discretion is required for the instituting of a marriage contract than the discretion required for the commission of a mortal sin. Smith answers their objection very much to the point by stating:

> By the same reasoning it may be said that a greater amount of discretion is required for the commission of one sin than for the commission of another. But the relative discretion of a person in marrying or in committing a mortal sin is not in question; the norm is concerned rather with a common degree of deliberation founded on a discretion which is in diverse proportion with reference to the instituting of a marriage contract and to the committing of a mortal sin.[99]

To be able to determine precisely the psychical requirements for matrimony, and to demonstrate at the same time that the authors quoted above may not differ as much in their opinions as may at first appear, it is essential to establish terminology precisely. In this study the writer will use the same terminology as employed by Smith in his study regarding the effects of ignorance upon matrimonial consent.[100] The two essential notions to be kept distinct are the notions of deliberation and discretion.

By deliberation is meant an act of the intellect which precedes the act of the will.[101] The power of deliberation in man is the power of the intellect which knows and considers an action as good or evil, something to be performed or omitted. In deliberation a person, as it were, considers an act with a view to determining whether it is to be performed or not.[102]

[97] *De Matrimonio,* n. 579—as cited by Smith, *op. cit.,* p. 52.

[98] *Canonical Procedure in Matrimonial Cases* (Milwaukee: The Bruce Publishing Company, 1938), p. 512—as cited by Smith, *op. cit.,* p. 52.

[99] Smith, *op. cit.,* p. 52, note 25.

[100] Smith, *op. cit.,* p.. 50-52.

[101] Cf. *supra,* p. 80.

[102] Cf. Sanchez, *De Matrimonio,* Lib. I, disp. VIII, n. 7.

The will being a blind faculty[103] acts upon the deliberation of the intellect. In consequence of the essential freedom of the will,[104] the resulting act of the will is termed a deliberate free act of man or a truly human act.[105] The least that can be required of the psychical powers of man to commit a mortal sin or to enter into matrimony is that the person can and actually does deliberate about the action which he is about to perform, so that the consequent action can be said to have been performed freely, in view of his antecedent deliberation. Therefore, if a person acts after sufficient deliberation, he can be said to have made a deliberate choice. The act of committing a mortal sin and the act of giving matrimonial consent both require that the act be free and deliberate. Consequently, the norm attributed to Sanchez, which equates the deliberation necessary for matrimonial consent with the deliberation necessary for the commission of mortal sin, is perfectly sound and acceptable.

By discretion, on the other hand, is meant what the writer would like to call the "content" or insight of the deliberation. It is the knowledge and appreciation of the object about which the mind deliberates before giving or not giving consent to a certain act. It is percisely here that different requirements are made for different acts. Discretion, therefore, concerns the question: How much does a person have to know about the nature, purpose, import, consequences, etc., of an act to make such an act imputable to him if he deliberately chooses to places the act?[106]

Quite naturally, the discretion necessary for an act to be imputable to a person depends upon the importance and complexity of the act involved and, consequently, the requisite discretion will vary with various acts.

Wynen, in a now famous Rota case,[107] gives a very simple yet clear example of the difference between the notions of

[103] Cf. *supra,* p. 79.

[104] Cf. *supra,* p. 81.

[105] Cf. Davis, *Moral and Pastoral Theology,* Vol. I, p. 11.

[106] Cf. Gasparri, *De Matrimonio* (1932 ed.,), II, n. 783.

[107] *S.R.R. Decisiones,* XXXIII (1941), pp. 149-151.

discretion and deliberation. The same example shows—and this was its primary purpose—the important distinction between evaluative and mere conceptual knowledge.[108] The following possible case was described by the court: A very young child deliberately sets fire to his father's barn. One can picture the child thinking about it; how exciting it will be; how to do it; why he wants to do it, etc. After such deliberations and planning the child obtains the matches and deliberately, knowingly, and willingly sets fire to the barn. Without a doubt, the act is a human act. The child knows what a barn is, he knows what a fire is, and he deliberately chooses to burn the barn. The child, therefore, must be considered responsible for the burning of that barn. It is a deliberated free act and as such, an imputable act. However, if the child does not know the seriousness of his action, if he does not realize what the action entails, if he has no idea of the value of the barn and of the serious damage resulting from his action, the act of burning the barn cannot be imputed to the child as a crime because of his lack of sufficient discretion.

In this hypothetical case the child had sufficient deliberation and conceptual knowledge to make the act imputable to him, but he lacked sufficient discretion or evaluative knowledge to make him responsible for the crime of arson. The deliberation must be considered to have been sufficient, but the content of that deliberation, the discretion, was insufficient.

Discretion, therefore, is the degree of evaluative knowledge necessary for a specific act, if done deliberately, to be imputable to a person precisely as that specific act. Discretion makes a last will and testament a valid last will and testament rather than a result of the human act of writing; it makes the burning of a barn by an adult the crime of arson rather than childish prank; it makes the crime imputable as such.

Every human act, whether it be a mortal sin, a crime, an

[108] Cf. *infra*, p. 73.

act of virtue, an act of marital consent—demands deliberation. It demands that the person have knowledge of what the act is, that he decides to place the act rather than not to place the act, and that he execute the act freely as a result of previous deliberation. It is in relationship to such deliberation that the requirements for matrimonial consent are equated with the requirements for the commission of a mortal sin.

The degree of discretion, however, which is necessary to make a particular act imputable to a person precisely as that particular act, will vary from act to act. Therefore, it will also vary between one mortal sin and another mortal sin or between a particular sin and matrimony. The necessary discretion must be proportionate to the importance, difficulty, complexity, gravity of effects, etc., of the specific act posited.

A clear understanding of the distinction between deliberation and discretion will help to correlate and explain the apparently contradictory and, often confusing views of the authors. In examining the opinions of the authors quoted above, their individual views will become clearer and less contradictory if one determines whether they are considering deliberation or discretion as separate components of the marital consent, or whether they are considering both simultaneously.

Curran believes that Sanchez was opposed to St. Thomas Aquinas.[109] Yet it seems that Sanchez was speaking only of the deliberation requisite for matrimony when he adopted the parallel to mortal sin as a criterion; and that St. Thomas Aquinas was treating of the degree of discretion necessary for the validity of martimonial consent when he required more for marital consent than he did for the commission of a mortal sin.[110]

De Smet concerned himself rather with the degree of dis-

[109] Cf. *supra,* p. 114.

[110] Cf. *supra,* p. 109; Amenieu, "Aliénation mentale en matière de nulité de mariage."—*D.D.C.*, I, 436; Castañeda Delgado, *Enajenación Mental Consentimiento Matrimonial,* pp. 53-55.

cretion requisite for matrimony than with the deliberation necessary to enter the matrimonial contract.[111]

Gasparri, in the quotation made by Curran, also examined the discretion required for matrimony rather than the deliberation. Both De Smet and Gasparri, in the citation indicated by Curran, took the necessary deliberation for granted when once it was shown that the requisite discretion was present. The conclusion drawn by Curran that Gasparri rejected the view of Sanchez in favor of the view of St. Thomas Aquinas is therefore, in the opinion of the present writer, not correct. Sanchez was concerned with the matter of deliberation alone, while St. Thomas Aquinas directed his attention to the matter of discretion. It is also the latter subject that was heeded by Gasparri when he stated: *"In primis ante pubertatem haec matrimonialis mentis discretio non praesumitur sed probari debet; e contrario post pubertatem praesumitur nisi contrarium evincatur, uti docet Codex in rel. Can. 1082, § 2."*[112]

Pickett realizes that some distinction is necessary. Rather than make a distinction between deliberation and discretion, he chooses a rather unfortunate distinction between intelligence and knowledge. By the term intelligence Pickett intends to convey the notion which is called deliberation in this study. His term knowledge, on the other hand, would seem to refer to the discretion necessary for a valid matrimonial consent.[113]

Bensch, as quoted by Pickett, refers only to the maturity of judgment, i.e., the discretion necessary for the giving of a valid consent. He demands, therefore, a degree of discretion which is normally found only in those who have attained the age of puberty. He concludes that the mortal sin norm must be rejected. However, as was seen above,[114] the mortal sin

[111] Cf. *supra*, p. 115.

[112] Gasparri, *De Matrimonio* (1932), II, n. 784; Gasparri cites Alexander II in c. 8, X, *De sponsatione impuberum*, IV, 2, and he adds: "Et communiter DD. ante Codicem."

[113] Pickett, *Mental Affliction and Church Law*, p. 146; Cf. *supra*, p. 118.

[114] Cf. *supra*, p. 119.

norm should be understood to refer only to the necessary deliberation and not to the requisite discretion for a valid matrimonial consent.[115] Castañedo Delgado[116] and Smith,[117] finally, make a distinction between discretion and deliberation in the same manner as done in the present study. Neither of these two authors finds any difficulty in accepting the mortal sin norm as far as the requisite deliberation is concerned. At the same time both hold that the mortal sin norm is not sufficient as such to determine the requisite degree of discretion. To determine the discretion necessary for matrimony the mortal sin norm must be considered insufficient.

Castañedo Delgado refers to Schmalzgrueber as making the same distinction between the discretion and deliberation required for the giving of a valid matrimonial consent. "Regarding the latter," he states, "Schmalzgrueber does not require more than is required for the commission of a mortal sin. As to the former, Schmalzgrueber exacts with St. Thomas a discretion of reason sufficient to know the conjugal state and the perpetual and indissoluble bond that arises from it."[118]

It is interesting to note that Castañeda Delgado refers to the deliberation necessary for a valid matrimonial consent as a maturity of the will, while he refers to the requisite discretion as a maturity of judgment.[119] However, since the will is a blind faculty,[120] it would seem better, *salve meliore iudicio*, to consider the requisite deliberation as an operation of the intellect, by which all angles of a question are appraised, rather than to speak of it as a maturity of will.

Even though it is imperative to keep the notions of deliberation and discretion distinct from one another for a correct understanding of the problem of the psychical capac-

[115] Bensch, *Influxus Amentiae in Validitatem Consensus Matrimonialis*, p. 294, as quoted by Pickett, *op. cit.*, p. 147.

[116] *Enajenación Mental y el Consentimiento Matrimonial*, pp. 53-54.

[117] *Ignorance Affecting Matrimonial Consent*, pp. 50-53.

[118] Castañeda Delgado cites Schmalzgrueber, *Sponsalia et matrimonium*, tit. 2, n. 23—*op. cit.*, p. 54, note 40.

[119] *Op. cit.*, p. 53.

[120] Cf. *supra*, p. 79.

ity for matrimony, it is at the same time important to remember that such a distinction is an artificial one in fact, in regard to the one act of consent.[121] It is the act of consent considered in itself as a whole which needs to be examined. That this act be valid, at least a certain minimum degree of deliberation is required. It would seem that it is because of the unity of the one act of giving consent that some authors find difficulty in accepting the mortal sin norm as far as the requisite deliberation is concerned. However, if one remembers that over and above the necessary deliberation there is also required at least a minimum degree of discretion in the one act of giving consent, then many of the apparent difficulties appear to vanish.

The mortal sin test alone is certainly insufficient to determine whether a particular marital consent is valid or not. The mortal sin norm refers only to one of the elements of the act of consent. The mortal sin test does not refer to the to the discretion, but only to the deliberation necessary for a valid marriage contract. The present writer sees no difficulty in subscribing to the norm set down by Smith when he states: "If the state of mind allows of a deliberation which is founded on a discretion proportionate to the concept of marriage, in the same degree that is required for the commission of a mortal sin, when the deliberation is founded on a discretion proportionate to the possible commission of the sin, then the mentally afflicted person must be deemed capable of eliciting a valid matrimonial consent."[122]

Up to this point it has been determined that for a valid matrimonial consent a person may not be ignorant at least regarding the essential nature, purpose and qualities of marriage.[123] It has also been determined that the deliberation necessary for a valid matrimonial consent can be equated with the deliberation necessary for the commission of a mortal sin.[124] The question which still remains to be an-

[121] Cf. *supra*, p. 104.
[122] Smith, *Ignorance Affecting Matrimonial Consent*, p. 52.
[123] Cf. *supra*, pp. 88-98.
[124] Cf. *supra*, pp. 98-128.

swered concerns the minimum degree of discretion necessary for a valid matrimonial consent. How much discretion or maturity of judgment does a person have to possess in order to be able to enter marriage validly? Before attempting to determine the requisite minimum degree of discretion, it may be useful to quote from the afore-mentioned[125] matrimonial case tried before the Sacred Roman Rota in 1941.[126] In this celebrated case the learned judge Monsignor Arthur Wynen made the following observations:

> In not a few judgments there is really a twofold cognitive function which can be and should be distinguished; the one merely representative or conceptual, the other, deliberative or evaluative; and this twofold function is principally in evidence in judgments which concern 'practicable things' (*agibilia*), in other words, in practical judgments. The merely conceptual cognition expresses what the object of cognition is; the evaluative cognition expresses what importance or worth it has, or what value it has. Generally, a man perceives both aspects together in the same act of cognition; especially an adult in those matters which pertain to ordinary, everyday experience. But neither factually nor conceptually do these two cognitions express the same thing; they express rather diverse aspects

[125] Cf. *supra*, p. 124.

[126] This case has since been made the subject of a juristic monograph by G. M. Fazzari, entitled: *Valutazione Etica e Consenso Matrimoniale* (Naples: M. D'Auria Editore Pontificio, 1951). The conclusions of Fazzari were the following: "Non è sufficiente l'uso di ragione del settennio col quale è compatibile, assolutamente parlando, la scienza del matrimonio richiesta dal can. 1082. Si richiede la possibilità di spontanea trasformazione della conoscenza della natura del matrimonio in valutazione del medesimo. La valutazione del matrimonio deve estendersi, anche se confusamente, a tutti gli aspetti sostanziali del matrimonio e particolarmente a quello tico. Non basta per la capacità psichica del consenso matrimoniale la possibilità di trasformazione della conoscenza della notura del matrimonio in valutazione, anche etica, intellettuale; è necessaria la possibilità di trasformazione della valutazione intellettuale in valutazione razionale, comprendente la conoscenza del valore e l'inclinazione spirituale per esso."—Cf. pp. 77-78

of the same object. Experience shows that the merely conceptual judgment is formed earlier and much more easily; an evaluative cognition is acquired later and with more difficulty. Furthermore, it is to be noted that the use of reason, which is required for every human act, regards both conceptual cognition and evaluative cognition, and demands a capacity both for the exercise of reason, and for the dominion of reason, that is, the capacity of a man to dispose of himself and of his action according to that twofold cognition of the object... Now it is one thing for a man to lack the requisite evaluative cognition, and another for him to pay no attention to it. A child of five years who sets fire to his father's hayloft, although he has conceptual cognition both of the hayloft and the fire, does not have evaluative cognition of the crime, that is, the objectively very serious violation of right order which he perpetrates; and consequently, this violation cannot be imputed to him. He does have, however, both conceptual and evaluative cognition of his act inasmuch as it is a wrongful childish deed, and accordingly, in this respect, his action is imputed to him and is deserving of punishment. But an adult who posits the same external act, generally has not only conceptual cognition, but also evaluative cognition of the crime he commits, but he pays no attention to it; because notwithstanding it, he proceeds to the commission of the crime, and therefore he should be fully accountable for it. And this essential difference between child and adult, as regards the imputability of their own acts, obtains even more in civil law and especially in the law of contracts than it does in criminal law... Whenever a man who because of his age is presumed to be endowed with the power of sufficiently evaluating something is said, nevertheless, to have acted without sufficient evaluative knowledge, that can arise either from the fact that he did not want, or from the fact that he was unable to evaluate or weigh the proposed action sufficiently. One who does not want to acquire this knowledge will generally not escape either the subjective imputability or the objective obligatory force of his act since he affects ignorance, and it is hardly ever possible to discern whether sufficient evaluative cognition was

> lacking—at least of a confused and implicit kind. But one who is unable to evaluate at least the substance of a proposed action is obstructed in his natural power of appreciation, either by an impediment which is merely temporary and transitory (drunkenness, delirium, violent fever, etc.) or by an habitual defect (whether congenital or acquired during the course of his life); this type of habitual defect is present in not a few mental diseases and psychic anomalies, among which in recent times has been numbered so-called constitutional immorality."[127]

At the risk of departing momentarily from questions of law, it is necessary to examine more closely the psychological process which takes place in the human mind when a judgment, particularly a practical judgment, is made. Moreover, it is also necessary to examine the influences that can affect a human judgment.

As was seen above,[128] the speculative and practical intellects are not different faculties, but the same faculty in so far as it directs what is apprehends to different ends. The speculative intellect directs its object solely to the consideration of truth, while the practical intellect directs what it apprehends to operation or action.[129] The object of the practical intellect, therefore, is truth relative to the activity of man.[130] The judgments proper to the practical intellect are ordered to human action, and they are distinguished according to their remoteness or proximity to operation. The more remote are called "speculative-practical" judgments in Thomistic psychology, and they are twofold: 1) universal principles of conduct, such as, good must be done and evil must be avoided, which is a principle of synderesis, the habit of first

[127] *S.R. Rotae Decisiones*, XXXIII (1941), pp. 149-151.

[128] Cf. *supra*, p. 73.

[129] Aquinas, *Summa Theologica*, I, q. 79, art. 11—as cited by Tyrrell, *The Role of Assent in Judgment, A Thomistic Study* (A Dissertation, n. 100 of the School of Philosophy, Washington, D.C.: The Catholic University of America Press, 1948), p. 118.

[130] Aquinas, *De Veritate*, q. 22, art. 10, ad 4—as cited by Tyrrell, *op. cit.*, p. 118.

moral principles; and 2) particular judgments by which it is asserted that, under specified conditions, a certain act should be done or avoided because of its connection with a universal principle. Most proximate to action are the "practico-practical" judgments which affirm that: I must perform, or stop this act, here and now.[131] In this study only the last type of practical judgments needs to be considered. It is the judgment which states: I must, here and now, give or not give, matrimonial consent.

The practico-practical judgment is referred to as a prudential judgment, and it enters intimately into the explanation of the freedom of the will, since it plays an integral role in the performance of free and deliberate human acts. Every act of the will, insofar as it is the rational appetite, must be specified by the intellect. The will is itself non-cognitive and, consequently, the intellect must offer an object to which the will can direct itself. When the intellect proposes a particular contingent good, the will is left undetermined and indifferent, so that if it is to act, it must determine itself.[132]

Freedom of choice is rooted, remotely, in the nature of the intellect, and proximately, in the practical judgment that specifies the act of choice itself. The ultimate act by which the will determines itself to a definite course of action is always accompanied by a practico-practical judgment which affirms that this act must here and now be done or not done. Up to that point the will is undetermined, and there remains the possibility of making more than one practical judgment. However, once the moral agent freely places this last judgment, his will is no longer indifferent but it is determined *ad unum.*[133] The last practical judgment is made by the intellect under the command of the will. It represents the cognitive aspect of the act of free choice. Choice resides

[131] Maritain, *Les Degres du Savoir* (4 ed., Paris; Desclée de Brouwer, 1946), pp. 618-627 and 879-896.

[132] Aquinas, *Summa Theologica,* I-II, q. X, art. 2—as cited by Tyrrell, *op. cit.,* p. 119.

[133] Cf. Tyrrell, *op. cit.,* p. 119.

formally in the will, since its object is the good, but it results from a concurrence of the intellectual and volitional powers. The climax, as it were, of human liberty is reached in the act of self-determination in which freedom is terminated, cognitively, by the practico-practical judgment and, appetitively, by the spontaneous choice of the will.[134]

The number of factors that can influence the mind to make a wrong judgment are numerous. Tongiori divides them into those which contribute to give the error the appearance of truth, and those which influence the will to move the intellect to the erroneous assent.

In the first category he includes prejudices of all kinds, undue appeal to authority or the contagion of testimony, the confusion of similar ideas, relations, facts, propositions or inferences. That which introduces the extraneous element into the mind can be either the imagination, which substitutes one thing for another in accordance with the laws of association, or it can be confusion which arises from forgetfulness, from the equivocal meaning of words, or from some obvious and easy inference. The condition which makes the introduction of this extraneous element possible is always some defect of attention or reflection. The reason for this mental indisposition on the part of the subject are: fatigue, a disturbed state of mind, a sensation or feeling that absorbs the attention, excitement, bad will. On the part of the object, they are: The multiplicity and likeness of the objects being considered, the length of the reasoning process, the subtlety, or breadth of the object, and in general, whatever makes attentiveness difficult.

Those factors which influence the will to command an imprudent assent can be classified under either of two headings: love of the object of the judgment, or love of assent itself. The former comes into play when the object of the false judgment corresponds to one's intimate desires, or favored opinions, or when it can contribute to attaining an intended purpose. The love of assent is brought into operation

[134] Aquinas, *De Veritate*, q. 24, art. 1—as cited by Tyrrell, *op. cit.*, p. 121.

because of several reasons, namely: impatience with the effort and bother required for prolonged reflection; vanity or excessive confidence in one's own perspicacity; the object's reputed unimportance; the need of acting quickly; and finally, a feeling of anxiety.[135]

Prudence is the habit which disposes one habitually to make right practico-practical judgments, and to overcome the various obstacles to right judgment. In his treatment of the virtue or good habit of prudence, St. Thomas declared that this habit belongs to the intellect rather than to the will.[136] The purpose of prudence is to guide and counsel judgment.[137] The act of circumspection and the faculty to deliberate are also operations of the habit of prudence.[138]

To give a valid matrimonial consent a certain degree of prudence in making practical judgments is required for the parties. Imprudent practical judgments are characterized by an assent given under the influence of passion, prejudice, mental illness, or other impelling factors. However, to determine the degree of prudence required for a valid matrimonial consent is not easy. The maturity or prudence of judgment must be proportionate to the act posited.[139] How should one determine the necessary proportion between prudence or maturity of judgment, i.e., discretion, and the object of the legal act of giving matrimonial consent?

Nature itself seems to give an indication where a norm may be found. It would seem that, when a person has

[135] Tongiori, *Institutiones Philosophicae* (4 ed., Brussels: H. Goemaere, 1868-1869), *Logica*, pp. 431-432; Cf. Naber, *Theoria Cognitionis Critica* (Rome: Gregorian University Press, 1932), p. 200.

[136] "Cognoscere autem futura ex praesentibus vel praeteritis, quod pertinet ad prudentiam, proprie rationis est: quia hoc per quandam collationem agitur. Unde relinquitur quod prudentia proprie sit in ratione."—*Summa tTheologica*, II-II, q. 47, art. 1—*Opera Omnia*, III, 178.

[137] *Ibidem*, art. 2.

[138] St. Thomas treats of prudence in the II-II of his *Summa Theologica*. In question 47 he devotes sixteen entire articles to the subject. —Cf. *Opera Omnia*, III, 177-203.

[139] Cf. *supra*, p. 82.

reached the physical capacity for matrimony, the necessary maturity of judgment could also be expected to be present in the normal case. This thought has been the basis for determining the requisite minimum age for matrimony. Would it be rash to assume that God has created man and regulated his growth in such a manner that, at the same time when man reaches the physical capacity for marriage, he also achieves the necessary psychical capacity, i.e., the requisite maturity of judgment and the actual knowledge necessary for the giving of a valid matrimonial consent?

The thought that the psychical development of man proceeds, as it were, parallel with his physical development led the Roman Law to hold that, when a person had reached puberty, he was also to be considered capable of marriage in every respect.[140] The same thought led Sanchez to say: "... It is clear that maturity supplies for a lack of age; therefore, a marriage must be considered valid before the age required by law, if the power of generation is present, and if there is sufficient discretion to bind oneself ... the reason why the law prescribes a certain age is because it presumes that children only at that time, and not before then, have both sufficient judgment for matrimony and the power of generation. However, if it is clear that both of these are present before that required age, then the presumption must give way to the objective truth."[141] Before the Code, the

[140] Freisen, *Geschichte des Canonischen Eherechts bis zum Verfal der Glossenliteratur* (Paderborn, 1893), p. 324.

[141] Secundo constat, in matrimonio malitiam supplere aetatem atque ideo validum esse matrimonium ante aetatem jure praescriptam initum, si tunc adsit potentia generandi et sufficiens discretio ad se obligandum. Idque expresse definitur ... et ratio est, quia ideo jus eam aetatem praescribit, quod praesumat tunc pueros et non antea, et judicio sufficienti ad matrimonium, et potentia generandi praeditos esse. Quando ergo antea haec adesse constat, cedit praesumptio veritati.—Sanchez, *De Matrimonio,* VII, disp. 104, n. 5.

The phrase *Nisi malitia supplet aetatem* can be traced to the Roman Law. In the Roman Law it did not refer to marriage. In its original context it denied the favor of the law to those youths who, with the intent to deceive, alleged that they were no longer bound by the *tutela* and were, as a result, free to make a contract, while later, to demand

Church accepted and canonized this same principle of the Roman civil law.

In Roman law it was specifically determined that at puberty a legitimate marriage could take place.[142]

Justinian (527-565) decreed that a physical inspection to determine the necessary maturity was unbecoming. He ruled that puberty was to be presumed when a boy had completed his fourteenth year and a girl her twelfth.[143] O'Dea concludes: "It was this presumption that appears to be the basis for the ecclesiastical law on the age of marriage and regarding the impediment of nonage."[144] This rule of law remained in effect until the Code of Canon Law introduced the present law. The Code of Canon Law states in Canon 1067: "A male before the completion of the sixteenth year and a female before the completion of the fourteenth year cannot marry validly."[145] The Church can and does regulate marriage for its subjects, not by touching the nature of marriage as a contract or as a sacrament, since these belong to the natural law or the positive divine law, but rather by determining external circumstances which make a person juridically incapable of marriage. The impediment of nonage is an impediment of positive law and not of the natural law. The natural law itself makes marriage invalid in the case of those who are unable to give marriage consent because they are either totally ignorant of the nature, end, or essential qualities of matrimony, or because they lack the

restitution, they claimed that they were still *impuberes* when they entered into the contract. Cf. C. (2;42) 3; Cf. O'Dea, *The Matrimonial Impediment of Nonage* (The Catholic University of America Canon Law Studies, n. 205, Washington, D.C.: The Catholic University of America Press, 1944), p. 11.

[142] Iustas autem nuptias inter se cives Romani contrahunt, qui secundum praecepta legum coeunt, masculi quidem puberes, feminae autem viripotentes . . .—Inst. (1.10), *in princ.*

[143] C. (5. 60), 3.

[144] *Op. cit.*, p. 12.

[145] Vir ante decimum sextum aetatis annum completum, mulier ante decimum quartum item completum, matrimonium validum inire non possunt.

ability to make an evaluative judgment regarding marriage. It does not seem rash to add that, at the time when puberty is reached, the absence of these psychical requirements cannot be presumed; in fact, the law presumes their presence.

The Code of Canon Law itself gives an indication of its attitude towards the psychical capacity required for valid matrimony in treating of ignorance which would invalidate marriage. In paragraph 2 of canon 1082 the law states: "This ignorance is not presumed after puberty."[146] Canon 88, § 2 rules: "A boy is held to have reached puberty at the completion of his fourteenth year, a girl at the completion of her twelfth year."[147] This paragraph of canon 88 uses the term *censetur* (is held), because it wishes to provide no more than a legal presumption with regard to the fact that puberty has been attained. The Code makes a similar presumption with regard to the attainment of the use of reason at the completion of the seventh year of chronological age.[148]

If the Code holds that the knowledge for matrimony is to be presumed present when puberty is reached, it must also accept the proposition that the deliberation and maturity of judgment necessary for matrimony is to be presumed upon the presence of puberty.

As Manning states:

> The real nature of the *praesumptio iuris* consists in this, that the law sets down some abstract situation as a premise. The premise may be one fact or a collection of facts and circumstances. Whenever this abstract situation or collection of facts materializes in a certain case the law states the result of the eventuality. This is not arbitrary and unreasonable on the part of the legislator. Obviously, it may be demonstrated that the law does not apply in this case in its conclusion, that the conclusion positively does not result as set forth in a legal statute. But the presumption enacted in the law

146 § 2. Haec ignorantia post pubertatem non praesumitur.

147 Minor, si masculus, censetur pubes a decimoquarto, si femina, a duodecimo anno completo.

148 Canon 88, § 3.

> still remains in spite of the fact that in the particular event it does not apply.
>
> In drawing these conclusions the legislator is guided by universal experience which teaches that in the majority of cases this is the result of these facts and circumstances. Exceptions to this rule may arise only rarely. Consequently, the exception to the rule is permitted to be demonstrated. If it is not demonstrated, either conclusively or only doubtfully, the law will maintain its conclusion in the particular event [sic].[149]

The following basic rule or norm to determine the maturity of judgment or discretion necessary for a valid matrimonial consent may now be constructed: when physical maturity or puberty is reached, a person must be judged to have the requisite maturity of judgment, or prudence in judgment necessary for a valid matrimonial consent.

In conclusion, it seems possible to determine the psychical capacity for matrimony as embracing the following constituent elements:

1) A person may at least not be ignorant of the essential nature, purpose, and qualities of marriage.[150]

2) To enter into a valid marriage contract, a person must have the power of deliberation. He must use that power in giving consent in the same manner as he would deliberate for the commission of mortal sin. Thus the act of giving matrimonial consent must be said to be a deliberated free act of the contractant.[151]

3) Besides the above given degree of deliberation, a person must have the necessary evaluative knowledge, i.e., discretion (insight), to realize the nature and implications of marriage. This discretion or prudence in judgment must be proportionate to the importance of the marriage contract.[152]

[149] Manning, *Presumptions of Law in Marriage Cases*, The Catholic University of America Canon Law Studies, No. 94 (Washington, D.C.: The Catholic University of America, 1935), p. 15.

[150] Cf. *supra*, pp. 88-98.

[151] Cf. *supra*, pp. 99-129.

[152] Cf. *supra*, pp. 130-135.

4) Finally, a norm to determine the minimum degree of maturity of judgment and of knowledge necessary for a valid matrimonial consent can be constructed as follows: The degree of knowledge and maturity of judgment necessary for matrimony is that degree of knowledge and maturity of judgment which is by virtue of general human experience normally, i.e., usually, found in young people when they have reached actual physical maturity or puberty.[153]

If it is shown that in a given case these requirements were not met, one must conclude that there was an essentially insufficient mental capacity to effect a valid matrimonial consent.

SCHOLION. CONCERNING THE REQUISITE FREEDOM FOR THE GIVING OF A VALID MATRIMONIAL CONSENT

Heretofore, the knowledge, deliberation and maturity of judgment necessary for valid matrimonial consent have been considered. One further element of the psychical capacity for matrimony must now be examined, namely, the necessary freedom of the will.

In the present scholion, therefore, the writer will attempt to determine whether a specific degree of freedom is required for valid matrimonial consent.

The question demands an explanation of what is meant when one speaks of freedom of the will and degrees of freedom. Consequently, the necessity of a brief discourse regarding these terms is indicated.[154]

[153] Cf. *supra*, pp. 135-139.

[154] It is impossible in a limited study such as the present one to enter into an elaborate examination of the problem of free will. The writer prefers, therefore, to refrain from discussing the definition of freedom as given by Molina in his *Concordia* (Paris, 1876), q. 14, a. 13, disp. II, *init.* Molina defined freedom as: "Illud agens liberum dicitur quod positis omnibus requisitis ad agendum potest agere et non agere." This definition of freedom, standard among Molinists, however satisfactory it seems at first sight, is in reality linked necessarily with the difficult problem of the *scientia media*, a discussion of which would lead too far away from the purpose of the present study. The writer will treat briefly of freedom of the will as it is understood in Thomistic

Free will is the opposite of necessity. It consists, therefore, in a lack of determination to one thing, or, in an indifference towards several things.[155]

Freedom of the will may be defined as the power of choosing between goods proposed as desirable by a changeable judgment.[156]

The relationship of the changeable judgment of the intellect and the act of free will may best be summarized by quoting the twenty-first thesis of the "Twenty-Four Theses" of Thomistic philosophy.[157] This thesis states:

philosophy. In examining the question of freedom, the writer will mainly employ the following sources: Garrigou-Lagrange, *Reality, a Synthesis of Thomistic Thought* (Translated by P. Cummins, St. Louis: Herder Book Co, 1953); Gredt, *Elementa Philosophiae Aristotelico-Thomisticae,* Volumen I, *Logica, Philosophia Naturalis* (Friburg: Herder, 1953); Renard, *The Philosophy of Man* (2. ed. Revised and Enlarged by Vaske, Milwaukee: The Bruce Publishing Company, 1955); Grenier, *Cursus Philosophiae,* Volumen Primum, *Introductio Generalis* (2. ed., Quebec, 1944).

155 Indifference is distinguished into passive indifference (indifference of potentiality) and active indifference (indifference of power). Passive indifference results from the imperfection of the agent. It is not conducive to action, but it is rather an obstacle to it. Active indifference, on the other hand, derives from the perfection of the agent. It is in virtue of such active indifference that an agent can choose to act or not to act. Such active indifference belongs to the very essence of liberty. Cf. Grenier, *op. cit.*, p. 449, n. 445.

156 Grenier, *op. cit.,* p. 450; Garrigou-Lagrange, explaining the Thomistic definition of free will states: "Now if, on the contrary [i.e., as opposed to the definition of freedom as given by the Molinists], we consider the specific object of free will, we will recall the words of St. Thomas: 'If we set before the will an object, which from any point of view is not good, the will is not drawn to it by necessity.' These words contain, equivalently, the Thomistic definition of free will which runs thus: Freedom is the will's dominative indifference in relation to any object which reason proposes as in any way lacking in good."—*Reality,* p. 189.

157 As a result of a special pronouncement (motu proprio, *Doctoris Angelici*) by Pope Pius X on June 29, 1914, regarding the teaching of the principles and major doctrines *(principia et maiora pronuntiata)* of St. Thomas Aquinas in all schools of philosophy, a number of philosophy professors met and drew up a list of the principles and major tenets of the philosophy of St. Thomas. This list was submitted

> The will follows, it does not precede the intellect. And the will necessarily wills only that object which is presented to it as good from every angle, leaving nothing to be desired. But the will chooses freely between good things presented by mutable judgment. Hence, choice follows indeed the last practical judgment, but it is the will which makes that judgment to be the last.[158]

In his consideration of this thesis, Garrigou-Lagrange explains how the will makes the last practical judgment to be the last.

He states:

> How does the will make the last practical judgment to be the last? It does this by accepting it as last, instead of turning in an opposed practical judgment. Intellect and will are thus reciprocally related, with a kind of matrimonial relation, since voluntary consent, ending deliberation, accepts the judgment here and now present as last. Intellectual direction is indispensable, since the will is of itself blind; nothing can be willed unless foreknown as good.[159]

Liberty or freedom can be divided into liberty of specification and liberty of exercise. Liberty of specification ob-

to the Sacred Congregation of Studies. On July 27, 1914, this Congregation declared that in its judgment the list of theses did indeed contain the principles and major tenets of St. Thomas. As a result, there arose considerable anxiety whether this approbation implied an implicit banning of the view of, e.g., St. Augustine, Scotus, Suarez, etc. Pope Benedict XV made it clear that the approval of the Congregation was not meant to close debate on various issues between divergent opinions of Scholastic and other Catholic philosophers. The Congregation itself, in 1916, declared that the twenty-four theses could be regarded as safe, directive norms, though nothing more. Cf. *AAS*, VI (1914), 383-396; *AAS*, VIII (1916), 156-157.

158 Intellectum sequitur, non praecedit, voluntas, quae necessario appetit id quod sibi praesentatur tamquam bonum ex omni parte explens appetitum; sed inter plura bona, quae judicio mutabili appetenda proponuntur, libere eligit. Sequitur proinde electio judicium practicum ultimum; at quod sit ultimum voluntas efficit:—*AAS*, VI (1914), 386.

159 *Op. cit.*, p. 190.

tains when an object can either be loved or be an object of hatred.[160] Liberty of exercise obtains when a subject can at will act or not act, perform an action or omit it.[161]

As was seen in a previous chapter, still another division of freedom is possible, namely, the distinction made between philosophical freedom and psychological freedom.[162] Philosophical freedom is the freedom which is required for a human act. It presupposes that a person have sufficient knowledge, advertence and rational deliberation. Philosophical freedom has its basis in the power of the intellect to make objectively indifferent judgments. By acting freely in this sense is meant that, at the time when the choice to act or not to act is made, man is able to choose the opposite. Freedom understood in the philosophical sense does not admit of degrees; a person either can or cannot make a choice. Either he can choose the opposite of what he actually chooses or he cannot do so. There are no intermediate degrees.

Psychological freedom, on the other hand, can be defined as the ease with which a choice is made. By it is understood the freedom from influences, circumstances, pressures, illnesses, etc., which make the exercise of philosophical freedom difficult. In this psychological sense, freedom allows for varying degrees.

Philosophical freedom is positive and active. It is the power or faculty by which the will determines itself to a specific action. Psychological freedom is passive and negative. It is the freedom from obstacles, pressures and impediments which make choices difficult.[163]

It must be clearly understood that philosophical freedom implies at least a minimal degree of psychological freedom. If, therefore, in a given action, as a result of compulsion, all, even the lowest degree of psychological freedom is excluded, then also philosophical freedom is excluded. If an

160 Grenier, *op. cit.*, p. 454, n. 451.

161 *Loc. cit.*

162 Cf. *supra*, p. 76.

163 *Ibidem*, p. 76, cf. Ford-Kelly, *Contemporary Moral Theology*, pp. 211-214.

act is to be a philosophically free act, there must be present at least the lowest degree of psychological freedom. The one type of freedom cannot exist independently of the other. The distinction, therefore, is a conceptual (logical) rather than a real distinction.

Psychological freedom, in at least its lowest degree, has to be required, for valid matrimonial consent. Without at least the lowest degree of psychological freedom, there cannot be any philosophical freedom, and, consequently, there cannot be a human act. In the present scholion the question, therefore, is not whether psychological freedom is required for the giving of valid matrimonial consent. What needs to be determined is whether more than the lowest degree of psychological freedom is required for matrimony, and if so, what is the specific degree of freedom necessary.

The objection might be raised that there is no need to treat of a necessary degree of psychological freedom if it has been determined that in a given case the minimum requirements of deliberation and discretion necessary for matrimony have been met. It may be argued, and perhaps correctly so, in support of this objection that with the use of reason unimpaired and with sufficient deliberation and discretion the will cannot be anything but sufficiently free. To answer this objection, the writer would like to quote at rather great length from a recent study by the moral theologians Ford and Kelly.[164] These authors state:

> Is it universally true that in the presence of sufficient advertence, there always follows automatically sufficient consent of the will? Moralists, canonists and scholastic philosophers have hesitated to admit that with the use of reason unimpaired, with intellectual perception intact, the will can be anything but sufficiently free.[165]

[164] *Contemporary Moral Theology*, pp. 220-247.

[165] Ford and Kelly, *op. cit.*, p. 220, note 15, observe: "Hence they repudiated the notion of 'moral insanity' as it was first proposed (in England) because they considered it clearly incompatible with free will. In psychiatric terminology the person who was formerly called 'morally insane' or 'constitutionally immoral' now seems to have become the

> They appeal to St. Thomas: 'To whatever extent reason remains free and not subjected to passion, to that extent the movement of the will which remains does not tend with necessity toward the object to which passion inclines.'[166]

'constitutional psychopath.' On moral insanity see Franciscus Roberti, *De Delictis et Poenis* (Rome: Catholic Book Agency, Piazza Ponte S. Angelo, 28, n.d.), vol. I, pars 1, n. 120 sq.; J. S. Cammack, S.J., *Moral Problems of Mental Defect* (New York: Benziger, 1939), p. 89 sq.; Coronata, *Institutiones Iuris Canonici* (Turin: Marietti, 1935), vol. IV, n. 1657; Vermeersch, *Theologia Moralis*, etc., vol. I, n. 83; Benedict Merkelbach, O.P., *Summa Theologiae Moralis* (3. ed.; Paris: Desclée, de Brouwer, 1938), vol. I, n. 99, note."

[166] The following important footnote is given: "'In quantum ergo ratio manet libera, et passioni non subjecta, in tantum voluntatis motus, qui manet, non ex necessitate tendit ad hoc ad quod passio inclinat.'—1a 2ae, q. 10, a. 1. Joseph S. Duhamel, S.J., comments on this passage: 'To state that man is always free in his actions unless passion or other impediments interfere with the cognitive element of the human act is not what St. Thomas says here; nor is it a justified conclusion from the words of St. Thomas, as we shall see later. It is also contrary to fact. Apart from the testimony of psychiatry on the existence of compulsive acts and irresistible impulses, I am sure that every priest has met with this experience: a penitent has admitted clear knowledge of and actual advertence to the sinful and gravely sinful nature of a proposed action, yet has also protested sincerely but stubbornly that he had little or no power to resist and is convinced that he is not guilty of sin or, at least, of mortal sin.' In a later part of the article Father Duhamel continues: 'Man is an *unum per se.* All his appetitive faculties are radicated in his own soul. For this reason a spontaneous impulse of his sensitive appetite can trigger a spontaneous impulse of his rational appetite toward the same sensitive good even when it is known to be morally evil. But his executive powers are also radicated in his own soul. For this reason it is also possible that the impulse in his sensitive appetite is so strong that, despite evaluative cognition of the sinful nature of the act to which there is the impulse, the executive powers carry out the act completely or partially on the level of an *actus hominis.* In this case no will act is posited to command the external action. St. Thomas wrote that, to the extent that reason remains free and not subject to passion, to that extent the *movement of the will that remains,* does not tend with necessity to that to which passion inclines. In compulsive actions there is no movement of the will that remains; we are in the sphere of the *actus hominis,* not of the *actus humanus.* It is one thing to say that every act of the will that follows unimpeded deliberation is completely free; that is true, and St. Thomas

> Since the will is blind, they say, it must follow the act of the intellect and correspond with it.[167]
>
> Furthermore, since the will is a spiritual faculty, passion and similar obstacles to human acts can affect it only through the intellect, only inasmuch as they can interfere with intellectual cognition.
>
> But, apparently, scholastic psychologists today would not consider that given the mere cognition of the right and wrong of an act the subsequent choice of the will is necessarily free.
>
> For instance, J. S. Cammack, S.J., who demolishes philosophically and psychologically the theory of moral insanity, is able nevertheless to say:
>
> It is almost universally accepted now that real moral action is not based on mere abstract knowledge, but on deeper 'sentiments' which provide adequate motives for action by organizing groups of emotions around, and in association with, certain intellectual perceptions.[168]
>
> Rudolf Allers describes the dissociation of emotional and intellectual elements that is character-

said that. But it is a very different thing to say that every external action of man that takes place despite clear attention to the sinful nature of the action is a (denominately) free action and under the complete control of the will; St. Thomas did not say that, and it cannot be proved.'—"Theological and Psychiatric Aspects of Habitual Sin. I. Theological Society of America (1956), pp. 130-63 at p. 134 and at pp. 138, 139. In Thomistic psychology the final free choice of the will must always be made in accordance with the *judicium ultimo-practicum.* But moralists should not forget that there are serious theoretical problems, disputed for many years among the scholastics, as to the nature of the mutual influence of intellect and will in the final production of the free act. No doubt the obscurities of our present discussion originate in part from these disputes."—Ford-Kelly, *op. cit.*, pp. 221-22.

[167] "See, for example, J. Noldin, S.J.,*Summa Theologiae Moralis,* vol. I, n. 61, *ad fin.*: 'Quoniam voluntas in suis actibus *directe* solum a cognitione dependet, ipsa, praelucente cognitione quae requiritur, semper expedita et libera est. Hinc fieri nequit, ut morali libertate *omnino* careat, qui actionis suae moralem bonitatem et malitiam *sufficienter* apprehendit.' " (Italics ours).—*Ibidem,* p. 222.

[168] J. S. Cammack, S.J., *Moral Problems of Mental Defect* (New York: Benziger, 1939), p. 95, note—Ford-Kelly, *op. cit.*, p. 222.

istic of schizophrenia. It is not intended that what he says here of the incapacity of the schizophrenic for human acts can be transferred to the case of every emotionally disturbed or compulsive person, but it illustrates a scholastic philosopher's willingness to admit that a person may be irresponsible while the operations of the intellect are still formally intact.

Though a normally functioning intellect is a *conditio sine qua non* of free consent, it is not the only factor influencing decision and volitional activity. Human acts are determined not only by reason but very much by emotional factors and by imagination (taking this term as used in Scholastic psychology). Schizophrenia is characterized especially by a dissociation of emotional and intellectual states; the normal emotional reaction to values or goods, by which the intensity of volition becomes reinforced, is destroyed. Influenced by abnormal emotional life and by a curious tranformation of the general ideas on reality, though the operations of the intellect are still formally intact, the will can no longer be said to be free in a schizophrenic personality. The schizophrenic process is not one which would attack this or that faculty or operation, but it is a definite and profound alteration of the whole personality. From the very moment this process has set in, normal personality ceases to exist. It is quite safe to advance as a general principle that whenever there is sufficient reason for supposing schizophrenic trouble to have existed at the time of contracting marriage, there was no possibility of free and rational consent.[169]

Dr. Allers speaks here of serious mental illness, and not of consent to sin but of consent to marriage, which may require a higher degree of discretion.[170]

At this point Ford and Kelly treat of the important distinction between evaluative and mere conceptual knowledge. As moral theologians concerned with moral responsibility

[169] Rudolf Allers, "Annulment of Marriage by Lack of Consent because of Insanity," *American Ecclesiastical Review*, 101 (1939), 325-343 at 336—Ford-Kelly, *op. cit.*, p. 223.

[170] Ford-Kelly, *op. cit.*, p. 223.

for mortal sin, they conclude their consideration by observing: "Hence despite sufficient conceptual knowledge that the act is a mortal sin, freedom and imputability should be measured not in proportion to that knowledge but rather in proportion to the evaluative knowledge. . . ."[171] They then continue:

> The second consideration is an analogy between the dependence of the intellect on the phantasm and the dependence of the will on the emotions. In scholastic psychology continual stress is laid on the extrinsic dependence of the intellect on the phantasm, or imagination. It is emphasized that a disturbance of the phantasm can result in a disturbance of reason—even a complete disturbance. The authors are at great pains to account for and theorize about the mysterious process by which the phantasm exercises its causality on the intellect, bridging the gap between the material and the spiritual.
>
> When the spiritual will, following upon the deliberation of the intellect, elicits an act which is philoshophically free, may there not be an analogous dependence on the emotions as far as its psychological freedom is concerned? In other words may not the internal act of choice itself depend to some extent, that is for its psychological freedom, on healthy emotional functioning, just as the intellect depends on the healthy functioning of the phantasm? The result would be that passion, emotion, and concupiscence could have their effect on the will more directly, and not merely through the operations of the intellect. The mystery would not be greater in the case of emotion acting on will than in the case of phantasm acting on intellect. The emotions and the will are both rooted in the same fundamental principle of operation ('radicantur in eadem anima').[172]
>
> Perhaps this or some other philosophical principle could be used in an attempt to solve the mystery. But whatever the explanation, there seems to be

[171] *Ibidem*, p. 224.

[172] Duhamel, "*art. cit.*," pp. 138-139—Ford-Kelly, *op. cit.*, p. 288.

> no insuperable philosophical objection to making the attempt.
>
> Furthermore, when the spiritual will, enlightened by the deliberations of the intellect, makes its choice and commands an external act of the body, is there not stil an analogous dependence of the free will on the emotions, on the sense appetites and instincts? Is there not here, also, a bridge to be crossed?—from the spiritual act of the will to the material acts of the bodily execution? Is there any philosophical objection to the assertion that emotional pathology can block that crossing, even though the intellectual operation of deliberation remains essentially unimpaired?
>
> In this view, emotional disturbance could destroy freedom not only by blinding the intellect beforehand and preventing deliberation, but also during and after the act of the will, in the sense that it could diminish psychological freedom or even effectively block the execution of the free will's commands, thus depriving the individual of the power of disposing of his activities.[173]

After treating rather extensively of what is called "the irresistible impulse," which they would prefer to call "a compulsive urge," Ford and Kelly consider the knowledge, deliberation and psychological freedom necessary for the commission of the mortal sin of masturbation. They then conclude the chapter entitled: *Freedom and Imputability under Stress* as follows:

> In the present chapter we have tried to clarify rather than to solve some of the formidable problems of subjective moral imputability. These problems confront the moralist on every side. Self-abuse was merely a concrete case which we used as an illustration. We believe that all theologians are agreed that for formal grave culpability there is required not only liberty of indifference, which we have referred to a philosophical liberty, but also a certain degree of the liberty from obstacles and pressures which we have referred to

[173] Ford-Kelly, *op. cit.,* pp. 227-228.

> as psychological liberty. This is implicit in the common teaching that objectively grave sins become only venially sinful *ob imperfectionem actus* in certain circumstances.
>
> The problem is to determine what degree of psychological freedom is required and not to put the mark so high as to negate the fundamental moral responsibility of the average man and woman. We must confess that the problem is obscure and baffling. Frequently we can only admit our ignorance. We believe, however, that given the traditional conceptions of sufficient deliberation and sufficient consent, and given the psychological knowledge we now have as to emotional and instinctive obstacles to human acts, we are staying well within the bounds of the theological requirements in concluding that we should judge much more leniently than we have in the past a great many individual cases of human misconduct and frailty. 'Though man may be more reasonable than the psychiatrist believe, he is less so than the philosophers think.'[174]

It is not the task of this scholion to judge the merits of the case as presented by Ford and Kelly. However, whether one accepts or rejects their approach to the problem of moral responsibility, it does seem necessary to determine whether, over and above the necessary deliberation and discretion, one must also require a certain minimum degree of psychological freedom for valid matrimonial consent in the same manner as Ford and Kelly require it for mortal sin.

Not admitting as a fact but merely as a possibility that the freedom of the will can be adversely influenced, even though the deliberation and discretion of the intellect remain unimpaired, the following question can be formulated. What degree of freedom, i.e., psychological freedom, is required for the giving of valid matrimonial consent? It is the opinion of the present writer that no definite degree of psychological freedom is to be required. It is sufficient for valid matrimonial consent if the parties at the time of giving consent, i.e., at the marriage ceremony, possess and exercise the

[174] *Ibidem*, p. 247.

philosophical freedom (and hence freedom from compulsion) to deliberately choose to give or not to give consent. No degree of difficulty or ease in making such a choice (degree of psychological freedom) would, therefore, in the writer's opinion, invalidate matrimonial consent, provided that sufficient deliberation and discretion are actually exercised in the giving of consent.

If a specific minimum degree of psychological freedom would be required for the giving of valid matrimonial consent, one would be faced with the same problem which moral theologians as yet have been unable to answer. Ford and Kelly very searchingly describe the problem as follows:

> To put the matter fancifully, if one were given marks on malice and culpability where bad actions are concerned, or on virtue and merit where good actions are concerned, or on degrees of freedom where both are concerned, the marks might range all the way from one percent to ninety-nine percent. Zero percent would mean no human act at all; and we avoid one hundred percent because it seems more appropriate to angels and devils than to men. Still speaking fancifully, what is the passing mark for mortal sin? Certainly not ninety-nine percent freedom. The full deliberation of the moralists does not demand that much. Is it ninety percent? Seventy-five percent? Sixty percent? Who can say? Some would put it higher, others lower. Only God knows the exact answer. We might also ask whether the passing mark of freedom is higher for bad actions than for good ones. Should we require ninety percent freedom to be worthy of eternal punishment, but only sixty percent freedom to be worthy of eternal reward?[175]

Even if it could be decided definitely what degree of psychological freedom were required for certain acts, how would one measure the degree of psychological freedom? As Ford and Kelly state: "Only God knows the exact answer." However, if one is to determine the juridic status of a person in a case which involves the question of psychological freedom

[175] Ford-Kelly, *Contemporary Moral Theology*, p. 209.

for a valid matrimonial consent, some norm must be found to determine and prove in the external forum whether a particular person is psychically capable of giving valid matrimonial consent.

Quite clearly the act of giving matrimonial consent must be a philosophically free act. In other words, a person must be able to choose not to consent if the actual giving of consent is to be a legally imputable act or a legally valid act.

Is it necessary, however, to hold that, as in the case of mortal sin, the choice to give or not to give matrimonial consent must be easily made? Is it required for the validity of marriage that at the moment of giving consent it would actually be easy for the parties not to give consent? This ease in choice would be required if one were to regard as necessary a definite degree of psychological freedom. It may be true that such a definite minimum degree of psychological freedom is required for the commission of a mortal sin.

The writer holds that, because of the gravity and seriousness of matrimony, the necessary deliberation in making the choice and the philosophical freedom in the actual choosing, can and must be compared with the requirements for mortal sin.[176] However, he does not hold that matrimonial consent should be compared with consent to mortal sin, with respect to a requirement of a definite degree of psychological freedom at the precise moment of giving consent, i.e., at the marriage ceremony.

Again, it is important to keep in mind that the ease or difficulty in giving consent must be understood here as resulting from direct influences on the will other than the influence of the rational deliberation of man. Such influences would be the emotions, passions,[177] mental illnesses, drugs, environment, heredity, etc. These influences would, pos-

[176] Cf. *supra*, p. 124.

[177] In modern terminology, the word passion is usually reserved for signifying violent emotions, while mild emotions are referred to as feelings. Essentially, however, passion, emotion and feeling are the same, namely, the operations of the sense appetites.

sibly—and the possibility is here postulated—directly cause a choice to become more or less difficult or easy.[178]

The writer believes that the requirements with regard to psychological freedom cannot be the same for matrimony as for mortal sin. In mortal sin, one consents to a morally bad action, while in matrimony, one does not. It would appear that the requirements of psychological freedom must be different for bad, good, or indifferent actions, as a basis of their imputability as human acts. Difficulty of not doing a good action, consequently, the ease of doing a good action, does not take away the merit of that action. It does not destroy or even diminish its imputability. Virtue need not be odious or difficult to be meritorious. Ford and Kelly observe:

> Facility of operation is not by itself a criterion of imputability in general. A high degree of difficulty will exclude serious guilt or blame. But the converse is not true. Given a high degree of facility or complete absence of obstacles, it does not follow that there is no room left for high merit and praise. A man's good actions are imputable to him even if he loves what is commanded. Neither difficulty nor facility is the criterion of philosophical freedom, and the degree of psychological freedom is not the measure of imputability *ad meritum*.[179]

Difficulty of not doing a bad action, consequently, the ease of doing a bad action, on the other hand, does diminish the imputability of that action. Clearly, therefore, the requirements on the part of the pyschological freedom of the will must be different for morally good, morally bad, and moral-

[178] There seems to be no question that man's freedom to make a choice can be influenced by some agent other than the intellect to such an extent that the action posited is no longer a human act but becomes instead merely an act of man. This psychic situation is verified in the case of the so-called irresistible impulse. If such an impulse can be proven to exist and to be truly irresistible, then there is no philosophical freedom present and, consequently, there is no morally or legally imputable act. It would actually be a force which totally overcomes all freedom and no choice would actually be made.

[179] *Op. cit.*, p. 210.

ly indifferent actions. The requirements cannot be the same for all important actions, as one might at first suspect.

Moreover, if one holds[180] that, e.g., the passions or emotions of man can diminish the degree of man's psychological freedom even to a minimum without at the same time affecting his powers to deliberate and evaluate, then one could reason as follows: If a definite degree of psychological freedom were required for the giving of a valid matrimonial consent, then a marriage based on a great love could be invalid by reason of a lack of psychological freedom. Hope and fear are passions or emotions of man. If one grants the theory that these passions and emotions, over and above their effect on deliberation and discretion, can also directly affect the will,[181] then both love and fear can diminish the degree of psychological freedom in man. Hope, like fear, is one of the passions or emotions of man. Hope and fear both belong to the irascible appetite of man. Their operations are not at rest, but they are in motion towards a good, in case of hope; or from an impending evil, in case of fear. They have their origin respectively in love and hate; and hope, based on love, will cease only when, in case of fear, the danger no longer exists or when, in case of hope, the desired object is attained. Both influence the psychological freedom of a person insofar as fear moves the will away from the object hated, while hope moves the will to the object loved. Would it not be necessary to conclude that if fear, based on hate, can influence the psychological freedom of man to such an extent as to invalidate matrimonial consent, that also hope,

[180] Cf. *infra,* p. 158.

[181] The influence of fear, as understood here, is regarded as affecting the operation of the will directly, apart from its causing a trepidation of the mind. The effect of fear on a person's power of deliberation is here taken for granted. Consequently, fear is taken here not in its accepted canonical sense, but in a psychological sense as defined by Allers: "The emotional response to the awareness of a great danger the nature of which is known, even if imperfectly, and which is conceived as imminent and, at the same time, as not absolutely unavoidable.—'Some Medico-Psychological Remarks on Canons 1068, 1081, and 1087,' " *The Jurist,* IV (1944), 351-380.

based on love, can invalidate matrimonial consent? In a marriage based on fear, the invalidity would arise from the difficulty of the will not to choose marriage, which is the only escape from the threatening danger; in a marriage based on hope, and therefore on love, the invalidity would arise also from the difficulty of not choosing marriage. Difficulty of not choosing marriage is the same as ease of choosing marriage.

Obviously, the conclusion that a marriage based on hope would be invalid because of a lack of psychological freedom caused by great love is untenable. Yet in both cases to choose not to marry is very difficult. Hence, in either case there is little psychological freedom though the cause for its lack is entirely different. The cause of the lack of psychological freedom, however, is not important. What must be determined is whether a diminution of psychological freedom (even the near total absence of it) does invalidate matrimonial consent. The obvious conclusion from the juxtaposition of opposite emotions or dispositions (fear and love) and by an argument *a pari* is that in both cases enough psychological freedom for the validity of marriage is present.[182]

This opinion that philosophical freedom (freedom from psychic compulsion) plus the necessary deliberation and discretion is all that is required for valid matrimonial consent, and that no specific degree of psychological freedom is necessary is confirmed by a Rota decision. In this case,

[182] If marriage because of fear is to be considered invalid, it is not because of a lack of necessary psychological freedom in the giving of consent, but rather because of the positive regulations of the lawgiver. Cf. Canon. 1087, § 1—Invalidum quoque est matrimonium initum ob vim vel metum gravem ab extrinsico et iniuste incussum, a quo ut quis se liberet, eligere cogatur matrimonium.

§ Nullus alius metus, etiamsi det causam contractui, matrimonii nullitatem secumfert.

For a good treatment of the positive law theory as opposed to the natural law theory with regard tot he invalidating effect of fear on matrimonial consent cf. Chatham, *Force and Fear as Invalidating Marriage: The Element of Injustice* (The Catholic University of America Canon Law Studies No. 310, Washington, D.C.: The Catholic University of America Press, 1950), pp. 95-98.

the validity of the marriage was attacked on the grounds that consent was given under the influence of a drug, namely, morphine. The court refused to accept the conclusions of the expert witness. In giving the decision of *non constare de nullitate,* the Rota comments:

> We say the *peritior* erred because he demands too much for valid contracting, not merely the use of reason, but sound critical acumen, prudence, wisdom, good judgment, etc. Also, he asks more of the will than is necessary. Granted, for the sake of argument, that the lady, without an injection of morphine, would not have given consent, this does not make her consent invalid. For it matters not how she is led to consent, whether altogether from within or also from some external incitement; it is required and suffices for validly contracting that the contracting party places a positive act of the will and legitimately manifests it.[183]

In the same case, the court rejected the opinion which would hold for the possibility of a direct influence on the will without at the same time affecting man's intellectual powers. The court stated:

> Auctores moderni, qui statuunt *ipsam voluntatem* alicuius hominis, pleno usu rationis gaudentis, laborare posse certis morbis, non sunt imbuti sanis principiis philosophicis neque cognoscunt naturam actus cognitionis et voluntatis, ideoque facile in errores perducuntur. 'Voluntas enim movet intellectum ad deliberandum, i.e., ad rem secundum diversos respectus considerandam, et ipsa est causa, ob quam intellectus ultimo manet in tali determinato iudicio; posset enim ad alia intellectum diverte. Voluntas igitur electione sua determinando ultimum iudicium practicum, libere dat sibi ipsa formam sui actus, et ita libere determinatam volitionem elicit. Si vero propter inadvertentiam aut propter phantasiae perturbationem (ex vehementi passione aut alia ex causa, ut ex morbo) a deliberando impeditur intellectus, ita ut non possit sub diversis respectibus rem considerare, per accidens eius iudicium est ad unum determinatum, et voli-

[183] *S.R.R. Decisiones,* XXIX (1937), 195-196.

tio exinde dimanans libertate caret' (Gredt, *Elementa Philosophiae arist.-thom.*, ed VI, pag. 476)

Omnes igitur morbi, quibus directe afficiatur una voluntas, incolumi seu sano intellectu reiiciendi sunt. Nam voluntas tunc tantum deficere potest, si intellectus morbo afficiatur; sed nec intellectus quidem directis morbis laborare potest, cum defectus rectae cognitionis proveniant ex perturbatione sensuum, phantasiae, etc., quibus intellectus, per se potentia spiritualis, ad agendum indiget.[184]

The Rota at the same time specified the following volitional requirements for valid matrimonial consent:

Quoad voluntatem autem requiritur, ut contrahens et valeat libere sese determinare ad consensum eliciendum, et velit obligationes cum matrimonio coniunctas suscipere. Facultas volitiva sufficit, si contrahens actu gaudeat libertate ponendi vel non ponendi actum; neque obstat, si simul adsunt motiva vim deligendi et sese determinandi roborantia. Voluntas autem sufficiens adest, si sufficienter cognita

[184] *S.R.R. Decisiones,* XXIX (1937), 171-176, nn. 2-7. In yet another, similar case (25 Feb., 1941) the Rota made a thorough examination of the theory of the so-called "constitutional immorality" or "moral insanity" developed in the nineteenth century, according to which some persons are to be considered as not responsible for actions which otherwise would be voluntary and imputable. In examining this theory, the court mentions Treccani, Pinel, Esquirol, Marcel, Falret, Prichard, Morel, Maudsley, Lombroso, Krafft-Ebing, and Tanzi-Lugaro, and proceeds to evaluate the theory with reference to the teachings of scholastic psychology. The observations of the Rota can be summarized as follows: The theory of "constitutional immorality" or "moral insanity" is of dubious value. Moreover, according to its exponents themselves it allows for varing degrees; the individuals supposed to be subject to this abnormality diverge from the normal state by almost infinite graduations. It is, therefore, very difficult to prove with certainty that a given individual, who is otherwise sane, is so affected by it as to be incapable of a human act, or of any specific act such as the act of giving matrimonial consent. For these reasons, which in accordance with canon 1804, § 2, are stated at some length in the decision, the court, notwithstanding the unanimous opinion of the experts, considered that the absence of matrimonial consent was not sufficiently proved. The decision was, therefore: *non constare de nullitate.*—Bouscaren, *Canon Law Digest,* III, 430-431.

> matrimonii natura, contrahens reapse vult matrimonium inire sicuti ceteri homines, licet omnes et singulas obligationes suscipere explicite non intendat.[185]

Such considerations compel one to conclude that no specific degree of psychological freedom is required to enter a valid matrimonial contract; further, psychological freedom as it affects matrimonial consent cannot be compared to psychological freedom as it affects consent required for mortal sin. Even if it could be proven that the freedom of the will can be directly and adversely influenced by emotions, passions, illnesses, drugs, etc., without any influence on the power and actual use of the power of deliberation, even then that consent is sufficiently free for marriage which is the result of a free choice (philosophical freedom). The ease or difficulty with which the choice is made (psychological freedom) does not affect matrimonial consent as long as the necessary knowledge, deliberation, and discretion are present. Hence, no definite degree of psychological freedom is required but only that psychological freedom is necessary and sufficient which insures a person's basic power of choice (philosophical freedom).

[185] *S.R.R. Decisiones,* XXIX (1937), 171-176.

CHAPTER VI

MENTAL ILLNESS AND MARRIAGE

The psychical capacity necessary to enter a valid marriage contract was closely examined in the previous chapter. The present chapter will consider the absence of this necessary psychical capacity by reason of mental illness or mental deficiency.

The present chapter has two purposes: first, to show that a person because of mental illness or some other mental deficiency or disturbance may lack the necessary psychical capacity for marriage. Second, to indicate the procedure to prove at law that a person at the time of marriage did not possess this necessary psychical capacity.

It is at this point that marriage cases involving mental illness will present the most difficulties; here the field of medicine and psychiatry meets with the field of law. These sciences, however, should only meet; they should not overlap.

ARTICLE 1. NECESSARY SEPARATION OF MEDICINE, PSYCHIATRY, AND LAW

The matter to be determined at law is: what was the legal responsibility of a person for a given legal act, for the act of giving matrimonial consent? Was this particular person psychically capable of giving valid consent to the contract of marriage? Was he possessed of sufficient knowledge, freedom and maturity of judgment validly to bind himself for life to the serious obligations and duties assumed in the contract of marriage? Before the law, therefore, the question is not whether this person was mentally ill or mentally defective. Neither is the law interested in determining the causes, symptoms, methods of treatment, classifications, etc., of the many mental disorders and disturbances known to the medical and psychiatric profession. At law, the question *per se* is not: What was wrong or abnormal with this person? The formal question at law is: Was the matrimonial consent of this particular person at the time of marriage so defective that it must be declared invalid?[1]

The *res* to be examined at law is not primarily the person, but specifically the person's act of giving matrimonial consent. Hence, the mental state of the person is of interest to the law only insofar as this mental state influences the person's act of giving consent. In theory, it would be possible to prove, in a given case of mental illness, that the marital consent of a person was defective because of the lack of, for instance, sufficient maturity of judgment, without necessarily proving that the person was mentally ill. By way of corollary, it is even less necessary to show the precise type of mental illness afflicting the person at the time of marriage.

In one case of mental illness, the Sacred Roman Rota decided for the invalidity of a marriage without determining the nature of the mental illness involved. The medical experts who had been summoned to assist the court, proferred various and divergent diagnoses; the doubt regarding the precise nature of the illness was left unsolved; the Rota nevertheless decided in favor of the invalidity of the marriage.[2]

It is certainly not the task of the law to judge whether a person was mentally ill according to the norms of medicine or psychiatry.[3]

On the other hand, determining whether a particular act was a valid act is a matter of law. This question cannot be answered by a medical doctor or psychiatrist, even though both may be most eminent in their own particular fields.

If one is to avoid confusion and hopes to preserve mutual respect between those in the field of medicine or psychiatry

[1] In case of doubt with regard to a marriage to be contracted, the principle of can. 1082, § 2 obtains; cf. can. 1827.

[2] *S.R.R. Decisiones*, XXIX (1937), 756-770.

[3] Psychiatry is defined as a branch of medicine which is focused upon the nature and treatment of mental disturbances; cf. Vanderveldt-Odenwald, *Psychiatry and Catholicism* (2. ed., New York: McGraw-Hill Book Company, Inc., 1957), p. 1.

and those in the field of law, it is necessary to keep these distinctions in mind. The doctor or psychiatrist is qualified to diagnose a person mentally ill; he is not qualified to determine the legality or validity of the act of a person. He is expert in the field of medicine or psychiatry. He is not an authority in the field of law.

The judge or legal expert is qualified to decide upon the legality and validity of an act. He is not qualified to diagnose a person as mentally unbalanced or ill. He is an expert in the law; he would be presumptuous to consider himself an authority in medicine or psychiatry.

Quintana Reynés, as quoted by Pickard,[4] vehemently complained of the extremist position of judges who, "in a manner certainly unbecoming their apparent education, place almost no confidence in expert proof . . . relying altogether on what they call their 'enlightened common sense' and regarding as of equal inconsequence the mastery of every kind of science, including those which they have not so much as greeted in their already rancid studies."[5] "Fortunately," as Pickard observes, "the attitude which Quintana Reynés so scathingly criticised is today rare."[6]

This is not to say that it is useless for those engaged in the field of law to study and be acquainted with modern psychiatry. Knowledge in the field of medicine and psychiatry stands the jurist in good stead, but he is not and is not expected to be an expert in this field.

It would seem, therefore, unnecessary in a legal study such as the present one, to enter into a medical or psychiatric investigation of the various types of mental illnesses, their causes, symptoms, and methods of treatment. Such a study of mental illness from a medical point of view would tend to confuse rather than clarify the legal issue at hand. It would seem to be an exercise in futility if a judge in a given

[4] Pickard, *Jurdicial Experts: A Source of Evidence in Ecclesiastical Trials*, p. 199.

[5] Quintana Reynés, *La Prueba en el Procédimiento Canónico* (Barcelona: Bosch, 1942), p. 141.

[6] Pickard, *op. cit.*, p. 141.

case would attempt to learn or understand all about the possible mental illness or abnormality of the person whose case is submitted to the court. Apart from the fact that the judge is not expected to be qualified in the field of psychiatry, it is usually only the very doubtful cases which are brought before him for adjudication. Cases in which one of the parties was openly and obviously insane at the time of the actual marriage are extremely rare, for few people will marry a recognized lunatic; and even fewer priests or civil authorities could be persuaded to officiate at such a marriage. Cases of doubtful mental illness or disturbance demand much more than a mere good grasp of psychiatry. Such cases demand that one be an expert in the field if one is to be able to give a scientific and reliable opinion regarding the mental health or illness of the person involved. These cases require not only a good abstract knowledge of psychiatry, but they also require much practical experience and great skill in examining the person and the evidences regarding his condition.

The Sacred Roman Rota itself indicates that it does not want to, and that it should not, enter into the field of medicine or psychiatry. This court of the Church continues to use the strictly legal terms of *amentia* and *dementia* in cases in which the validity of a matrimonial consent is questioned on the basis of a supposed mental illness or deficiency. In using this terminology, the court is not failing to keep up with modern science and proven facts. The remark has been made: "It is a common charge against all courts, civil and ecclesiastical, that they run a generation or two behind the times, that they are so rigidly determined to abide by the principle *stare decisis* that they are relatively blind to newly discovered facts, and theories, and circumstances which might justly challenge precedent."[7]

The continued usage by the ecclesiastical courts of the

[7] "Mental Disease and the Ecclesiastical Courts," address delivered by the Right Reverend John J. Hayes, Officialis, Diocese of Bridgeport, at the seventeenth annual National Meeting of the Canon Law Society of America, held October 25-26, 1955, at Hershey, Pennsylvania, as reported in *The Jurist*, XVI (1956), pp. 267-284 at p. 268.

ancient terms of *amentia* and *dementia* indicates admirable prudence on the part of the law. It in no way indicates a failure to recognize the advances made by the medical sciences. Had the courts adopted the rich and confusing and often changing terminology of the growing and eager psychiatric profession, the result would have been legal chaos. At the same time, the adherence of the courts to the ancient terminology regarding insanity shows the court's realization of the limits of its own field of competence.

According to the jurisprudence of the Sacred Roman Rota, "those persons who are insane in all matters are termed *amentes*, while those who are insane only with regard to one or other point are classified as *dementes*. In the particular matter regarding which they are insane, the *dementes* are equated with the *amentes*. The *amentes* are always to be considered incapable of contracting marriage validly, while the *dementes* are incapable of marriage only if their insanity concerns marriage itself."[8]

The division of mental illness into *amentia* and *dementia* is a very rudimentary and even useless one as far as the medical or psychiatric professions are concerned. Doctors and psychiatrists have every right to object to its use as medical terminology. In the same way one may rightly object to the usage of such terms as mental disease, insanity, unsound mind, mental incompetence, etc., if these terms were intended to be used as medical terminology.[9] These

[8] "Juxta jurisprudentiam SRR amentes dicuntur insanientes quoad omnia, dementes vero, qui quoad unum alterumve punctum insaniunt; quoad rem, circa quam insaniunt, amentibus aequiparantur; amentes semper incapaces sunt ad matrimonium valide contrahendum, dementes vero dumtaxat, si eorum insania respicit rem matrimonialem. Haec generica divisio infirmitatum mentalium sufficit, quia in foro de his quaestionibus tractatur tantum, quatenus de valore actuum humanorum vel de eorumdem imputabilitate dijudicandum est."—Holböck, *Tractatus De Jurisprudentia Sacrae Romanae Rotae* (Graz:Styria, 1957), p. 101.

[9] Regarding the usage of the term mental disease, Cavanagh and McGoldrick state: "Disease always implies some pathology of the body or organism, some biological alteration of the state of the human body. It is correct, therefore, to refer to diseases of the body, but it would seem to be incorrect for this reason to refer to diseases of the mind.

terms, however, are not medical terms. They are strictly legal terms and have reference solely to the legal acts of persons.

Rudolph Allers observes regarding the use of the term *amentia*: "This is the general term for all kinds of mental ailments causing an incapacity of responsible action and correct thought."[10] Pickard adds: "So general is the term that it would embrace not only the many types of mental illness, as one generally understands them, but also characteristic types of mental deficiency. Thus, feeblemindedness may be of such a pronounced degree that it renders a person absolutely ignorant of the meaning of marriage even in its minimum canonical sense."[11]

The simplicity, yet sufficiency, of the terms *amentia* and *dementia* as employed by the ecclesiastical courts may perhaps be explained as follows: The law approaches the act of a person in quite a different manner from the approach used by the medical or psychiatric profession. A doctor's approach could be described as follows. A person, his actions, emotions, etc., are closely examined. Upon examination a patient is diagnosed as being, e.g., psycho-neurotic, psychotic, mentally defective, or psychopathic.[12]

At best, such language is figurative, but due to a particular circumstance such a figure of speech is dangerous. The 'circumstance' referred to is the prevalence of the materialistic concept of mental disorder. The 'danger' referred to is the error of considering the mind as an organic, bodily entity indistinguishable from the gray matter or brain. If the mind were actually identified with the biological brain, if the processes of thought and volition were secretions of the gray matter, then it would perhaps be permissible to call mental disorders mental diseases and to mean it literally. Such, however, is not the case. The brain is indeed a necessary condition of mental life, but it is by no means the mind."—*Fundamental Psychiatry* (2. ed. Revised, Milwaukee: The Bruce Publishing Company, 1958), p. 309.

[10] "Annulment of Marriage by Lack of Consent because of Insanity," *The Ecclesiastical Review*, LI (1939), 325-343, at p. 340.

[11] Pickard, *Judicial Experts: A Source of Evidence in Ecclesiastical Trials*, pp. 161, 162.

[12] Vanderveldt and Odenwald makes these distinctions: "The psychotic mind is separated, wholly or in part, from reality. As a result

In case the patient is judged to be psychotic (in layman's language "insane"), the doctor will attempt to determine the precise type of psychosis involved. He will, as it were, classify the patient, for instance, as being a schizophrenic, whether simple, hebephrenic or catatonic; or he may decide that the patient is a manic depressive or paranoid, etc. The classification will depend on the school of thought, back-

of a major loss of contact with reality, most psychotics are unable to make a living or to conform to the rules of society. Some psychotics maintain a relatively adequate contact with reality in most respects but are victims of hallucinatory or delusional systems within a special area; these individuals usually manage to get along in society without being institutionalized. Indeed, some of them are highly efficient in their own line of work so long as no unfamiliar factor enters their environment. Psychotics, some all of the time, some part of the time, live in a world of fantasy wherein every wish is satisfied: the one who wants power becomes Napoleon or the Pope or God; the woman who wants a child 'gets a child daily'; the man who wants money is suddenly a multimillionaire. To them these fantasies conflict in no way with the facts of their life.

"Psychoneurotics, on the other hand, maintain contact with reality but are disabled by their inability to cope with the problems through normal means. Since they remain in contact with reality, they are usually able to make a living, to care for their families, and to perform successfully valuable work. Occasionally, their neurosis is completely debilitating because their entire attention and energies are taken up in carrying out their neurotic maneuvers. Whereas many psychotics, having lost the 'hurt instinct,' suffer little from their condition, psychoneurotics suffer intensely and continuously.

"Psychopathic patients present a picture of symptoms which sometimes resemble those of a neurotic, sometimes those of a psychotic, and sometimes a mixture of both. The psychopath, although very close to psychosis, never experiences the full-blown psychotic attack. While psychopathic personalities sometimes do suffer like the psychoneurotics, yet most of the time they do not suffer, because they live a life of unreality similar to that of the psychotics.

"Mental deficiency is, primarily, an impairment of the intellectual functions. The person with normal intelligence is able to use his memory, his power of concentration, and his ability to judge and to reason in an orderly, socially acceptable way, without undue emotion or bizarre operations of the mind. The feebleminded person lacks these abilities to a varying degree."—*Psychiatry and Catholicism* (2. ed., New York: McGraw-Hill Book Company, Inc., 1957), p. 287 and p. 315.

ground, skill, etc., of the doctor. Quite often a patient may present more or less pronounced symptoms of various types or forms of mental illness; and it may, as a result, be quite difficult to establish precisely the exact nature of the illness.[13]

It is only after he has made a more or less definite diagnosis of the mental disturbance involved that a psychiatrist is able to state that a certain act is to be called the act of a psychopath, schizophrenic, etc. Quite obviously, such an approach requires a very extensive knowledge of the many mental illnesses and disturbances, their causes and symptoms.

The legal approach to a given act is exactly the reverse of the medical approach. From the strictly legal point of view, there are only these three possibilities:

1) If a given act and all the other acts of a person are judged to have been posited with sufficient knowledge, freedom, and maturity of judgment to make them valid legal acts, then they are termed the acts of a sane person.

2) If a given act and all the other acts of a person are judged to have been posited without sufficient knowledge, freedom, and maturity of judgment to make them valid legal acts, then they are termed the acts of a person who suffers from *amentia*. The person is classified as being *amens* at law. The term *amentia*, therefore, refers to the condition of a person whose every legal action lacks the requisite psy-

[13] Regarding the problem of classification, Noyes in his work, *Modern Clinical Psychiatry* (4. ed., Philadelphia: W. B. Saunders Company, 1954), remarks on page 158: "From a descriptive standpoint the problem is simplified if mental disorders are divided into groups based on clinical and behavioral differences. It is well, however, to avoid thinking in categories of disease entities and seek only to present a factual digest of the origins and types of reaction. While classifications are necessary for statistical and other purposes, at times there has perhaps been too great a disposition in psychiatry to consider that its objective was attained when a classificatory diagnosis had been made. The principal value of classification is not in the categorizing of a disease entity but in quickly eliminating those considerations which will be least useful in understanding the patient and in directing attention to those which are likely to be relevant."

chical requirements to make them valid or legally imputable acts.

3) If a given act and some, but not all, of the other acts of a person are judged to have been posited without sufficient knowledge, freedom, and maturity of judgment to make them valid legal acts, then they are termed the acts of a person who suffers from *dementia.* The term *dementia,* therefore, refers to the condition of a person who has sufficient psychical capacity for some legal acts while he has insufficient psychical capacity for other legal acts. The person is said to be *demens* at law. The *demens* is put on a par with *amens* in those legal acts which are posited with insufficient knowledge, freedom, or maturity of judgment; he is, however, equated with the sane person in all those legal acts which do meet the minimum psychical requirements to make them legally imputable acts.[14]

As will be seen later,[15] the law will call upon medical and psychiatric experts for advice and help in determining whether a particular act of a person possessed the pyschical requirements to make the act legally imputable. The law does not ask the help of experts to determine whether a particular person was or is a schizophrenic, paranoic, psychopath, etc. The law does not need to establish such a diagnosis at all, for mental illness in medical terminology and classification falls outside the scope of interest of the law as outside its area of competence. However, the law does want to determine whether a particular act is the act of a person who is considered *amens, demens* or sane.

In this study, therefore, such terms as *amentia, dementia,* insanity, mental illness, mental incompetence, unsound mind, etc., do not intend to convey any medical information whatsoever. These are not, and are not meant to be medical terms; they are strictly legal. They refer to the acts of a

[14] *S.R.R. Decisiones,* I (1909), 164; XIII (1921), 48; XIII (1921), 86; XX (1928), 60; XX (1928), 260; XXVII (1935), 282; XXIX (1937), 757; XXXII (1940), 82; XXXIII (1941), 653; XXXIII (1941), 668; XXXVIII (1946), 571.

[15] *Infra,* p. 205.

person rather than to his professionally considered mental state or condition.[16]

The only distinction of legal import, therefore, in cases of mental illness or insanity is the time-honored distinction of the law between *amentia* and *dementia*.

Psychiatrists may perhaps hold that it is impossible for a person to be insane with respect to one thing and not with respect to another. From the medical point of view, this may be correct for, medically speaking, the whole personality is disturbed and, consequently, all the acts of the patient are the acts of a mentally sick or disturbed person.[17] At law, however, it is possible that a person is not capable of meeting the psychical requirements for one particular act, while at the same time he is able to meet the requirements for another legal act.

It may be interesting to note the observations made by Dr. Noyes regarding the (medically) traditional distinction between psychoneuroses and psychoses. His remarks clear-

[16] "Legislatores omni aevo medicorum placita non sunt sequuti in multiformi divisione ac variis nominibus, quibus placuit ac placet mentales infirmitates dispescere ac significare. Cum enim finis legis diversus sit ab eo, quem sibi medici proponunt in variis huiusmodi morbis indagandis, consequens fuit quod lex eam tantum divisionem ac nomina acciperet, quae fini sibi proprio responderent, quaeque diversas species vel subspecies sub se complecterentur. Ita in Romanorum iure mentio simpliciter fiebat de dementibus, sub cuius nomine veniebant mentecapti et furiosi; quam terminalogiam accepit quoque vetus Decretalium ius, distinguentes eius Commentatores [sic], inter furiosos vere tales, et furiosos sub umbrata quiete. Etiam sequiori tempore et penes civiles nationes ab hac classificatione et denominatione non est recessum, unde in foro usuvenit distinctio, quam etiam medicilegistae passim acceperunt, inter dementiam naturalem, quae complectitur mentecaptos a nativitate vel infantia, ab extremo gradu imbecillitatis, usque ad simplicitatem spiritus, et dementiam adventiciam vel accidentalem, quae post adeptum iudicium supervenit, Legislator noster, in novo Codice, ad hanc distinctionem subtilius attendere non videtur, et loquitur simpliciter de amentia, sive in ordine ad consensum matrimonialem, (can. 1982), quam ad delicti incapacitatem, cui opponit debilitatem mentis ad minorem delicti imputabilitatem (can. 2201 §§ 1-4)."—*S.R.R. Decisiones*, XX (1928), 60, n. 6.

[17] Noyes, *Modern Clinical Psychiatry*, p. 95.

ly demonstrate the vast and basic difference between the medical approach to mental illnesses and disturbances and the juridical approach. He states:

> For a long time psychiatrists have placed much emphasis on a supposed distinction between psychoses and psychoneuroses . . . To a constantly greater extent it is being felt by psychiatrists that there are no such differences in the fundamental nature of psychogenic disorders as to warrant the present rigid and meticulous distinction between psychoses and psychoneuroses. Many agree with Bowman (Bowman, Mark M., and Rose, Milton: A criticism of the terms "psychosis," "psychoneurosis," and "neurosis." Am. J. Psychiat., 108:161-166, 1951) that the distinction is without scientific basis and has been based on rough descriptive differences in symptomatology, also that precise and universally accepted definitions of the two terms have never been established. There is, in fact, a continuity between "normality," neurosis, and psychosis.
>
> While one must doubt if there is any scientific basis for the distinction between "psychoses" and "psychoneuroses" yet nomenclatures that have become so thoroughly established traditionally must contain some value. The value in this distinction has been largely legal, social and administrative and based arbitrarily on symptomatology. Since differences in symptomatology readily conduce to the establishment of a diagnostic categories the distinction has also been of value as a teaching aid. The matter of classification, too, may be of importance in selecting the type of therapy. Many criteria have been suggested upon the basis of which the differentiation between psychoses and psychoneuroses should be made. The great variations in those proposed suggest, as Bowman has pointed out, that the distinction is not basic but superficial. Some psychiatrists have designated the psychoses as "major reactions" and the psychoneuroses as "minor reactions," the distinction being made on the extent of the involvement of the personality. Other psychiatrists look upon psychosis and psychoneurosis as different stages in the same mental process. While it must probably be conceded that there is

> very little scientific basis for the distinction between the psychoneuroses and other psychogenic disorders there is nevertheless a sufficient difference in their clinical nature to justify the distinction on pragmatic grounds. In general the diagnosis of psychosis implies a greater severity of symptoms than in psychoneurosis.[18]

The distinction between psychosis and psychoneurosis, therefore, appears to be based solely on a descriptive difference in symptomatology. "There is," Noyes states, "a continuity between 'normality,' 'neurosis,' and 'pyschosis.' " From the medical point of view, this statement appears to be sound or at least tenable.

In legal terminology, however, such a continuity between normality, *amentia* and *dementia* is impossible. Each term has a vastly different and essentially distinct meaning at law.

In medical terminology, as just indicated, there is only a difference in degree or in the extent of the involvement of the total personality and, therefore, there is only a superficial and not a basic distinction between psychosis and psychoneurosis. But it is precisely on this degree of severity and extent of involvement that the essential legal distinction is based between a person who is psychically capable of performing a certain legal act, and one who is not psychically capable of doing so. This is the essential distinction between the legally sane and legally insane person (*amens*). It is on the basis of the same degree of severity of disturbance and extent of involvement that a person is judged psychically capable of positing one legal act and psychically incapable of placing another legal act, i.e., the distinction found in legal *dementia*.

These observations make evident the absolute necessity of distinguishing between the medical and the legal notions of insanity or mental illness if one is to avoid serious and frustrating confusion in dealing with cases of mental illness and marriage.

[18] Noyes, *Modern Clinical Psychiatry*, pp. 446-447.

Article 2. Invalid Matrimonial Consent by Reason of Mental Illness or Defect

A person cannot validly contract marriage if, at the moment of giving matrimonial consent, he does not possess sufficient knowledge,[19] the necessary freedom,[20] or, finally, that degree of maturity of judgment which is proportionate to the matrimonial contract.[21] Legally it is immaterial whether the psychical deficiency arises from mental illness or from mental deficiency, or from any other cause. This statement forms the obvious conclusion to the previous chapter in this study. The law does not look formally to the classification of mental disability, but only to its end result, its effect.

That mental illness or mental deficiency can destroy a person's psychical capacity for marriage is self-evident. For instance, an idiot who has a mental age of two or three years or less, who is incapable of any education, and who is unable to guard himself against even common physical dangers[22] is evidently incapable of giving valid matrimonial consent. In the same way, a schizophrenic is not able to bind himself to the marriage bond while in a catatonic stupor, which leaves him mute and immovable, or merely repeating the words or actions of others.[23]

Cavanagh and McGoldrick give the following definition of a psychosis: "Psychoses are either temporary or prolonged deviations from normalcy in judging, reasoning, and willing, which are the result of an individual's failure to adequately solve his conflicts and which may result in disturbed or inappropriate emotions, delusions, seriously irregular conduct, and deep-seated personality disorganization and other symptoms."[24] Among the other symptoms they mention defective insight, which makes the patient in-

[19] Cf. *supra,* p. 88.

[20] Cf. *supra,* p. 99.

[21] Cf. *supra,* p. 130.

[22] Cavanagh-McGoldrick, *Fundamental Psychiatry,* p. 528.

[23] Vanderveldt-Odenwald, *Psychiatry and Catholicism,* p. 291.

[24] Cavanagh-McGoldrick, *op. cit.,* p. 311.

capable of realizing that his mind is affected; loss of contact with reality, which makes him move as though he were in a dreamland of imagery and complexes; lack of orientation, i.e., the inability to realize circumstances of time, place and persons; distortion of the psychic functions, by which the intellect is left incapable of performing some or all of its functions or is capable of doing so only defectively. The powers of understanding, reasoning, memory and imagination all may be adversely affected.[25] If such are the effects on a person's psychical powers, it is not difficult to show that mental illness can indeed leave a person psychically incapable of giving valid matrimonial consent.

To prove, in a particular case, that a mental illness or a mental deficiency had actually destroyed a person's capacity for matrimonial consent is usually much more difficult and at times even impossible. This would require proving, first of all, that an illness or deficiency was present at the precise time when the matrimonial contract was entered into; secondly, proving that the illness or deficiency at the time of marriage had already reached such a degree of severity that it made matrimonial consent psychically impossible.[26]

In dealing with the question of the invalidating effect of mental illness on marriage, it must be born in mind that mental illness is not an impediment to matrimony. The only reason that mental illness may invalidate marriage is because of its effects on a person's psychical ability to consent validly to the matrimonial contract.[27]

There is no incompatibility between an existing marriage bond and a supervening mental affliction. They may and do exist simultaneously, sad as this situation may be. An abnormal mental state, therefore, does not of itself offer any sufficient reason for the dissolution of an existing marriage bond. The bond remains intact, even though the mental af-

[25] *Loc. cit.*

[26] Cf. can. 1082 and 1086, § 1.

[27] Cf. Fässler, *Die Schizophrenie als Ehenichtigkeitsgrund im Kanonischen Recht*, p. 54.

fliction may render impossible the fulfillment of marital obligations.

Mental illness has an invalidating effect on marriage only when it renders the consent defective, that is, when it is directly opposed to the eliciting of matrimonial consent and, in consequence, to the establishing of a marriage contract.

In cases of mental illness, it is necessary to determine whether the psychical deficiency actually existed at the time of the marriage ceremony. The fact that a person was mentally ill before or after the marriage ceremony has legal import only insofar as it may help in determining the person's psychical capacity for marriage at the precise moment of giving consent to the matrimonial contract. Hence, in practice, many difficulties present themselves with regard to the problem of the so-called "lucid interval." In theory, there is no special difficulty. A lucid interval should be understood to be a period of time in which a mentally ill person actually has sufficient knowledge, freedom, and maturity of judgment to contract a valid marriage.[28]

The question whether a lucid interval actually can exist in a true mental illness seems to be a problem to be considered by the psychiatrists rather than by the jurists. It is the problem of the psychiatrist because the possibility of a true lucid interval is intimately connected with the nature of mental illness itself, which is the precise object of study by the science of psychiatry.[29]

Theoretically, a lucid interval is definitely admissible at law. At law, the term conveys the notion that a person who, at one time, was considered psychically incapable of marriage by reason of mental illness, improved to such an extent that for a limited period of time he could meet the psychical requirements for marriage, while later his condition again deteriorated to such an extent that marriage again became impossible for him. A lucid interval should not be confused with a full and definite recovery. Neither should a

[28] Cf. Smith, *Ignorance Affecting Matrimonial Consent*, p. 47; Holböck, *Tractatus De Jurisprudentia Sacrae Romanae Rotae*, pp. 107-108.

[29] *Supra*, p. 160.

lucid interval be confused with the mere absence of the external symptoms of mental illness or insanity.[30]

A true lucid interval, therefore, requires that there be a definite improvement in a person's knowing, willing and judging even though the mental illness itself remains. The improvement makes it possible for the person to meet the minimum psychical requirements for marital consent during a certain limited time. Afterwards his condition deteriorates so that marriage again becomes impossible for him. If his condition would not again deteriorate, there would be question of a definite improvement rather than of a lucid interval.

A supervening mental illness which arises after the marriage has taken place does not invalidate an existing marriage bond. On the other hand, the fact that a person had been afflicted with a mental illness or disturbance prior to the marriage ceremony does not *ipso facto* make a subsequent marriage impossible. The person may have been cured of his mental illness, or he may have improved to such a degree that he is actually able to meet the necessary psychical requirements for marriage.

The liceity or even advisability of entering into a marriage contract during a lucid interval or after complete or partial recovery from a mental illness, there being no question as to validity of matrimonial consent, falls outside the scope of this study. It is a moral rather than a canonical problem.[31]

At law, the matter of paramount importance is the time of the illness: It must be proven that at the precise moment when the marriage was contracted, the person was psychically incapable of matrimony by reason of mental illness or disturbance.

[30] Lucida intervalla non sunt confundenda cum "conspectu umbratae quietis," sicut Glossa dicit, in quo saepe furiosi sunt constituti, aut cum mera absentia externarum manifestationum amentiae, neque cum plena et definitiva sanatione infirmi.—*S.R.R. Decisiones* XXII (1930), p. 133.

[31] Cf. Smith, *Ignorance Affecting Matrimonial Consent*, p. 49; Gougnard, *Tractatus de Matrimonio* (7. ed., Mechliniae: H. Dessain, 1931), p. 150.

McGowan described the problem regarding the exact time at which the mental illness must be proven to have been present in order to have its invalidating effect on matrimony. Treating of the manic depressive psychosis he declared:

> In Manic Depressive Psychosis, generally speaking, we have a totally different situation with regard to the presence of lucid intervals than we do in Schizophrenia.
>
> Between the episodic attacks of Manic Depressive Psychosis, the person is clear mentally and is capable of making valid decisions. The exception is in another malignant form of the illness which is referred to as the *Circular Type*, or Circular Insanity. In this condition the afflicted person goes from an attack of the Manic Type into an attack of the Depressed Type with no free interval between these two types, and acute symptoms of either one or the other are always present. Here there are, of course, no lucid intervals.
>
> With reference to the Manic Depressive Psychosis, it is necessary to point out that since this disease is characterized by recurrence and complete recovery, it is not enough to prove a person had this illness before his marriage but it must be proved that signs of a psychosis of serious degree were present at the time of the marriage or at least up to a time very shortly before the marriage, and again very shortly after the marriage.[32]

Just as the question of time does not present any difficulties in theory, neither does the question of the degree of mental illness offer any particular problem. In practice, however, to prove a degree of severity of the mental illness sufficient to invalidate matrimonial consent, may often be quite difficult.

In theory, the question: How serious does the mental illness or deficiency have to be to make matrimonial consent impossible, can be answered as follows: If the mental ill-

[32] "Fundamentals of Psychiatry in Relation to the Ecclesiastical Tribunal," *The Jurist*, XVI (1956), pp. 251-266.

ness is of such a degree of severity that it affects a person's knowledge, freedom, and maturity of judgment to the extent that the psychical requirements for matrimony cannot be met, then mental illness invalidates matrimonial consent.

If a person is truly mentally ill or retarded but only to such an extent that he still remains capable of meeting the minimum psychical requirements for marriage, then he can certainly enter into a valid matrimonial contract. At law, such a person is considered sane even though by medical standards he is mentally ill or disturbed.

Again the question of liceity or advisability of entering into marriage in such a state or with a person in such a condition is outside the scope of this study.

McGowan described the problem of the degree of mental illness as follows:

> Medically speaking, Schizophrenia is generally considered to be a continuous, chronic, maiming illness with never a recovery in the fullest sense. The general rule is "Once a Schizophrenic, always a Schizophrenic."
>
> Since, generally speaking, Schizophrenia is a continuous, incurable, deteriorating disease-process, once it has been proved that this disease existed in a serious stage of development, it is presumed, medically speaking, to continue to be present in the same serious stage unless it is proved, by certain and evident arguments, that all traces of Schizophrenic thinking, feeling, and acting have completely disappeared.
>
> However, since we are dealing with a disease of unknown cause and for which we have no specific treatment, we cannot make a universal rule to this effect.
>
> It must be remembered the illness may be present in greater or less degree of seriousness or that it may be halted at any stage or there may be some apparent improvement, if not recovery.
>
> Therefore, each individual case has to be judged on its own merits, and the presence and the serious-

ness of the stage of the disease at the time of marriage have to be determined in the individual case.[33]

Article 3. Juridic Proof of Invalid Matrimonial Consent by Reason of Mental Illness or Defect

The theory regarding the invalidating effect of mental illness or mental deficiency on matrimonial consent does not present any serious difficulties. This theory, as established in the foregoing, can be summarized simply as follows: For a valid marriage contract, it is required that the contractants at the time of the marriage ceremony possess a certain minimum degree of psychical capacity. That is to say, both parties must know the essential nature, purpose and qualities of marriage.[34] Moreover, both parties must have at least the philosophical freedom to be able to choose or not to choose matrimony.[35] This minimal practical capacity is usually found in a person at puberty. Consequently, if a person has psychical capacity in the same degree as the average adolescent at puberty, that person is to be considered as being able to give valid matrimonial consent. Such a person must be considered capable of matrimony even if, by medical standards, he is regarded as being mentally ill or disturbed. On the other hand, if a person by reason of mental illness does not meet this same norm, he must be judged incapable of giving valid consent.

Mental illness, or any other mental disturbance or defect, can, and often does, affect a person's knowing, willing and judging to such an extent that the mentally ill or defective person lacks the psychical requirements for matrimony and fails to measure up to the psychical standard or norm, i.e., the mental capacity normally and usually present at puberty. If a person in such a condition nevertheless would attempt to enter into a marriage contract, the contract itself must be considered invalid at Church law.

In practice, however, difficulties often arise when a mar-

[33] *Ibidem*, p. 257.
[34] *Supra*, p. 139.
[35] *Supra*, p. 158.

riage case based on a plea of mental illness or deficiency is presented to the court for adjudication. Then questions of degree of severity, of time, and of the possibility of a lucid interval often present perplexing problems. Yet these difficulties often are not as insurmountable as may at first appear. If both the court and the psychiatrist recognize their own limitations, and if they remain strictly within their own areas of competence, most of the practical problems can be readily resolved.

A judge,[36] to declare a marriage invalid by reason of mental illness or defect, must have moral certitude that a mental illness or defect was certainly present at the time when the marriage was contracted, and that it was present to such a degree that it made the contractant incapable of entering into marriage, according to the standard of incapacity stated above.[37]

SECTION A. MORAL CERTITUDE

Canon 1869 states that the judge must have moral certitude about the matter to be defined in the sentence before pronouncing that sentence. He must arrive at this certitude by examining the acts and proofs which he must evaluate according to his own conscience, unless the law expressly makes some specific demand concerning the efficacy of some particular proof.[38] If the judge cannot arrive at this certi-

[36] The term judge here refers to any one of the three judges of the collegiate tribunal. These judges issue a joint sentence, arrived at by means of a majority vote according to Canon 1577, § 1. Each of the judges arrives at his own conclusion independently, with moral certainty derived from the acts of the process and the incorporated proofs; cf. c. 1869, §§ 1-2. Each of the judges has equal discretionary authority in this matter, each evaluating or appraising the evidence according to his own conscience (cf. c. 1869, § 3 and c. 1871); (cf. Bottoms, *The Discretionary Authority of the Ecclesiastical Judge in Matrimonial Trials of the First Instance*, p. 161.

[37] *Supra*, p. 140.

[38] § 1. Ad pronuntiationem cuiuslibet sententiae requiritur in iudicis animo moralis certitudo circa rem sententia definiendam.

§ 2. Hanc certitudinem iudex haurire debet ex actis et probatis.

§ 3. Probationes autem aestimare iudex debet ex sua conscientia, nisi lex aliquid expresse statuat de efficacia alicuius probationis.

tude after a diligent examination of the cause, he must decide in marriage cases that the invalidity of the marriage has not been proven (*non constare de nullitate in casu*).[39]

Any extensive examination or consideration of the nature of moral certitude, and the manner in which it is obtained, is clearly outside the purpose of the present study. It will not be amiss, however, to repeat here some of the salient points from the Allocution of Pope Pius XII to the Sacred Roman Rota concerning moral certitude.[40] The Supreme Pontiff declared:

> There is an absolute certainty, in which all possible doubt as to the truth of the fact and the unreality of the contrary is entirely excluded... In contrast to this degree of certitude common speech often designates as certain a cognition which strictly speaking does not merit to be so called, but should rather be classed as a greater or lesser probability, because it does not exclude all reasonable doubt, but leaves a foundation for the fear of error....
>
> Between the two extremes of absolute certainty and quasi-certainty, or probability, is that *moral certainty . . . of* which We principally wish to speak. It is characterized on the positive side by the exclusion of well-founded or reasonable doubt, and in this respect it is essentially distinguished from the quasi-certainty which has been mentioned; on the negative side, it does admit the absolute possibility of the contrary; and in this it differs from absolute certainty. The certainty of which We are now speaking is necessary and sufficient for the rendering of a judgment, even though in the particular case it would be possible either directly or indirectly to reach absolute certainty....
>
> Sometimes moral certainty is derived only from an aggregate of indications and proofs which, taken singly, do not provide the foundation for true certitude, but which, when taken together, no

[39] Cf. can. cit., § 4.

[40] *AAS*, XXXIV (1942), 338 ff. The English translation has been taken from Bouscaren, *Canon Law Digest* (Milwaukee: Bruce Publishing Co.; 1954), III, pp. 605 ff.

> longer leave room for any reasonable doubt on the part of a man of sound judgment . . . Consequently, if in giving the reasons for his decision, the judge states that the proofs which have been adduced, considered separately, cannot be judged sufficient, but that, taken together and embraced in a survey of the whole situation, they provide the necessary elements for arriving at a safe definitive judgment, it must be acknowledged that such reasoning is in general sound and legitimate.
>
> In any event, this certainty is understood to be objective, that is, based on objective motives; it is not a purely subjective certitude, founded on sentiment or on this or that merely subjective opinion, perhaps even on personal credulity, lack of consideration or inexperience . . . To make sure of the objective nature of this certainty, procedural law establishes well defined rules of inquiry and proof.
>
> . . . But since moral certainty, as We have said, admits of various degrees, what degree can or should the judge demand in order to be able to proceed to judgment? In the first place, he must always make sure that there is in reality an objective moral certainty, that is, that all reasonable doubt of the truth is excluded. Once this is assured, he should, as a rule, not require a higher degree of certainty, except when the law prescribes it especially in view of the importance of the case. At times, it is true, even though there be no such express provision of the law, it may be prudent for the judge not to be satisfied with a low degree of certitude, in cases of great importance. Yet, if after serious consideration and study, a grade of certitude is attained which corresponds to the requirements of law and the importance of the case, there should not be insistence, to the serious inconvenience of the parties, that new proofs be adduced so as to attain a still higher degree of certitude. To require the highest possible certainty, notwithstanding that a sufficient certainty already exists, is without justification and should be discouraged.

In a case before his court in which a plea is made of defective consent by reason of mental illness or defect, the judge does not have to decide whether a person is or was mentally ill or defective. Much less does he have to obtain moral certitude regarding the precise nature of the particular ailment involved. Rather, the judge, using the ordinary means provided in procedural law, must obtain moral certitude to decide only whether, in the given case, one of the parties did or did not have sufficient knowledge, freedom, and maturity of judgment, to contract marriage validly.

SECTION B. JUDICIAL EVIDENCE IN MARRIAGE CASES BASED ON A PLEA OF MENTAL ILLNESS OR DEFECT

In relation to the judge, judicial proof can be considered objectively or subjectively. In the objective or broad sense it can be taken to be the presentation of proofs for the purpose of convincing a judge, or the proofs themselves available for presentation. In the subjective or restricted sense, judicial proof is understood to be the effect of the presentation of evidence when it brings about moral certainty in the mind of the judge about a matter which is to be defined by the sentence of his court.[41]

The Instruction *Provida Mater* of the Sacred Congregation of the Sacraments, dated August 15, 1936,[42] in Title IX, *de probationibus,* lists five types of judicial evidence used in marriage trials: 1) the deposition of the parties; 2) the testimony of witnesses; 3) the opinion of experts; 4) documents; 5) presumptions.

[41] Bottoms in his study, *The Discretionary Authority of the Ecclesiastical Judge in Matrimonial Trials of the First Instance,* observes on page 75: "Taken in the objective or wide meaning, proof *(probatio)* seems to agree with what is called 'judicial evidence' in the Anglo-American systems of law.... In Anglo-American common law, judicial evidence is defined as 'any knowable fact or group of facts, not a legal or a logical principle, considered with a view to its being offered before a legal tribunal for the purpose of producing the effect of persuasion, positive or negative, not of law or of logic, on which the determination of the tribunal is to be asked.'" Cf. Wigmore, *The Principles of Judicial Proof as given by Logic, Psychology and Generel Experience and Illustrated in Judicial Trials* (Boston: Little, Brown & Co., 1913), p. 5.

[42] *AAS,* XXVIII (1936), 312-370.

In the present study, the following question must be answered: How can it be proven at law that the mental condition of one of the contracting parties in a contested marriage was of such a nature, at the time of the marriage, that it rendered the party incapable of meeting the psychical requirements necessary for a valid matrimonial consent?

The judge must examine carefully and in detail the quality of the thinking, willing, judging, acting, and feeling of the person involved at the time of the marriage ceremony. The daily actions of the person, his conversation, tone of voice, his manner of dress, idiosyncrasies, regard for others, his conduct in company, and similar indications can provide valuable help to the judge in coming to moral certitude regarding the psychical capacity of that person.[43]

The actual judicial investigation into the psychical capacity of a person at the time of marriage will be considered here under three separate headings: 1) the evidence derived from the testimony of the parties and witnesses; 2) the evidence obtained from documents and presumptions; 3) proof derived from the testimony of the judicial expert.

a. The Evidence Derived from the Testimony of the Parties and Witnesses

Two general classes or categories of cases are presented to the courts for adjudication. One class are those in which there is no history of treatment for mental illness prior to the date of the marriage. The second class are those cases in which medical records are available to indicate mental illness or abnormality and, at times, even hospitalization for mental illness prior to the wedding date. Normally, it will be much more difficult to determine whether an illness which is discovered only after the marriage actually existed before the marriage, and whether is existed to such a degree as to make marital consent impossible.

In evaluating the testimony of witnesses, the judge needs to be aware of the following possible circumstances which may color the testimony of the witnesses, especially of the

[43] *S.R.R. Decisiones*, VIII (1916), p. 211.

close relatives of the party involved. These same circumstances may also influence the testimony of the parties themselves.

a) The members of the immediate family of the person or even of the intended marriage partner may not recognize many and clear indications of mental illness or disturbance. b) The members of the family may recognize that something is wrong, but they are not willing to admit to the possibility of a "mental case in the family." c) the standards of the family and the environment may be low and, as a result, what should indicate abnormality is accepted as being merely personal eccentricity. d) The future spouse, being in love and preoccupied with his own emotions prior to the marriage, often does not recognize the indications of mental illness in his future marriage partner. If he does recognize them, he believes his intended marriage partner to be merely "mixed up or nervous," and he thinks that she will "settle down" or "straighten out" after they are married. At times such "nervous," "strange," or "mixed up" persons are even urged to get married by members of their immediate family, who sincerely believe that marriage may be exactly what is needed to help them over their so-called "nervousness."

Noyes makes the following observations regarding the interview of the psychiatrist with the relatives of the patient:

> It is usually well to obtain a history from more than one relative or friend. This is desirable not only that the history as given by the first informant may be supplemented, but because emotional factors such as feelings of shame and guilt may lead an informant to conceal certain facts or overemphasize others ... With the lapse of time the informant tends to omit incidents which he did not consider significant, and if he be a near relative of the patient he is prone to conceal important data, perhaps because of regret for previous attitudes toward the patient, because of fear the patient may resent the disclosure of the information, or because in his eagerness for the patient's recovery he is inclined to gloss over facts which he believes the

> physician may consider ominous. Often the informants lack the objective, detached attitude which will permit them to recall or state correctly the intra-family attitudes and relationships under which the patient was raised.[44]

Though these observations were made concerning the testimony of family witnesses in a psychiatric examination, they may apply in a somewhat similar manner to the testimony and attitudes of relatives in a judicial investigation.

Monsignor Hayes, quoting Monsignor Fidecicchi, stated:

> It happens frequently that the family and friends of the sick person do not notice the confusion of his mind, especially at the beginning of the insanity. Whence it follows that it is not unusual for a person to seem capable of carrying on his ordinary duties well—and yet he must be considered unfit for marriage—sometimes the violently insance remain in a state of apparent quiet and yet their actions are not those of their own mind.[45]

Another important factor is that at times a person who is mentally ill or seriously disturbed may be able to act quite sanely in common, everyday life. One of the Rotal sentences points to this fact by insisting that a distinction must be made between the acquired habits of daily routine and those acts that require deliberation and decision. The former are performed almost automatically and mechanically and do not absolutely require a sane mind; the latter require the use of a sane mind and a deliberate act of the will.[46]

These circumstances may at times lead to apparent contradictions between the testimonies offered by, e.g., the parents and the fellow employees of a particular person and the

[44] Noyes, *Modern Clinical Psychiatry,* p. 133.

[45] Hayes, art. cit., *The Jurist,* XVI (1956), p. 283.

[46] *S.R.R. Decisiones,* XIV (1922), 312-320: Distinguendum est, aiunt, inter actus qui ex habitu iam acquisito et usu fere quotidiano fiunt, et eos qui deliberato consilio faciendi sunt; illi fere automatice perficientur datis opportunis adiunctis et stimulis, nec sanam mentem absolute requirunt; hi autem nonnisi praehabita cognitione rationali per deliberatum voluntatis usum exerceri possunt. Cf. also *S.R.R. Decisiones,* XXVII (1935), 284.

opinion given by the psychiatric experts. Apparent contradictions are to be expected. Such contradictions alone should not lead the judge to suspect the honesty of the witnesses or the capabilities of the experts.

Witnesses are not called upon to give their opinion regarding the mental health or illness of a person, much less regarding a person's capacity to marry. Their task is to testify to facts. As Pickard states:

> Of the witnesses, on the other hand, no specialized skill, knowledge, or art is required. Honesty and the proper functioning of the senses suffice, for the witness testifies only to what he has seen, heard or learned through the ordinary use of his faculties. No opinion or judgment is asked of him, nor is any accepted if it is voluntarily given. He is to state facts of which he has personal knowledge, and is not allowed to testify with reference to his reasoned conclusion or his inference from the fact of which he has knowledge.[47]

The witnesses are called to testify to facts which indicate external symptoms of abnormality which they themselves have observed. If witnesses undertake to give opinions and conclusions without designating specific acts or signs, they are being allowed by the court to depart from their role as witnesses and to judge the case, which is clearly not within their province as witnesses.[48]

In hearing the witnesses, the judge will direct his questions, therefore, to the external symptoms of mental illnesses or mental disturbances. He will particularly endeavor to establish facts indicating the duration and degree of departure from normal behavior on the part of the person involved in the case.

[47] Pickard, *Judicial Experts: A Source of Evidence in Ecclesiastical Trials*, p. 62.

[48] Quando agitur de probanda aliqua qualitate animi, tunc testes debent testificari per actus exteriores, quos viderint; nam exteriora indicant secreta animi. Unde cum testes nullam assignent rationem, nec etiam referant aliqua signa vel actus extrinsecos, dicuntur iudicare, non autem testificari.—*S.R.R. Decisiones,* XX (1928), 71.

It may be helpful to cite at this point Cavanagh and McGoldrick who state:

> Peculiarities of some kind or another are not uncommon in otherwise normal individuals. Although these unusual characteristics may produce an eccentric type of personality, a complete personality inventory is necessary before they can be regarded as evidences of mental abnormality. The maladjustments of normal people differ from those of the mentally ill, either in duration or degree of departure from the average performance. Case studies give convincing proof that mental abnormality is frequently an exaggeration of a normal process . . . It might be said that the mentally ill are just like ourselves, only more so. The above is also the conclusion reached by outstanding psychiatrists and psychologists.[49]

The judge, therefore, in hearing the testimony, should pay particular attention to facts which reveal the degree and the duration of departure from normal knowing, willing, and judging as it unfolds in the testimony of the witnesses.

Noyes divides the symptoms of mental illness into the following categories: 1) disorders of perception; 2) disorders of thinking; 3) disturbances of consciousness; 4) disorders of appreciation; 5) disorders of orientation; 6) disturbances of affectivity; 7) disorders of behavior; 8) disorders of attention; 9) disorders in memory.[50]

It is of practical value here to present a rather elaborate treatment of the various symptoms of mental illness.[51]

1) Disorders of Perception.

Under disorders of perception, one finds illusions and hal-

[49] *Fundamental Psychiatry,* p. 26.

[50] *Modern Clinical Psychiatry,* pp. 97-129.

[51] Knowledge regarding such symptoms will aid the judge in coming to a decision in a given case. Moreover, detailed testimonies regarding such symptoms will be of invaluable help to the judicial expert when he is called upon to examine the acts of the case and to give his opinion in the case. Quite often he will have to base his conclusions on the facts learned from the testimonies of witnesses; cf. *Provida Mater,* Art. 147, § 2.

lucinations. Illusions are misinterpretations of things heard or seen. For instance, a person may actually hear the rustling of leaves but think that he hears voices.

Hallucination is a more serious form of falsification of perception because it has no basis in reality whatsoever. Mentally ill people at times converse or quarrel with "voices" which they believe to be hearing. At other times they may see people, animals (e.g., snakes in delirium) which actually are not present. Hallucinations conveying a command are often very convincing and compelling. Considerations of reality are of little weight in comparison to the influence of such hallucinations of hearing or vision. Hallucinations of sight are less frequent than auditory ones. They often excite great fear in a person and should be considered a very serious distortion of reality.[52]

2) Disorders of Thinking.

At times, there can be present disorders in the production of thought or in the progression of thought. In certain mental disorders there occurs a disturbance in the progression of thought characterized by a rapid digression from one idea to another. Ideas follow each other very rapidly, but they do not lead to any particular goal or conclusion. Such a flight of ideas makes it impossible for a person to sustain his attention for any length of time or to keep it directed to any definite goal.

Opposed to flight of ideas there may be present what is called "retardation of thought." Thoughts and, consequently, speech are slow and laborious. Retardation is often found in repressive phases of mental illnesses. Repression or "blocking" occurs when there is an exclusion of specific psychological activities or contents from conscious awareness by a process of which the individual is not directly aware.

Another type of disorder in thinking is termed "perseveration," by which is meant an abnormally persistent repetition or continuance in expression of a particular idea.

[52] *Ibidem,* p. 100.

This clinging to one thought is often found, for instance, in catatonia, i.e., a condition in which the person sits quietly or completely mute or motionless, immovable, with a staring countenance, the eyes fixed on a distant point and apparently completely without volition and without any reaction to sensory impressions.

Another disturbance in the flow of thought is that known as "circumstantiality." Circumstantiality leads a person from one unnecessary and trivial detail to another before he finally reaches the thought which he intends to express. The progression of thinking can also become so disorderly that one idea runs into the next one without any logical connection whatsoever. The patient suffering from this symptom often speaks incoherently and in disjointed phrases.

"Blocking" is a disturbance in thought which completely stops all thinking and, as a result, all speech. It can be observed when a person stops speaking abruptly in the middle of a sentence without any apparent reason for the sudden silence.[53]

In the case of some persons, symptoms of mental illness are found in the content of their thoughts. When a person places too much importance or value upon one or another idea or thought, there is present what has been termed an "overdetermined or overvalued idea." When an overvalued idea is present, it tends to blind the individual to all else, so that only those observations and memories are selected which suit its purpose or confirm it. Anything which conflicts with this overvalued idea is denied admission to consciousness. The personality, including its thinking and feeling aspects, becomes absorbed by the idea so that the overvalued idea becomes one of the most important determinants of the person's behavior.

Delusional ideas may appear by which reality is transformed to make it compatible with the emotional needs of the person. Delusions of grandeur, of self-accusation, or of persecution may twist a person's thinking and acting to a serious degree. Through ideas of reference, remarks or

[53] *Ibidem,* pp. 101-102.

actions on the part of others, although in no way referring to the mentally disturbed person, are interpreted by him as being related to himself and often as expressing accusation or depreciation. He constantly hears people talking about him, whispering behind his back, etc.

Other symptoms of mental illness which manifest themselves in the thought content of a person are hypochondria, i.e., exaggerated concern of physical health; obsessions, which are thoughts which keep recurring against the conscious desire of a person, and which cannot be influenced by logic or reasoning; phobias, which are obsessive fears of dirt, bacteria, cancer, crowds, heights, etc.[54]

3) Disturbances of Consciousness.

Confusion, bewilderment, perplexity, disorientation as to time and place, all can be indications of the presence of a serious mental disturbance. Consciousness can be beclouded to such an extent that to think clearly, to perceive, or to respond to one's surroundings, becomes difficult or impossible. To make a person whose consciousness is beclouded understand a question, it may be required to shake him, to shout the question many times before the question penetrates and evokes a response.

Other disturbances of consciousness are stupor and delirium. In stupor there is either a suspension of all thinking, or there is in intense preoccupation with just one thought. In delirium there is a clouding of consciousness, bewilderment, restlessness, confusion, disorientation, incoherent and dreamlike thinking, illusions, and hallucinations, and excessive fear.[55]

4) Disorders of Apperception.

"Involving much more than a disturbance of consciousness are the disturbances of that complex function known as apperception, by which through active, attentive thought one analyzes, synthetizes, integrates, evaluates, and absorbs

[54] *Ibidem,* pp. 103-109.
[55] *Ibidem,* pp. 109-112.

experience."[56] By apperception new ideas are formulated and related to ones already familiar, with the result that one is able to understand or grasp new situations, events and experiences. In disturbances of apperception a person has great difficulty in grasping questions and comprehending accustomed situations and experiences.

5) Disorders of Orientation.

If a person does not or only with great difficulty is able to recognize and localize himself as to time, place, circumstances and relationship to others, he is said to manifest the symptom of "disorientation."[57]

6) Disturbances of affectivity.

By affectivity is meant the feeling-life of a person. Noyes states:

> Fully to evaluate the significance of affect or feeling-tone in mental disorders, one must not confine its consideration to that of pathological variations, since, directly and indirectly, it exercises profound influence upon the thought and behavior of every individual. Not only is the thought content composed largely of affectively valued ideas but judgment is constantly distorted and rendered unreliable by those ideas that are overvalued for emotional reasons.[58]

The most frequent of the disturbances of affectivity are the following: "euphoria," which is a feeling of happiness, well-being, confidence and assurance even though the circumstances of the person may be such that they should produce the very opposite reactions. Euphoria, therefore, imparts a false sense of security in the mentally unbalanced person.

In "exaltation" there is an intense happiness and elation accompanied by an attitude of grandeur, which again is not warranted by the actual circumstances.

Depression, on the other hand, is a constant unpleasant

[56] Noyes, *op. cit.*, p. 112.
[57] *Ibidem*, p. 113.

tension as a result of which every experience is accompanied by mental pain or sorrow. Conversation becomes quite difficult for people who manifest this symptom of depression in a serious degree. They become totally dejected and hopeless in their attitude and manner. The depression may, and often does, impair a person's memory, attention, and power of concentration. Even bodily movements may become very slow and difficult for a depressed patient.

Tension, anxiety, fear, and panic are still other disorders of affectivity.

In tension the patient has a continual feeling of uneasiness, restlessness, dissatisfaction, dread, and discomforting expectancy. Often such a person is tremulous and jerky in his movements, has difficulty in concentrating, and often complains of tightness and unpleasant sensations in the head.

Anxiety and fear both are responses and signals of danger. Fear is a response to an actual, present, external danger; and it does not persist if the external danger is eliminated by conquest or flight. Anxiety differs from fear because it does not refer to any specific danger. It is an irrational dread of situations and people.

Noyes remarks:

> Anxiety with its threatening feelings from within, occupies a most important place in the dynamics of human behavior . . . Anxiety is one of the most distressing and intolerable of mental states with the result that adjustmental defenses designed to avoid, disguise or relieve it become exceedingly important determinants of behavior.[59]

He adds:

> It has been said that the degree of anxiety from which a person suffers, its various modes of expression, and the varying types of defenses which people utilize against it, constitute a means of dif-

[58] *Op. cit.,* p. 114.
[59] *Ibidem,* p. 118.

> ferential diagnosis between healthy and mentally sick people.[60]

Panic is a fear based on prolonged tension. There is often a very great difficulty in clear thinking and, at times, a sense and appearance of bewilderment. Noyes observes: "The situations giving rise to panic are ones in which some long-standing insecurity of the personality has created tension and become particularly threatening. Homosexual and, occasionally, disowned heterosexual tendencies are the most frequent factors."[61]

Indifference or "apathy" is one of the most frequent forms of an affective disturbance. There is an inadequate reaction to those experiences which normally give emotional pleasure or pain. People suffering from apathy often demonstrate a lack of drive or interest. Such qualities as gratitude, sympathy, hope, anticipation, grief, regret, pride or shame, no longer seem to be possessed by these people. Often they may appear to be completely out of touch with reality.

In others there is an inappropriateness of affect. They are happy when they should be sad; discouraged, when there is good reason for hope, etc.

"Depersonalization" is an affective disturbance in which feelings of unreality and of changed personality are the principal symptoms. These symptoms of unreality can be of two kinds. A person may no longer feel like himself. He sees himself as being unreal rather than changed into another person. He may feel that his body is dead or "frozen," that his thoughts are strange, or he may feel as if he were a machine or robot. Naturally, such a person has great difficulty in concentration and clear thinking.

In the second kind of depersonalization, the person feels not that he himself has become unreal; but, rather, that his surroundings and the world in general have changed. People and objects appear unreal, far away, and lacking in normal color and vividness. The sick person appears to be per-

[60] *Loc. cit.*

[61] *Ibidem*, p. 119.

plexed and bewildered due to the strangeness and unreality of things around him. He cannot concentrate and may have a sensation that "My brain is dead or has stopped working."[62]

7) Disorders of Behavior.

Certain disorders are found in the action field of the disturbed or mentally ill person. There may be overactivity, underactivity, or even total lack of activity. In overactivity the goal of the activity is constantly changed and, consequently, is never reached. In underactivity there are many prolonged delays before beginning the intended activity, and once begun the action is done very slowly and with painful effort.

Repetitious activity found when there is a tendency to repeat the same thing in the same manner for an indefinite period of time. Such activities may result in peculiar mannerisms, grimaces, gestures, peculiarities of gait, etc. The same words or sentences may be repeated over and over again.

Other disturbances of activity include automatic obedience, which is manifested if the person automatically fulfills commands and requests, repeats what is heard or imitates what is seen. "Negativism," on the other hand, consists in a constant refusal to obey or in doing exactly the opposite of what is requested. Negativism may result in mutism, refusal to eat or drink, immobility, etc. "Compulsion," finally, is a morbid and irresistible urge to perform an apparently unreasonable act, e.g., touching things, walking on cracks, constant handwashings, counting cars or telephone poles, etc.[63]

8) Disorders of Attention.

The inability to focus the attention a sufficient length of time to render adequate examination possible is known as

[62] *Ibidem*, pp. 113-121.

[63] They are not meaningless acts, but through the operation of the mechanisms of displacement, substitution and symbolism serve as defenses against anxiety; cf. *op. cit.*, pp. 123-124.

"distractibility." At other times as, for instance, in profound depression, there may be too great a tenacity of attention, so that nothing can divert the attention away from the depressive mental content of a person's thoughts.[64]

9) Disorders in Memory.

There are three basic disorders of memory: abnormally pronounced memory or *hypermnesia;* loss of memory or *amnesia;* falsification of memory or *paramnesia.* Abnormally pronounced memory is usually limited to specific periods of time or to certain specific events. Amnesia not only refers to past events but also to intended actions or plans. A person, for instance, completely forgets what he intended to do, his regular duties, appointments, etc. Finally, in paramnesia, or the falsification of memory, a mentally disturbed person fills the gaps in his memory by confabulation. Such a person fabricates events without any basis in fact. He himself, in speaking of these falsifications, believes them to be true and factual.[65]

It must be observed that many of the symptoms just described are found to a certain extent in all normal, mentally healthy people. It is only when they occur excessively, either in time or degree, that they become signs of abnormality.

It is precisely on facts regarding these symptoms that a judge must question the parties and witnesses in marriage cases in which a plea of insanity is made.

A judge inquires into the occurrence of any of these signs of mental illness not to diagnose the particular mental illness involved, as a doctor would, but only to come to a sound opinion regarding the psychical capacity of a person necessary to give a valid matrimonial consent.

As will be seen later,[66] an extensive and in these cases often necessarily lengthy inquiry into the various symptoms, idiosyncrasies, and abnormalities of a person will help the

[64] *Ibidem,* p. 125.
[65] *Ibidem,* pp. 125-129.
[66] Cf. *infra,* p. 216.

medical expert in his attempt to establish the psychical capacity of that person at the time of marriage.

The medical expert is called upon to examine the acts of the person which engender the suspicion of insanity.[67]

The "acts of a person which engender the suspicion of insanity" must be described in the judicial *acta* of the cause, which the psychiatrist must examine and study to be able to give his reasoned opinion.[68] The testimony of the parties and the witnesses, therefore, should be as detailed and specific as possible, especially regarding the time of occurrence in relation to the date of marriage, and regarding the severity of degree of any unusual or abnormal happenings or symptoms. Seldom, if ever, will there be too much factual evidence in these cases.

The purpose of the testimony of the parties and witnesses is twofold. First, it is the evidence which helps the judge to obtain moral certitude in the case; second, it is often the only source of factual information on which the expert can form his reasoned opinion. In those cases in which there is no history of treatment for mental illness prior to the marriage, the testimony of the parties and of the witnesses is of invaluable help, in fact, of necessity.[69]

In cases in which there is a history of treatment for mental illness prior to the marriage, more and usually very

[67] Etiam in causis defectus consensus ob amentiam, requiratur suffragium peritorum, quia infirmum, si causus ferat, eiusve acta quae amentiae suspicionem ingerunt, examinent secundum artis praecepta; insuper uti testes audiri debent periti qui infirmum antea visitaverint. —c. 1982.

[68] *Instructio Provida,* Art. 147, § 2.

[69] It would be impossible in a limited study such as the present to go into the details of the procedural law with regard to the hearing of the parties and witnesses. The writer has intended merely to indicate what should be the content of their testimony in cases of marriage involving mental illness. For a more extensive treatment of judicial examinations in general, cf. Bottoms, *The Discretionary Authority of the Ecclesiastical Judge in Matrimonial Trials of the First Instance;* Clune, *The Judicial Interrogation of the Parties,* The Catholic University of America Canon Law Studies, n. 269 (Washington, D.C.: The Catholic University of America Press, 1948).

valuable evidence is often available. Such evidence can often be obtained from doctors who had previously examined the person whose marriage is now being impugned. The law itself commands that in cases of mental illness the testimony be taken from those doctors who have, previous to the introduction of the case, examined the party in question.[70]

Even though these doctors or psychiatrists must be called in cases of marriage involving mental illness to give their testimony, they are not invited to testify as canonical experts,[71] but rather as ordinary, though often very important, witnesses. The reason for excluding as experts those who have previously examined the party in the same matter which is the foundation of the matrimonial cause is that they will likely have fixed opinions, based upon their previous examination. They may also have formed bonds of friendship with one or both of the parties involved and, consequently, be led to judge, even unconsciously, in a manner favorable to one of the parties.[72] The testimony of these professional men, however, will often have great weight, especially if their previous examination was made under unquestionable circumstances, and especially if their examination took place shortly before or after the wedding ceremony itself.

These professional men are not called upon to give their opinions in the case, because they remain ordinary witnesses. Rather, they testify to facts which they discovered in their examination of the person. Consequently, they, like all other witnesses, are called upon to testify regarding the

[70] Can. 1982; *Provida,* Art. 143, states: In causis impotentiae vel amentiae excluduntur quoque a periti munere qui coniugem privatim inspexerunt; hi autem in casu impotentiae possunt (cfr. can. 1978), in casu amentiae debent (cfr. can. 1982), induci uti testes. It should be noted that this rule applies not only to those who have examined the party before the marriage ceremony itself, but also to those who have examined the party after the attempted marriage took place but before the case was introduced into court.

[71] Cf. *infra,* p. 206.

[72] Cf. Wernz-Vidal, *De Processibus,* pp. 451-452, n. 493.

quality of the thinking, willing, judging, acting, and feeling of the person at the time when the examination took place. However, as Torre observes, the testimony of such extra-judicial experts can, in case of necessity, be given the force of proof which normally is accorded only to the testimony of the judicial experts. "For," he states, "the judge remains the '*peritus peritorum.*' "[73]

It must be born in mind that when doctors or psychiatrists are called to testify in these cases, they must first obtain a release from the serious obligation of profesional secrecy. In cases of insanity it is the guardian of the mentally ill person who must release the psychiatrist from his professional duty to the patient.[74] If the doctor or psychiatrist still feels that he cannot in conscience reveal some or all that he has learned profesionally, the court cannot force him to testify.[75]

It seems to be belaboring the obvious to state that the testimony of a professional man who examined a person precisely in his own field of knowledge can be of invaluable help to the judge in coming to a conclusion in the case. On the other hand, such a previous examination made by a doctor or psychiatrist does not, per force of a rule of evidence, have the probative force of the examination by the canonical expert designated by the presiding judge. It is not a canonical examination.[76]

[73] "Si hoc in casu forte peractae fuerint peritiae extra judiciales a peritis indubiae famae ac pollentibus maxima dignitate, credibilitate, sensibus religionis, tunc attenta oppositione illius partis Tribunal decernere potest quod peritiae ratae habeantur a medicis et illis tribuatur vis probationis juxta principium quod judex est peritus peritorum."—Torre, *Processus Matrimonialis* (Editio Tertia, Neapoli M. D'Auria, 1956), p. 295, art. 143 .

[74] Doheny, *Canonical Procedure in Matrimonial Cases,* I, 388; cf. also *Provida,* Art. 77; can. 1650.

[75] Can. 1755, § 2, n. 1; *Provida,* Art. 121, § 2, n. 1.

[76] Heston, "Some Practical Hints on the Preparation of 'Super Rato' Cases for the Sacred Congregation of the Sacraments," *The Jurist,* XVII (1957), 284. The court can accord such examination the force of a canonical examination. Cf. Torre, *op. cit.,* p. 295, art. 143.

b. The Evidence Obtained from Documents and Presumptions

The principle of canon 1812 that proof by documents, either public or private, is admitted in all kinds of trials, unmistakably asserts the possibility of use of this means of evidence in ecclesiastical procedure.[77]

In many cases of mental illness and marriage, documentary evidence will be entirely lacking. When, however, documents are presented or can be obtained, they must be given their proper consideration in the trial.

Documents of particular value are those which may in some cases be obtained from medical or hospital records. At times such records give valuable evidence regarding a person's psychical capacity. These records are and have the value of private documents.[78]

Doctors and hospitals, because of the obligation of professional secrecy, may hesitate or even refuse to provide such records for use in court. Before the court requests such documents for juridical inspection, therefore, it should first obtain from the patient involved, if he has sufficiently recovered, or from his guardian a release from the professional secrecy in favor of the doctor or hospital.[79] Doctors and hospitals, however, cannot be forced to produce these documents. If, as may happen quite often, they would still

[77] Can. 1812. In quolibet iudicii genere admittitur probatio per documenta tum publica tum privata.

[78] A public document is a writing which relates an act that was executed by, or in the presence of, a public official acting as such, and then was properly committed to writing by the same official, or at least was signed by him. A private document, on the other hand, is one which is drawn up either by a private person in any form, or by a public person who does not act in his official capacity, or who has omitted some formality which is required for making the instrument a public one. Cf. Willett, *The Probative Value of Documents in Ecclesiastical Trials*, The Catholic University of America Canon Law Studies, no. 171 (Washington, D.C.; The Catholic University of America Press, 1942), pp. 4-9.

[79] Cf. *supra*, p. 197.

refuse, they cannot be forced to do so.[80] Even if the doctor or hospital refuses to produce the records or documents involved, they may, at times, allow the court-appointed medical expert to examine such records. Such an examination may be of great help to him in reaching his scientific opinion in the case. His knowledge obtained from such records is to be included in the judicial acts.

Another source of evidence in marriage trials based on a plea of mental illness is the "presumption." A brief consideration of the juridic doctrine of presumption will prove invaluable, especially because of its relation to canon 1082.[81]

First of all, it must be noted that no presumption can exist as such except upon the basis of a specific fact-situation which must be proven.[82]

The judge, in evaluating the judicial evidence and in drawing conclusions from the acts of a process and the proofs incorporated therein, has the discretionary authority to deduce personal presumptions, commonly called "*praesumptiones hominis.*"[83] Such presumptions, in turn, may be of help to him in reaching the necessary moral certitude to come to a decision.

A presumption is defined as a probable conjecture in an uncertain issue.[84] Presumptions serve as an indirect source of proof. It should be remembered that presumptions must always yield to proven facts. Indeed, presumptions require

[80] Can. 1823, § 1. Nemo tamen exhibere tenetur documenta, etsi communia, quae communicari nequeunt sine periculo damni ad normam can. 1755, § 2, n. 2 aut sine periculo violationis secreti servandi.

§ 2. Attamen si qua saltem documenti particula, quam produci intersit, describi possit, et in exemplari exhiberi sine memoratis incommodis, iudex decernere potest ut eadem exhibeatur.

[81] For a more complete study on presumption as a source of evidence in marriage trials see Manning, *Presumptions of Law in Marriage Cases*, The Catholic University of America Canon Law Studies, No. 94 (Washington, D.C.; The Catholic University of America, 1935).

[82] Cf. can. 1748 and can. 1828.

[83] Can. 1828: Praesumptiones, quae non statuuntur a iure, iudex ne coniiciat, nisi ex facto certo et determinato, quod cum eo, de quo controversia est, directe cohaereat.

[84] Can. 1825, § 1.

the support of circumstances and evidence sufficient to raise them to the level of moral certitude in the judge, since this is demanded for every judicial sentence.

Presumptions which are stated within the law itself, called *praesumptiones iuris,* constitute full proof until the contrary is proven,[85] for the law takes the position that the subject matter of the presumption is existing and true.[86] A presumption of law has a twofold effect. First of all, it constitutes full proof until the contrary becomes established.[87] Secondly, the entire burden of proof to the contrary must be borne by the one who challenges the presumption.

The presumptions of law applicable in marriage cases in which the validity of the consent is questioned on a basis of mental illness or disturbance are the following: 1) The all-important presumption of canon 1014. This states that a marriage once contracted is presumed valid until its invalidity is actually proven. This canon may well be termed the pivotal point of all matrimonial procedure, for no matter on what grounds a marriage is attacked, the plaintiff will be immediately confronted with this law. In its wording and its operation it is a typical *praesumptio iuris,* i.e., the plaintiff is forced to prove that this so-called matrimonial contract now questioned has not the semblance of marriage and never took place; or that because of some invalidating reason, it was null *ab initio.*[88] 2) Canon 1082, § 2, establishes a second very important presumption of law, namely, the presumption that after puberty has been reached, persons must be presumed to have sufficient knowledge to give a valid matrimonial consent.[89] 3) Internal consent is presumed to be present when there is a manifestation of consent through external signs in the marriage ceremony.[90] 4) A marriage uncontested during the lifetime of the parties

[85] Can. 1747, n. 2; can. 1827.

[86] Cf. can. 1827.

[87] Cf. can. 1869, § 4 and can. 1748.

[88] Manning, *op. cit.*, p. 53.

[89] Cf. *supra*, p. 88.

[90] Can. 1086, § 1.

is, upon the death of either or both of the parties, to be presumed as valid in such a manner that no proof to the contrary is admissible unless it serves in vindication of some incidental question, such as the claims of legitimacy or the succession in behalf of the children.[91]

A personal presumption (*praesumptio hominis*) is defined by Schmalzgrueber as a conjecture not expressed in or based on a law, but drawn from the circumstances of the case and accepted as true until the contrary is demonstrated.[92] Since it is not expressed in a law or rule of law, it is simply the offspring of the individual human mind. According to the degree of directness with which personal presumptions are drawn from certain and determinate facts connected with the case, and, consequently, also according to the degree of force with which they compel the mind, personal presumptions are known as light, grave, or dominant.[93] If the judge entertains personal presumptions which are light, weak, or rash, and which do not spring from certain and definite facts directly connected with the case, or which are unduly extended in their scope, he cannot utilize such presumptions as offering judicial evidence.[94]

Regarding the probative value of personal presumptions, Bottoms observes:

> Grave and even dominant personal presumptions have not as a general rule the value of full proof, and alone will ordinarily not be sufficient to offset the effect of the legal presumption for the validity of a marriage; but they may have the value of partial proof, even against presumptions of law.[95]

[91] Can. 1972.

[92] Schmalzgrueber, *Ius Ecclesiasticum Universum,* Lib. II, Pars III, Tit. XXIII, n. 4.

[93] Cf. Regula 81, *Regulae Servandae in Processibus Super Matrimonio Rato et Non Consummato—AAS,* XV (1923), 408.

[94] Can. 1828.

[95] Bottoms, *op. cit.,* p. 220; he cites the following Rota decisions: *S.R.R., Dec.,* IV (1912), 87; *S.R.R., Dec.,* IV (1912), 240; S.R.R. *Dec.,* XIII (1921), 265.

The Rota in a decision handed down in 1941 clearly sets forth the relationship between presumptions of law and personal presumptions.[96]

> Haec tamen 'disputatio iuris' concludi non potest, quin dicantur quaedam verba etiam circa 'praesumptiones homines,' ne scilicet Patres Turni praesentis suo silentio approbare videantur quae hac de re in sententia Turni antecedentis inveniuntur. Patres appellati qui adeo contrarii sunt praesumptionibus hominis, sub influxu fuisse videntur alicuius libelli cui titulus *Incipit Lamentatio Vinculi,* auctoris anonymi, ubi inter alia sub n. 64 proclamatur falsum principium: 'Contra iuris praesumptionem praesumptio hominis vix admittitur.' Si hoc principium esset verum, tunc in re matrimoniali, in qua plures habentur praesumptiones iuris in favorem validitatis matrimonii, non intelligeretur, curnam tantum praesumptio hominis et non etiam aliae probationes contrariae excludi deberent. E contra, nulla praesumptio iuris-non confundenda cum praesumptione iuris et de iure-praetendit se esse normam generalem pro omni casu, sed potius semper admittit probationem contrariam. Ultro conceditur quod apud Wernz-Vidal dicitur: 'Quemadmodum in aliis probationum generibus contrarietas quaedam existere potest, cum v. gr. testis testi contradicat, ita in praesumptionibus conflictus non raro vitari nequit' (Vol. VI, n. 521). Et si duae praesumptiones inter se contrariae secum comparantur, norma generalis est quod 'fortior praesumptio vincat necesse est minorem. Hinc cum praesumptio iuris fortior sit praesumptione facti, generi per speciem derogetur' (loc. cit.).
>
> Sed *'si praesumptio hominis validior et verisimilior est, contra iuris etiam praesumptionem praevaleat'* (Schmalzgrueber, in lib. II, tit. 23, *De Praesupt.,* n. 38); nam omnis praesumptio iuris per se est generalis et superari potest per quamlibet certam probationem contrariam, in specie, per praesumptionem hominis violentam, 'quae ex multis vel uno valde efficaci, et veritati proximo indicio

[96] *S.R.R. Decisiones,* XXXIII (1941), 370.

formatur, et vehementer movet cogitque ad credulitatem, ita ut moraliter non relinquat dubium' (Schmalzgrueber, 1, c. n. 5). Audiatur adhuc Lega, qui docet: 'Si vero praesumptio (scilicet hominis) est gravissima seu vehemens, tunc ipsa sufficit ad causam definiendam in foro ecclesiastico. In Decretalibus habentur textus, quibus statuitur vehementem praesumptionem efficere plenam probationem; uti vehementi praesumptioni innixus processit Salomon ad sententiam in suo celebri iudicio. In nostro iure canone 1869 ponitur regula, iudicem debere rem definire iuxta moralem certitudinem ex actis iudex hauriat vehementem praesumptionem, huic sententiam suam plane conformare valet. *Hoc etiam pro causis gravioribus, quales sunt matrimoniales, vim habet, maxima tamen cum cautela et dummodo* quodlibet positivum dubium ex adverso sit eliminatum' (*Commentarius in Iudicia ecclesiastica iuxta Codicem I.C.*, cura Bartocetti editus, Romae 1939, Vol. II, p. 821.').

It pertains to the judge alone to determine whether the personal presumption be light, grave, or dominant, what force of proof it has, and what degree of certainty is derivable from it.[97]

In matrimonial cases of insanity, a valid *praesumptio hominis,* based on Rotal jurisprudence,[98] is had when it is established, through the reports of experts or through other evidence, that, both before and after the marriage contract took place, a type of mental illness existed which of its nature is perpetual and incurable. In that case, there is a presumption that the insanity existed also at the time when the contract took place.[99] A possible period of external quiet

[97] *S.R.R. Decisiones,* V (1913), 18; *S.R.R. Decisiones,* VII (1915), 125.

[98] *S.R.R. Decisiones,* IV (1912), 87; *S.R.R. Decisiones,* IV (1912), 240; *S.R.R. Decisiones,* XIII (1921), 265.

[99] In upholding this presumption Pickard, *op. cit.*, page 198, note 24, cites a Rota case of 1931 and also the doctrine of Gasparri. "Si constet de amentia antecedenti et subsequenti, deducitur et amentia concomitans. Mentecapti namque habent et quae vocantur lucida intervalla, in quibus possunt etiam quandoque valide contractus inire et proinde etiam matrimonium, etsi hodie iuxta complures medicos etiam in ipso

or lack of external symptoms of insanity is presumed to be a period of remission, i.e., a temporary abatement or cessation of the symptoms of an illness, which illness itself, nevertheless, remains present. Such a period of external quiet must not be presumed to be a truly lucid interval.[100]

Regarding what has been called the "troublesome question of the lucid interval" and the presumptions concerning it Wanenmacher makes the following observations:

> If the person is shown to have been insane some time before the marriage was contracted, but it has not been shown that he thereafter enjoyed lucid intervals, it is presumed that the insanity endured. If he had been insane at some time before the marriage, but the insanity has afterward permanently left him, and it is doubted whether he was sane or insane at the time the marriage was contracted, the presumption holds for sanity if the marriage was contracted a long while after the known spell of insanity; but militates against sanity if the marriage was entered upon shortly after the time when the party was known to be insane. If he is shown to have been insane at some time before marriage and again after marriage, there may be question whether the marriage was performed during one of those periods that are commonly called "lucid intervals." Now this term is used to denote either the complete, even though

lucido intervallo habeatur latens quaedam amentia. Quare cum amentia sit morbus natura sua perpetuus et insanabilis, in dubio, num matrimonium tempore amentiae initum fuerit, an in lucido intervallo, censetur fuisse tempore amentiae contractum."—*S.R.R. Decisiones* XXIII (1931), p. 153, n. 8; cf. also Gasparri, *De Matrimonio*, II, n. 785; A summary of Gasparri's teaching can be found in a recent case in which the marriage was declared null because of psychasthenia. "Adducatur denique principium a cl. Gasparri . . . idest, cum morbus est certus, et certe matrimonium antecedens, et certe facultates mentis laedens, defectus consensus etiam in casibus apparentis normalitatis praesumi debet, donec contrarium stricte probetur."—*Nullitatis Matrimonii*, coram R.P.D. Boleslao Filipiak, *Ponente*. Recorded in *Monitor Ecclesiasticus*, An. LXXXI, Ser. VI, Pasc. III, a. 1956, p. 456, n. 4.

[100] *S.R.R. Decisiones*, I (1909), 92; *S.R.R. Decisiones*, VIII (1916), 209; *S.R.R. Decisiones*, XXV (1933), 408; *S.R.R. Decisiones*, XXVI (1934), 710; cf. also Gasparri, *De Matrimonio*, II, n. 785.

> but temporary, cure of insanity, or it denotes the mere lessening of insanity to such a degree that the disease, though still present, is outwardly quite imperceptible. If it is doubted whether at the time of the marriage, the person in question was really cured temporarily, so that he could validly marry, or rather labored under a hidden spell of insanity, the presumption holds the lucid interval to have been a mere lessening, rather than a cure, for the disease is of its nature enduring, and this is all the more to be maintained since modern medical opinion tends to view all such lucid intervals as the mere screening of a latent insanity, and the modern civil laws do not generally hold contracts valid, when entered upon during such intervals.[101]

To the present writer the question of the lucid interval actually does not present too serious a problem, at least not a legal problem. The question of the possibility or probability of a lucid interval is not a question of law, but a question of scientific fact to be determined in each case by the proper science, medicine and, especially, psychiatry. It is on the facts or evidences presented by science that the presumptions of the judge must be based.[102] It is precisely for that reason that medical experts or psychiatrists must be employed in all marriage cases based on a plea of mental illness.

c. *The Evidence Obtained from the Testimony of the Judicial Expert*

The Code of Canon Law itself demands the use of experts in all matrimonial cases of alleged lack of consent due to mental illness.[103]

[101] Wanenmacher, *Canonical Evidence in Marriage Cases* (Dolphin Press, Philadelphia, 1935), p. 296, n. 465.

[102] But cf. can. 1804.

[103] Can. 1982: Etiam in causis defectus consensu ob amentiam, requiratur suffragium peritorum, qui infirmum, si casus ferat, eiusve acta quae amentiae suspicionem ingerunt, examinent secundum artis praecepta; insuper uti testes audiri debent periti qui infirmum antea visitaverint; *Provida*, Art. 139: In causis impotentiae et defectus consensus ob amentiam requirendum est suffragium peritorum (cfr. cann. 1976-1982).

From the wording of canon 1792[104] the following definition of an expert at Canon Law may be deduced: A judicial expert is a person endowed with a particular skill or knowledge, who is legitimately called into a judicial process to assist the judge in establishing some fact or in determining the true nature of a thing by conducting an examination and by giving a report in accord with the principles of his art or profession.

Article 4. The Judicial Expert in Marriage Cases Based on a Plea of Mental Illness or Defect

Because of the importance of canonical experts in cases of mental illness and marriage, the final article in this study will be devoted to a closer study of the task of the experts and to a consideration of the value of the proof derived from their judicial report.[105]

At Church Law one does not find the spectacle of experts testifying to contradictions because they are "for the defense" or "for the plaintiff."[106] The expert is the helper or adviser of the court and not of the parties in the case. It is his task to be the medical or psychiatric mind of the judge.

[104] Peritorum opera utendum est quoties ex iuris vel iudicis praescripto eorum examen et votum requiritur ad factum aliquod comprobandum vel ad veram alicuius rei naturam dignoscendam.

[105] It cannot be considered the purpose of the present study to present an extensive treatment of canonical experts. Experts will here be treated only specifically in their relation to marriage cases based on a plea of mental illness. For a complete study on judicial experts cf. Pickard, *Judicial Experts: A Source of Evidence in Ecclesiastical Trials*, The Catholic University of America Canon Law Studies, no. 389 (Washington, D.C.: The Catholic University of America Press, 1958).

[106] Pickard, *op. cit.*, p. 80, note 9, observes: "The German (§§ 404, 405) and Austrian (§ 351) Codes assign to the judge absolute power in appointing the experts. The Italian Penal Code (art. 253) allows the parties to appoint experts upon whom they agree; should they disagree, the judge decides who is to be appointed. In the United States the parties to the suit generally select their own experts, with the result that quite often one can read of cases wherein experts for the defense testify contradictorily to the experts for the prosecution."

Consequently, it is only the court which can and must appoint him.[107]

SECTION A. APPOINTMENT AND NECESSARY QUALITIES OF THE EXPERT

Canon 1982 states: "In cases of lack of consent by reason of insanity, the opinion of experts is required. These shall, according to the norms of their art, examine the person, if the case demands it, or his acts when they arouse the suspicion of insanity: Moreover, experts who previously attended the patient are to be heard in the capacity of witnesses." Article 151 of the Instruction *Provida* decrees: "In cases of insanity, one or, in line with the gravity of the case, two doctors are to be appointed, who are particularly versed in the science of psychiatry. Nevertheless, precaution must be taken to exclude those who do not profess sound (Catholic) doctrine in this matter."[108]

Clearly, it is not a matter of choice whether experts should or should not be employed in marriage cases based on a plea of mental illness. They must be employed no matter how evident the insanity may be in the eyes of the judge. Experts are required because the law does not expect the judge to be qualified to evaluate mental abnormalities without the aid of a qualified professional man.

It would seem that the use of experts is required only for the liceity and not for the validity of the trial and the ensuing sentence. Pickard,[109] citing Torre, defends this posi-

[107] Can. 1793, § 1: Iudicis est peritos eligere vel designare. However, only the Ordinary himself, with the consent of the woman party, is to appoint men physicians for the physical inspection of the woman in cases of impotence or non-consummation.—Cf. Suprema Sacra Congregatio S. Officii Decretum, *De Quibusdam Cautelis Adhibendis in Causis Matrimonialibus Impotentiae et Inconsummationis*, n. 3, (12 iunii, 1942)—*AAS*, XXXIV (1942), 200-202 (hereafter cited with the opening words, *Qua Singulari*).

[108] "In causis amentiae unus vel, pro casus gravitate, duo medici deputentur, qui in scientia psychiatrica peculiariter sint versati, cauto tamen ut excludantur qui sanam (catholicam) doctrinam hac in re non profiteantur."

[109] *Op. cit.*, p. 71.

tion by stating: "There is not one recorded case in the Rota wherein a plea of nullity of the sentence was upheld because of the failure to employ experts when the law commanded it."[110] "Indeed," he continues, "decisions of that body make it quite clear that the *peritia* is required not as a requisite for validity, but as a condition for licitness."[111] Referring to Doheny,[112] Pickard bases the proof for his view on the understanding of canon 1869. He reasons that according to this canon the judge must have moral certitude before bringing a verdict in a particular case. He must evaluate the proofs according to his own conscience unless the law explicitly stipulates a provision regarding the efficacy of some particular proof. Ordinarily, the opinion of the expert is only one of the many means which the judge employs to arrive at the necessary moral certitude. From these observations Pickard concludes that if the judge in an exceptional case inadvertently or unknowingly would undertake the examination of the mental status of the party without the help of an expert and would, therefore, fail to secure his opinion in the case, yet if he does in some other fashion attain to moral certitude, his decision must be regarded as being valid though perhaps gravely unlawful.[113] This conclusion is further strengthened by canons 1892 and 1894. These canons list the various causes which might invalidate a judicial sentence. The failure of examination by qualified experts is not included among these invalidating causes. The question itself, however, seems to be more a theoretical than a practical one, because it is difficult to imagine that any judge would actually attempt to settle any of these cases without summoning the expert help of a doctor or psychiatrist

The presiding judge must consult with the defender of the bond before appointing experts.[114]

[110] Torre, *Processus Matrimonialis* (3. ed., Neapoli: M. d'Auria, 1956), p. 288, art. 139.

[111] *Loc. cit.;* cf. *S.R.R. Decisiones,* VII (1915), 211, n. 12.

[112] *Canonical Procedure in Matrimonial Cases,* I, 383-384.

[113] Pickard, *op. cit.,* p. 71.

[114] *Provida,* Art. 141; Concerning the controversy whether the audi-

The parties are allowed to present to the judge the names of the experts of their choice.[115] The judge, however, has the authoritative discretion to employ those who have been suggested by the parties or to select other qualified men.

The appointment of the expert is made by means of a decree, which must contain the name(s) of the expert(s) chosen; the individual points with which the *peritia* is concerned,[116] and the interval of time allowed to the expert to make his investigation and to present his opinion.[117] This decree is sent to the expert and to the parties in order that any possible objections may be filed against the appointment.[118] The expert has no obligation to lend his assistance to the tribunal. Obviously, he should not be appointed to the office of judicial expert until he has expressed his willingness and intention to accept. Practically, the expert is chosen because of his outstanding moral and professional qualities. Realizing that they are chosen because of their outstanding qualities, most professional men will feel honored in being asked for their professional assistance.

However, the task of the expert is often a very demanding and time-consuming one. Canon 1805, therefore, specifies that the expenses entailed and the fee for the expert should be determined by the judge with fairness and equity

tor could also appoint the judicial expert see Pickard, *op. cit.*, pp. 78-80 and Bottoms, *op. cit.*, pp. 129-130. To enter into a discussion of this controversy falls outside the scope of the present study. Article 141 of the Instructions *Provida* seems purposely to reserve the appointment of the expert to the presiding judge rather than to the auditing judge, in order to lend greater importance and authority to the appointment.

In view of the word *audito* of canon 1793, § 2, and article 141 of *Provida*, it seems that a failure to consult the defender of the bond would not invalidate the appointment, but would simply render it illicit; cf. Regatillo, *Institutiones*, I, pp. 159-160, n. 210 at canon 105, for the two opinions on the interpretation of the word *audito*.

115 Lega (ed. Bart.), *Iuducia Ecclesiastica,* II, p. 749, n. 2.

116 Canon. 1799, § 1.

117 Can. 1798; Can. 1799, § 2.

118 Can. 1796, § 1; Instructio, *Provida,* Art. 145.

in conformity with the custom and practice of the particular place.[119]

There seems to be some confusion about the number of experts to be employed in cases of mental illness and marriage. The law demands the use of only one expert. Canon 1982 states that in cases of *amentia,* the opinion of experts is required. In the same way Article 139 of the Instruction *Provida* rules: "In cases of impotency and lack of consent due to insanity the opinion of experts is required."[120] Both these texts use the word experts in the plural form. However, Art. 151 of the same Instruction *Provida* explicitly states that in case of insanity one, or according to the importance of the case, two medical men who are particularly expert in the science of psychiatry, are to be appointed.[121]

The rule of Lega would seem to be safe and advisable in practice. He held that the judge should appoint only one expert if he thinks that one may suffice. If he discovers, upon the report of the first expert, that the question is not clearly resolved, he should appoint a second expert. In this way, he will keep expenses at a minimum, and at the same time he will avoid any unnecessary delay which would result from the employment of superfluous experts.

Moreover, Lega observes that discordant opinions of the experts often bring more complication than clarification to the issue.[122]

Regarding such possible confusion Hayes observes:

> Mental disease has many and wide and unpredict-

[119] Peritorum expensas et honoraria iudex, receptam uniuscuiusque loci consuetudinem prae oculis habens, ex bono et aequo taxare debet, salvo iure recursus ad normam can. 1913, § 1.

[120] Can. 1982: Etiam in causis defectus consensus ob amentiam, requiratur suffragium peritorum.... Article 139: In causis impotentiae et defectus consensus ob amentiam requirendum est suffragium peritorum.

[121] *Provida,* Art. 151: In causis amentiae unus vel, pro casus gravitate, duo medici deputentur, qui in scientia psychiatrica peculiariter sint versati, caute tamen ut excludantur qui sanam (catholicam) doctrinam hac in re non profiteantur.

[122] Lega (ed. Bart.), *Iudicia Ecclesiastica,* II, pp. 749-750, n. 3.

> able ramifications. Various psychiatrists may hold widely different opinions on the nature or origin or course of the same disease. They may disagree violently upon many matters with which the disease is concerned. But much of this disagreement may from our point point of view be simply irrelevant. Our concern is with the one simple question: "Was the person capable of giving consent?" Doctors who might agree on this one point affirmatively or negatively might differ on everything else, yet we would have the consensus we ideally seek from the experts.[123]

A case adjudicated by the Sacred Roman Rota demonstrates the great divergence of opinion possible among experts as to the precise nature of a particular mental disorder.[124] One expert diagnosed the particular illness involved to be a case of paranoia; the other expert rejected this diagnosis and at first considered schizophrenia as the illness involved, but later advanced the opinion that it was a case of hysterical constitutional deviation. To settle the dispute a third expert was called into the case. He considered the whole case atypical and would not venture a precise diagnosis. All three agreed, however, that the person definitely suffered from a serious mental disorder and, consequently, was to be considered incapable of matrimonial consent.

Quite clearly, the greater the number of experts called in a given case, the greater is the danger of confusion. The one criterion for the judge in determining the number of experts to be appointed in a given case is the effort to reduce all the judicial evidence to proof in the strict sense. Normally, the evidence presented by one expert should suffice. If the judge feels that the matter is too involved or serious to rely on one expert's opinion, then he may appoint two or even more.[125]

The value of the evidence obtained from expert testimony does not depend primarily on the number of experts heard,

[123] Hayes, art. cit., *The Jurist,* XVI (1956), 280-281.
[124] *S.R.R. Decisiones,* XXIX (1937), 756-770.
[125] Lega (ed. Bart.), *op. cit.,* II, p. 750, b), c).

but rather on the qualifications of the experts heard and on the facts on which they have based their profesisonal opinions.

Canon 1795, § 1 states: "All other things being equal, there are to be appointed to the office of expert those who have been approved as qualified by the competent authority."[126] The competent authority to approve the qualifications of the expert is the judge or some other ecclesiastical magistrate, e.g., the Ordinary.[127]

In marriage cases, those who are chosen to be experts must, in addition to having a diploma or a certificate of capability,[128] be experienced and outstanding in their proper art or science, and commendable for their religious and upright lives.[129]

To the question whether the expert should be a Catholic, the answer usually given[130] is: preferably, yes; that is,

[126] Ad periti munus, ceteris paribus, deligantur, qui competentis magistratus auctoritate idone fuerint comprobati.

[127] Coronata, *De Processibus*, p. 270, n. 1326. Noval contends that there must be a public or an official approbation, written or unwritten. If unwritten the approbation may be either express or tacit, "for those who have degrees or can present official approbation cannot always be obtained."—Cf. Noval, *Commentarium Codicis Iuris Canonici*, Liber IV, *De Processibus*, Pars I, *De Iudiciis* (Augustae Taurinorum, Romae: Marietti, 1920), n. 518 at can. 1795, § 1. The competent authority would be some college, university or association empowered by the civil government to issue academic degrees or certificates of fitness in a particular art or science. Cf. Lega (ed. Bart.), *Iuducia Ecclesiastica*, II, p. 751, n. 6. An academic degree furnishes a presumption of capability. It is the office of the ecclesiastical judge or Ordinary to determine whether this presumption of capability derived from an academic degree or civil certificate, stands or falls. Cf. Pickard, *op. cit.*, p. 89.

[128] In the United States, the fact that a psychiatrist is a member in good standing of the American Psychiatric Association can be taken as sufficient evidence of capability. The fact, on the other hand, that the psychiatrist has an M.D. degree is, per se, no proof of capability in the field of psychiatry.

[129] Cf. can. 1979, § 1, 2; *Catholica Dotcrina*, Reg. 87, 89; *Provida*, Art. 142, § 1; Art. 150, n. 2; Art. 151.

[130] Pickard, *op. cit.*, p. 90; Wanenmacher, *Canonical Evidence*, p. 181; Augustine, *A Commentary on Canon Law*, VII, 243.

ceteris paribus, the expert should be a Catholic. However, the most important consideration is whether the expert is truly outstanding as a professional and experienced person in his field, and that he is a religious, trustworthy, upright person. A proficient, upright non-Catholic is to be preferred to a good Catholic of little or no ability. The Instruction *Provida,* on the other hand, states: "In cases of insanity, one, or according to the importance of the case, two physicians are to be appointed, who are expert in the science of psychiatry, due precautions being taken that those who do not profess sane (Catholic) doctrine in this matter, be excluded."[131] Pickard observes: "Since there is no distinct body of knowledge known as 'Catholic psychiatry,' one must conclude that the canon [*sic*] intends to speak negatively, i.e., it excludes from the office of expert those who profess theories obviously contrary to Catholic teaching; e.g., those who deny the freedom of the will, and those who deny the existence of the spiritual soul of man."[132] The eminent Rotal judge P. Felici remarks, regarding the necessary qualifications of the experts: *"In eligendis ergo peritis psychologis et psychiatris, ratio in primis habeatur de ipsorum vita, moribus, institutione philosophica et religiosa: coniuncta quidem cum recta institutione scientifica et rerum hominumque usu."*[133]

SECTION B. THE FUNCTION OF THE EXPERT AT CHURCH LAW

The testimony of the experts and the testimony of the parties and witnesses are distinct though similar. For this reason some authors define the expert as a particular type of witness.[134] Others prefer to refrain from calling the ex-

[131] Art. 151.

[132] *Op. cit.,* pp. 91-92.

[133] Felici, "De Investigatione Psychologica in Causis Definiendis," Apollinaris, XXXII (1959), 205.

[134] Noval, *De Processibus,* Pars I, *De Iudiciis,* n. 513; cf. also F. X. Wernz, *Ius Canonicum, ad Codicis Normam Exactum* opera P. Vidal (7 vols. in 8, Vol. VI, *De Processibus,* editio altera, a Felice Cappello recognita, Romae: Apud Aedes Universitatis Gregorianae, 1949), VI, n. 489; Lega, (ed. Bart.), *Iudicia Ecclesiastica,* II, 744, n. 1.

pert a witness because of the peculiar nature of his testimony.[135] The Code of Canon Law treats the office of experts separately, thereby indicating that expert testimony is different from the testimony of ordinary witnesses.[136] Roberti takes a position between the two opinions by stating: "The office of an expert stands midway between that of a witness and that of a judge."[137] Like a witness, the expert gives judicial testimony; like a judge, he draws conclusions and gives his own opinion, which an ordinary witness may not do. Employing his specialized skill or art, the expert endeavors to determine a fact and the precise nature of that fact. Through his reasoning process, based on the principles of his profession, he arrives at a conclusion which he declares in his judicial report. The essential difference, therefore, between an expert and a witness consists in the fact that the expert presents his own opinion in the case at hand. This opinion is based on professionally investigated facts and on scientific knowledge and experience. The witness, on the other hand, simply testifies to a fact which he has observed. He does not draw a conclusion nor is he allowed to give his opinion in the case.[138] However, the judgment of the expert is scientific and not judicial.[139]

The task of an expert in marriage cases based on a plea of mental illness can, therefore, be summarized as follows. After the court has heard the parties and witnesses in a case, the expert is summoned to give his opinion of the psychical capacity of the person whose marriage is being examined. He is asked to present his own opinion about the psy-

[135] Cf. Regatillo, *Institutiones Iuris Canonici* (4. ed., 2 vols., Santander: Sal Terrae, 1951), II, n. 545; Coronata, *De Processibus*, n. 1324; Beste, *Introductio in Codicem* (3. ed., Collegeville, Minn., St. John's Abbey Press, 1946), p. 821, at can. 1792; Doheny, *Canonical Procedure in Matrimonial Cases*, I, 382.

[136] C.I.C. Lib. IV, Tit. X, Caput III, *De Peritis*, canons 1792-1805.

[137] F. Roberti, *De Processibus* (2 vols., Romae, 1926), Vol. II, pars I, n. 357.

[138] Cf. *supra*, p. 185.

[139] L. Quintana Reynés, *La Prueba en el Procedimiento Canonico* (Barcelona: Bosch, 1942), p. 131.

chical capacity for marriage of this person at the time when the marriage was entered into. Therefore, he must determine, to the best of his ability, whether the person at the time of the marriage did have that degree of knowledge, freedom and maturity of judgment which the law requires for valid matrimonial consent. Consequently, he must be carefully instructed regarding the knowledge, freedom, and degree of maturity of judgment required by the law for valid matrimonial consent.

The expert is not asked to give a judgment on the validity or non-validity of the marriage itself. He is asked to give a judgment on the actual psychical capacity of the person at the time when the marriage ceremony took place.

To obtain this scientific opinion, whether the person in question did or did not meet these requirements for marriage, the expert needs to make either or both of the following examinations: 1) a personal examination of the party involved, 2) an examination of the acts of the case, especially of the testimonies of the parties and of the witnesses.

It is quite evident that a personal examination will be of great help to the expert in determining the mental condition of the party at the time of the marriage. Such an examination would *per se* prove only that a mental illness existed at the time of the examination itself. However, this diagnosis would enable the expert to look for specific symptoms of the same illness at the time of the marriage. For judicial purposes the point of supreme importance is, however, to determine the mental state of the party at the time of the marriage rather than at the time of the trial.

Quite often it is impossible to make the personal examination even if it is desirable. A person may have been cured of his mental illness or disturbance, and he may now refuse the mental examination; or he has been committed to a mental institution. "The modern tendency, at least in the United States, is to exclude rigorously all persons from examining the patients in insane asylums ... Whenever such an impasse is reached in a trial, it might be advisable for the court to secure the service, as experts, of the officials of the particular institution where the insane person is interned."[140] Before the judge orders a personal examination, therefore, he would do well to first consult the psychiatrist regarding the advisability or possibility of such a personal examination.[141]

Quite often it will suffice to have the expert make a careful examination of the judicial *acta,* i.e., the testimonies of the parties and witnesses, previous medical records, and the testimony of doctors who had examined the person previously. The judge is bound to allow the expert to study the *acta* of the case. The Instruction *Provida* states: "All the acts of the case, which appear necessary or opportune in the judgment of the *instructor,* should be sent to the experts to enable them to form their opinion correctly."[142] The judge may even, at the suggestion of the expert, and after hearing the defender of the bond, call in more witnesses, recall those already heard, obtain previous medical records, and in general amplify the evidence enough to give the expert a sufficient basis for study.[143]

After completing his examination, the expert must report his findings to the court in accord with the instructions received from the judge and within the time specified. The

[140] Doheny, *Canonical Procedure in Matrimonial Cases,* I, 392.

[141] Allers points out: "A personal inspection of the defendant does not reveal anything bearing immediately on the pending decision. The one thing a personal examination will show is the diagnosis, of which there is as a rule no doubt, since the expert may in most cases rely on the diagnosis made in the hospital for the insane or by the specialists who advised the patient's confinement."—"Annulment of Marriage by Lack of Consent because of Insanity," *Ecclesiastical Review,* CI (1939), 325-326. On the other hand Allers states: "Personal examination of the feeble-minded is more important than the evidence collected from the witnesses.... If careful examination shows a person to be feeble-minded today, it proves that this person was feeble-minded before and will not improve."—*Ibid.,* p. 340.

[142] Peritis, ut iudicium suum recte facere possint, omnia causae acta, quae instructori necessaria aut opportuna videantur, remittenda sunt. —Art. 147, § 2.

[143] Cf. Canons 1749; 1781; 1786; *Provida,* Art. 95; art. 107.

report, made in written form,[144] must contain an account of the examination, the method employed, the facts discovered, the conclusion drawn from the examination and the reasons which led the expert to his conclusion.[145]

After the expert has submitted his report in writing, he must appear in court for the threefold purpose of identifying his report, confirming it by oath, and answering any questions proposed to him by the court. Pickard observes: "Generally, before his acceptance of the office, the expert will have agreed to appear in court in order to confirm and elucidate his report. In keeping with the note of courtesy that should prevail throughout the judicial process, especially in the court's dealings with the expert, the judge should consult the convenience of the expert before assigning a time for the confirmation of the written report."[146]

The questions addressed to the expert will concern the general and particular circumstances and difficulties of the case in question. Often technical phrases in the written report will need explanations; or further elucidation of the arguments on which the expert bases his opinion may be required.

Again it is important to realize the precise purpose of the expert's examination and report. Quite naturally, the expert will present to the court his opinion regarding the nature and perhaps the causes of the mental illness or disturbance involved. However, these are of importance to the court only insofar as they help to come to an understanding of the psychical capacity for marriage of the person in question at the time when the marriage ceremony took place.

It is rather puzzling that certain authors deny the expert the right to offer his opinion regarding the psychical capacity of a person for giving valid matrimonial consent. It is precisely the opinion of the expert regarding the psychical capacity for matrimonial consent which is asked for by the

[144] *Provida,* art. 148, § 1.
[145] Can. 1801, § 3; *Provida,* Art. 148, § 1.
[146] *Op. cit.,* p. 172.

law in canon 1982 and in article 139 of the Instruction *Provida Mater.*

For instance, Pickard states:

> The experts employed must report to the court their opinion regarding the nature and the degree of the mental illness in the particular case. They should define what was the mental state of the contracting party at the time of the marriage ceremony. The judge should, then, instruct them to report whether the insanity (amentia) was permanent or transitory, and whether lucid intervals may have intervened. It is, however, outside the province of the expert to give his opinion regarding the validity of the marriage consent. Rather, this is the duty of the judge, who is sometimes called the "*peritus peritorum*" ... The judge, then, instead of asking the experts whether they consider the marital consent to have been given validly or invalidly, should rather ask whether the defendant was fully responsible for his actions. "If the expert's answer does not seem definite enough, the case may be made clearer by asking the expert whether he would consider the defendant responsible had he committed a crime, or whether he would deem him capable of attending to his personal affairs. The judge is a layman in psychiatry, but the expert is usually entirely unacquainted with the spirit and terminology of the law."[147]

It is precisely such an approach which makes marriage cases based on a plea of mental illness as cumbersome and interminable as they often are. It is precisely the task and the duty of the expert to present his opinion and the reasons for that opinion regarding the ability of the person in question to have met the psychical requirements of the law for a valid marriage consent at the time when the marriage was contracted. As was seen above,[148] these requirements are usually and normally realized or fulfilled at physical puberty.

[147] *Op. cit.*, p. 164; Pickard quotes from Allers, "Annulment of Marriage by Lack of Consent because of Insanity," *Ecclesiastical Review*, CI (1939), 341.

[148] Cf. *supra*, p. 139.

The expressed opinion of the expert regarding the psychical capacity of a person is obviously not a judicial sentence. The opinion of the expert is one of the means by which the judge hopes to attain the moral certitude necessary for him to reach a definite sentence.

It would seem to be confusing the matter and frustrating the purpose of the employment of the expert to ask him, as Pickard suggests, whether he would consider the defendant responsible had he committed a crime. In reality the person has not committed a crime. He has, instead, attempted to enter a marriage. As was shown before,[149] the psychical requirements for crime, sin, and matrimony are not and cannot be the same. It is the psychical ability or capacity of a person to enter a valid matrimonial contract at a particular time which needs to be determined at law. It is the law which determines the psychical requirements. It is the expert who is asked to give his scientific opinion whether a person could meet these requirements. Finally, it is the court, which, using the testimony of witnesses and the expressed opinion of the expert, comes to moral certitude if warranted by the evidence, and passes a judicial sentence in the case.

There is, therefore, no question of the expert exercising in any way the office of the judge. He presents an opinion based on professional discovery and examination of facts and on principles of his science. He does not, and he cannot give a judicial sentence.[150]

Allers[151] summarized the task of the expert as follows:

> The decision whether in a given case the facts justify the annulment of matrimony rests with the tribunal. But the facts have to be attained, partly at least, by the experts. Medical and psychological or psychiatric examinations have to furnish the material for the judges to consider. Moreover, the value and significance of statements made by either party or witnesses must be evaluated in the light

[149] Cf. *supra*, p. 158.

[150] *S.R.R. Decisiones*, XXIII (1931), 464, n. 4.

[151] "Some Medico-Psychological Remarks on Canon 1068, 1081, and 1087," *The Jurist*, IV (1944), 351.

> of psychological and psychiatric science. It is part of the expert's task to synthetize the data gleaned from examination, or, eventually, a medical case-history with those contained in the depositions, and to see whether or not there results a homogeneous picture, in accordance with scientific knowledge. The opinion of the expert ought, accordingly, do more than simply mention a diagnosis and declare that the *pars conventa* was or was not capable of consent... A more detailed analysis and explanation ought to be given so as to furnish to the judge adequate material whereupon to base his final decision.

The fact that an expert gives his opinion to the effect that a certain person on a specific date could or could not meet the psychical requirements of the law for entering into matrimony does not make the expert a judge any more than if he testified that a certain person was or is physically impotent. In matrimonial cases of impotency, experts are engaged by the tribunal to give a scientific opinion and the reasons for their opinion, regarding the physical capacity of a person to consummate the marriage contract.[152] The same holds true in cases regarding non-consummation.[153]

In cases of impotency and non-consummation, the judge instructs the expert regarding the canonical notions of impotency or non-consummation. The expert then examines the person in question and gives to the court his opinion on the facts, viz., whether the person was or is impotent in the legal sense, or whether the marriage was ever consummated. In giving his scientific opinion, he is not usurping the office of the judge by declaring a marriage invalid by reason of impotency. He merely gives his opinion whether he believes the person to be or have been impotent in the legal sense. He does not attempt to take over the office of S. Roman Congregation or of the S. Roman Rota and render a decision upon a *ratum et non-consummatum* marriage. He merely supplies scientific evidence upon which the decision can be at least partly based.

[152] Canons 1976; 1792; 1804; *Provida,* Art. 139.

[153] *Catholica Doctrina,* Reg. 20, 64, 84.

The same holds true in cases of mental illness and marriage. Consequently, it is of the utmost importance that the expert be instructed as to the precise psychical requirements necessary at canon law for giving valid matrimonial consent.[154]

SECTION C. THE PROBATIVE VALUE OF EXPERT TESTIMONY

Since a judge is to pronounce judgment only when he has achieved moral certitude,[155] and since the moral certitude must be drawn from all the evidence in a given case,[156] it is evident that the juridical value of the expert's testimony will vary from case to case.[157] "In one instance it may supply the vital part which welds together the other bits of evidence into a tightly coherent picture of moral certitude. In another it may be one of the small, rather inconsequential contributors to the completed portrait of certitude; or it may contribute absolutely nothing."[158]

The judge is not bound to pronounce sentence according to the opinion of the expert, not even if several experts would hold an identical opinion.[159] However, respect and deference must be shown to the opinion of the expert. It is for this reason that the judge in giving his decision must state the reasons and arguments which motivated him in his rejection or acceptance of the conclusion reached by the expert.[160] Thus, while ordinarily he would and should accept the judgment of the expert regarding whose competence and honesty he is satisfied,[161] for what in his prudent juristic discretion he considers it to be worth, the judge remains the

[154] Cf. *supra*, p. 139.

[155] Can. 1896, § 1; *Provida*, Art. 197, § 1.

[156] Can. 1896, § 2; *Provida*, Art. 197, § 2.

[157] For a more complete treatment of the value of the evidence derived from the *peritia*, cf. Pickard, *Judicial Experts*, and Bottoms, *The Discretionary Authority of the Ecclesiastical Judge in Matrimonial Trials of the First Instance.*

[158] Pickard, *op. cit.*, p. 193.

[159] Canons 1804; 1869, § 1-3; *Provida*, Art. 154, § 2.

[160] Can. 1804, § 2; *Provida*, art. 154, § 2.

[161] *S.R.R. Decisiones*, I (1909), 87, n. 6.

final voice in the solemn decision on the validity of the marriage contract, which is, after all, his sacred and often difficult task. *"Nam periti non sunt conjudices sed consiliarii tantum, nec eorum voto quantum vis erudito et concordi alligatur judex."*[162]

It may be well to conclude these remarks regarding the evaluation of the proof afforded by expert testimony with the words of His Holiness, Pope Pius XII, who, in his Allocution to the Sacred Roman Rota in 1942, made the following observations regarding the well-defined legal rules of inquiry and proof as delineated in procedural law:[163]

> The conscientious observance of these norms is a matter of duty for the judge; but on the other hand, in their application he must remember that they are not ends in themselves. but means to an end, that is, to attain and guarantee a moral certainty with an objective foundation as to the reality of the fact. It should not come about that what the will of the legislator intended as a help and security for discovering the truth, become instead an obstacle to its discovery. If ever the observance of formal rules of law results in injustice or is contrary to equity, there is always a right of recourse to the legislator.
>
> Hence you see why, in modern, even ecclesiastical, procedure, the first place is given, not to the principle of juridical formalism, but to the maxim of the free weighing of the evidence. The judge must —without prejudice to the aforesaid procedural rules—decide according to his own knowledge and conscience whether the proofs adduced and the investigations undertaken are or are not adequate, that is, sufficient for the required moral certainty regarding the truth and reality of the matter to be decided.
>
> No doubt there may at times be conflicts between "juridical formalism" and "the free weighing of the evidence," but they will usually be only apparent

[162] *S.R.R. Decisiones*, XVI (1924), 128, n. 2.

[163] *AAS*, XXXIV (1942), 338 ff.; English translation from Bouscaren, *Canon Law Digest*, III, 605 ff.

and hence not difficult to resolve. Now, as the objective truth is one, so too moral certainty objectively determined can be but one. Hence, it is not admissible that a judge declare that personally, from the record of the case, he has moral certainty regarding the truth of the fact at issue, while at the same time, in his capacity as judge, he denies the same objective certainty on the basis of procedural law. Such contradictions should rather induce him to undertake a further and more accurate examination of the case. Not infrequently such conflicts are due to the fact that certain aspects of the case, which attain their full importance and value only when viewed as a whole, have not been properly weighed, or that the juridical-formal rules have been incorrectly understood or have been applied in a manner contrary to the mind and purpose of the legislator.

Finally, this study may well be concluded with the thoughts and words of Felici who wrote:

> Pauca delibavimus, at quae satis sint ad demonstrandam necessitatem rectae investigationis et prescrutationis psychologicae in iudice causam cognoscenti et definienti. Qui quidem iudex illud quoque sui officii censeat: efficere in seipso, gratia Dei adiuvante, optimam iudicandi psychologiam, ne citra bonas intentiones, suarum passionum veluti inconsciae incitationi subiaceat. Leges multa iudici praescribunt, multa vetant, ut, quantum potis sit, aliorum influxum devitet et fugiat atque uni Deo iustitiaeque serviae. At haec praescripta multum amittent vigoris nisi iudex curet intimos sui animi recessus, quantum fieri potest, perscrutari et cognoscere, passiones proclivitatesque suas ita moderari et, si opus sit, corrigere et emendare ut ad administrandam iustitiam aptae semper inveniantur. Praeiudiciis ne parcat quae vel nimia severitas vel nimia benignitas suggerat: iustitiam cum omni humilitate colat atque, suis commodis hominumque favoribus post-habitis, *solum Deum prae oculis habeat* ipsiusque summae gloriae iustitiam administret.[164]

[164] Art. cit., *Apollinaris* XXXII (1959), 216.

CONCLUSIONS

The following statements present, in summary form, the more important conclusions arrived at in the course of the composition of this dissertation.

1) A specifically human act is an act that issues from the will acting freely, with antecedent knowledge of the nature and end or purpose of the act and with accompanying advertence.

2) It is possible for a person to be able to posit a human or free act while at the same time his freedom, knowledge, deliberation and discretion have been limited to such an extent that the person is unable to posit a certain specific legal act.

3) Psychic capacity for legal acts is a relative notion. The psychic capacity necessary for a legal act must be proportionate to the importance and complexity of that act.

4) To enter a valid matrimonial contract, a certain minimum of actual knowledge is required:

a) The contracting parties must know that marriage is a permanent society of a man and a woman for the procreation of offspring. This knowledge, which need not be complete or perfect, must include the idea that for the procreation of children a physical cooperation of the marriage partners is necessary, and that in view of this physical cooperation the right to one's body is transferred in the matrimonial contract. However, knowledge of carnal copulation is not required for the validity of matrimonial consent. It suffices that the contracting parties know that they are obliging themselves to the performance of corporal acts.

b) The contracting parties must know that procreation of offspring is the purpose or end of matrimony, even though they may validly and licitly marry for any other honorable motive, as long as they know that marriage, as instituted by God, has for its purpose the procreation of children. Knowledge of procreation as the purpose of matrimony implies, at the same time, knowledge of the obligation of education of offspring and of the secondary purposes of matrimony.

c) The contracting parties must associate the ideas of permanence and exclusiveness with marriage even though a simple error in judgment regarding them does not invalidate matrimonial consent.

5) To enter into a valid marriage contract, a person must have the power of deliberation, and he must actually use that power in giving consent, in the same manner as the power of deliberation and the use of that power is required for the commission of mortal sin, so that the act of giving consent may be said to be a deliberated free act of the contractant.

6) Over and above the requisite deliberation, a person must have the necessary evaluative knowledge or discretion (insight) to realize what marriage is and what it implies. This discretion or prudence in judgment must be proportionate to the importance of the marriage contract.

7) The norm to determine the minimum degree of knowledge and of maturity of judgment necessary for a valid matrimonial consent, as required by canon 1082, is the following: The degree of knowledge and maturity of judgment necessary for matrimony is that degree of knowledge and maturity of judgment which is, by virtue of general human experience, normally, i.e., usually, found in young people when they have reached actual physical maturity or puberty.

8) If it can be proven that the freedom of the will can be directly and adversely influenced by emotions, passions, illnesses, drugs, etc., without any interference with a person's power and actual use of the power of deliberation, then matrimonial consent must be regarded as being sufficiently free for validity if the consent is the result of a free choice (philosophical freedom) independent of the ease or difficulty

with which the choice is made (psychological freedom), as long as the requirements of knowledge, deliberation and maturity of judgment have been met.

9) To avoid serious and frustrating confusion in dealing with cases of mental illness and marriage, it is absolutely necessary to keep distinct the medical and the legal notions of insanity or mental illness.

10) To declare a marriage invalid by reason of mental illness or defect, a judge must have moral certitude that a mental illness or defect was certainly present at the time when the marriage contract was entered into, and that it was present to such a degree as to make the contractant psychically incapable of giving a valid matrimonial consent according to the criterion stated in n. 7, above.

11) Even though the opinion presented by experts is ordinarily only one of the means which a judge employs in arriving at moral certitude in a given case, yet expert opinion often is of the greatest importance in cases of mental illness and marriage. Normally the expert will present to the court his opinion regarding the nature and perhaps the causes of the mental illness or disturbance involved. However, these considerations are of importance to the court only insofar as they help in arriving at an understanding of the psychical capacity for marriage of the person in question at the time when the marriage ceremony took place.

12) It is the task and the duty of the expert to present his opinion and the reasons for that opinion regarding the ability of a person to have met the psychical requirements of the law for a valid marital consent. In giving his scientific opinion, the expert is thereby not usurping the office of the judge in respect to declaring a marriage invalid by reason of mental illness.

BIBLIOGRAPHY

SOURCES

Acta Apostolicae Sedis, Commentarium Officiale, Romae, 1909-.

Acta et Decreta Sacrorum Conciliorum Recentiorum, Collectio Lacensis. 7 vols., Friburgi Brisgoviae, 1870-1892.

Acta Sanctae Sedis, 41 vols., Romae, 1865-1908.

Anselmi Episcopi Lucensis Collectio Canonum una cum collectione minore, recensuit Fredericus Thaner, Oeniponte, 1906.

Antiquae Collectiones Decretalium cum Antonii Augustini Episcopi Ilerdensis notis, Ilerdae, 1576.

Bruns, Hermann T., *Canones Apostolorum et Conciliorum Saeculorum IV-VII.* 2 vols., Berolini, 1839.

Codex Iuris Canonici Pii X Pontificis Maximi iussu digestus Benedicti Papae XV auctoritate promulgatus, Romae, 1917.

Codicis Iuris Canonici Fontes cura Emi Petri Gasparri editi, 9 vols., Romae (postea Civitate Vaticana): Typis Polyglottis Vaticanis, 1923-1939. (Vols. VII-IX ed. cura et studio Emi Iustiniani Card. Serédi).

Codex Theodosianus, ed. P. Krueger, Berolini, 1928.

Collectanea Congregationis de Propaganda Fide, 2 vols., Romae. 1907.

Corpus Iuris Canonici, Editio Lipsiensis 2., post Aemilii Ludovici Richteri curas ad librorum manu scriptorum et editionis Romae fidem recognovit et adnotatione critica instruxit Aemilius Friedberg, 2 vols., Lipsae, 1879-1881. Editio anastatice repetita, Lipsiae, 1928.

Corpus Iuris Civilis, 3 vols., Vol. I, *Institutiones,* ed. stereotypa 15, recognovit P. Krueger; *Digesta,* ed. stereotypa 15, recognovit Th. Mommsen, retractavit P. Krueger; Vol. II, *Codex Iustinianus,* ed. stereotypa 10, recognovit et retractavit P. Krueger; Vol. III, *Novellae Constitutiones,* ed, stereotypa 5, recognovit R. Schoell, opus Schoellii morte interceptum absolvit G. Kroll, Berolini, 1928-1929.

Decisiones Sacrae Romanae Rotae coram R. P. D. Ansaldo De Ansaldis, 8 tomes, Romae, 1711-1777.

Decretales D. Gregorii Papae IX, suae integritati una cum glossis restitutae, Romae, 1582.

Fontes Iuris Romani Antejustiniani, editio altera et aucta ediderunt Johannes Baviera, J. Furlani, S. Riccobono, C. Ferrini, V. Aramgio Ruiz, 1 vol. in 3 parts, Florentiae: S. A. G. Barbera, 1940-1943.

Hardouin, Jean, *Acta Conciliorum et Epistolate Decretales ac Constitutiones Summorum Pontificum*, 12 vols., 1714-1715.

Jaffé, Philippus *Regesta Pontificum Romanorum ab condita Ecclesia ad annum post Christum natum MCXCVIII*, 2. ed., correctam et auctam auspiciis Gulielmi Wattenbach curaverunt F. Kaltenbrunner, P. Ewald, S. Löwenfeld, 2 vols., Lipsiae, 1885-1888.

Lex Romana Cononice Compta, ed. C. G. Mor, Pavia, 1927.

Lex Romana Visigothorum, ed. Gustavus Haenl, Lipsiae, 1847-1849.

Liber Sextus Decretalium D. Bonifacii Papae VIII . . . cum suis glossis suae integritati restituta, et ad exemplar Romanum diligenter recognita, Augustae Taurinorum, 1588.

Monumenta Germaniae Historica—Leges, 5 vols., Vols. I-IV, ed. G. Pertz; Vol. V. ed. G. Pertz, G. Waitz, H. Brunner, Hannoverae, 1835-1889. Vol. III, *Lex Romana Burgundiorum.*

———, *Legum Sectio I*, Tomus I, *Leges Visigothorum*, ed. K. Zeumer, Hannoverae, 1902.

Pitra, Ioannes B., *Iuris Ecclesiastici Graecorum Historia et Monumenta*, 2 tomes, Romae, 1864.

Potthast, Augustus, *Regesta Pontificum Romanorum inde ab anno post Christum natum MCXCVIII ad annum MCCCIV*, 2 vols., Berolini, 1874-1875.

Quinque Compilationes Antiquae, ed. Aem. Friedberg, Lipsiae, 1882.

S.R. Rotae Decisiones, Romae, 1764.

Sacrae Romanae Rotae Decisiones coram R.P.D.F. Buratti, Romae, 1624.

Sacrae Romanae Rotae Decisiones seu Sententiae (ab anno 1909), Romae: Typis Vaticanis, 1912-.

Thesaurus Resolutionum S.C. Concilii, 167 vols., Urbini, 1718-1741; Romae, 1741-1908.

Reference Works

Aichner, Simon, *Compendium Iuris Ecclesiastici*, II ed., Brixen, 1911.

Aquinas, Thomas, *Commentaria Praeclarissima in IV Libros Sententiarum Petri Lombardi*, 2 tomes, Parisiis, 1659.

Aquinas, Thomas, *Summa Theologica*, diligenter emendata, Nicolai Sylvii, Billuart, C. J. Drioux notis ornata, 6. ed., 8 vols., Barri-Ducis, 1870.

Barbosa, Augustinus, *Collectanea Doctorum in Ius Pontificium Universum*, 5 vols., Lugduni, 1632.

Bellarminus, Robertus, *De Controversiis Christianae Fidei*, 2. ed., 3 tomes, Ingolstadii, 1591.

Bensch,T., *Wplyw Chorob Umyslowych na Waznosc Umowy Malvenskiej*, Lublin, 1936.

Bernard, Fernand, *The First Year of Roman Law*, trans. by Chas. P. Sherman, New York, 1906.

Beste, R. P. Udaricus, *Introductio in Codicem,* 4. ed., Napoli: M. D'Auria, 1956.

Bingham, Joseph, *The Antiquities of the Christian Church,* 2 vols., Londen, 1956.

Boich, Henricus, *Commentaria in Quinque Libros Decretalium,* Venetiis, 1576.

Bonaventura, *Opera Omnia,* 10 tomes, ad Claras Aquas prope Florentiam, 1882-1902.

Bottoms, Archibald M., *The Discretionary Authority of the Ecclesiastical Judge in Matrimonial Trials of the First Instance,* The Catholic University of America Canon Law Studies, n. 349, Washington, D.C.: The Catholic University of America Press, 1955.

Brennan, Robert E., *Thomistic Psychology,* New York: Macmillan Co., 1957.

Bry, Georges, *Principes de Droit Romain,* 6. ed., revue et corrigée par Paul Bry, 2 tomes, Paris, 1927.

Buckland, W. W. A., *A Textbook of Roman Law from Augustus to Justinian,* 2. ed., Cambridge: The University Press, 1932.

Cammack, J. S., *Moral Problems of Mental Defect,* New York: Benziger Bros., 1939.

Cangardel, Louis, *Le Consentement des époux au mariage,* Paris: Librairie du Recueil, 1932.

Cappello, Felix, *De Curia Romana iuxta Reformationem a Pio X sapientissime Inductam,* 2 vols., Romae, Ratisbonae, Neo Eboraci, Cincinnati, 1911-1912.

———, *Tractatus Canonico-Moralis de Sacramentis,* Vol. V, *De Matrimonio,* 6. ed., Taurini et Romae: Marietti, 1950.

Castañeda Delgado, Eudoxio, *La Locura y el Matrimonio* (Psiquiatria y Jurisprudencia de la Sagrada Rota Romana), Valladolid and Madrid: Editorial Sever-Cuesta, 1955.

———, *La Enajenación mental ye el Consentimiento Matrimonial a la luz de la Psiquiatria y de la Jurisprudencia de la Sagrada Rota Romana,* Tesis Doctoral en la Facultad de Derecho Canónico, Universitas Pontificia Salmanticensis: Valadolid, Editorial Sever-Cuesta, 1955.

Cavanagh, John R.-McGoldrick, James B., *Fundamental Psychiatry,* 2. ed. revised, Milwaukee: Bruce, 1958.

Cerato, P., *Matrimonium a Codice Iuris Canonici Integre Desumptum,* 4. ed., Patavii, Libr. Gregoriane Editi. Typis Seminarii, 1927.

Chatham, Josiah G., *Force and Fear as Invalidating Marriage: The Element of Injustice,* The Catholic University of America Canon Law Studies, n. 310, Washington, D.C.: The Catholic University of America Press, 1950.

Chelodi, Ioannes, *Ius Matrimoniale iuxta Codicem Iuris Canonici,* 3. ed., Tridenti Libr. Edit. Tridentum, 1921.

Cicognani, Amleto, *Canon Law*, 2. ed., revised, English version by J. O'Hara and F. Brennan, Reprint, Westminster: Newman Press, 1949.

Clune, Robert B., *The Judicial Interrogation of the Parties*, The Catholic University of America Canon Law Studies, n. 269, Washington, D.C.: The Catholic University of America Press, 1948.

Corbett, Percy Ellwood, *The Roman Law on Marriage*, Oxford, 1930.

Coronata, Matthaeus Conte, a, *Institutiones Iuris Canonici*, 2. ed., 5 vols., Taurini-Romae: Marietti, 1939-1947.

———, *Institutiones Iuris Canonici, De Sacramentis*, 3 vols., Turin: Marietti, 1943-1946.

———, *De Sacramentis*, Vol. III, 3. ed., Turin: Marietti, 1957.

Covarrubias, Didacus De, Toletanus, *Opera Omnia*, 2 vols., Coloniae Allobrogum, 1679.

D'Annibale, Josephus, *Summula Theologiae Moralis*, 3. ed., emendata et aucta, 3 vols., Romae, 1892.

Dauvillier, Jean, *Le Mariage dans le Droit Classique de l'Eglise, depuis le decret de Gratian (1140) jusqu'a la mort de Clement V (1340*, Paris: Librarie du Recueli Sirey, 1933.

Davis, Henry, *Moral and Pastoral Theology*, 6. ed., revised and enlarged, 4 vols., London-New York: Sheed and Ward, 1949.

De Lugo, Ioannes, *Disputationes Scholasticae et Morales*, 8 vols., Parisiis, 1868-1869.

Desforges, L., *Etude Historique sur la Formation du Mariage en Droit Romaine et en Droit Français*, Paris, 1887.

Devoti, Ioannes, *Ius Canonicum Universum et Privatum*, Romae, 1830.

De Becker, Iulius, *De Sponsalibus et Matrimonio Praelectiones Canonicae*, 2. ed., Lovanii, New York, 1903.

De Smet, Aloisius, *De Sponsalibus et Matrimonio*, Brugis, 1909.

Dictionnaire de Droit Canonique, commencé sous la direction de A. Villien et E. Magnin, continué sous la direction de A. Amanieu, publié sous la direction de R. Naz, Parisiis: Letouzy et Ané 1924—.

Dictionnaire de Théologie Catholique, 15 vols. with general tables, Paris: Letouzey et Ané, 1903—.

Doheny, William J., *Canonical Procedure in Matrimonial Cases*, 2 vols., Vol. I, 2. ed., revised, Milwaukee: Bruce, 1948.

Durandus, Gulielmus, *Speculum Judiciale*, 4 vols., in 3, Venetiis, 1577.

Esmein, A., *Le Mariage en Droit Canonique*, 2. ed., 2 vols., (Vol. I, rev. by R. Génestal and J. Dauvillier, 1935), Paris: Librarie de Recueil Sirey, 1929-1935.

Fässler, Hans N., *Die Schizophrenie als Ehenichtigkeitsgrund im Kanonischen Recht*, Freiburg in der Schweiz: Paulusdruckerei, 1951.

Fazzari, G. M., *Valutazione etica e consenso matrimoniale*, Naples: Editore M. D. D'Auria, 1951.

Ferraris, Lucius, *Prompta Bibliotheca Canonica, Iuridica, Moralis, Theologica, nec non Ascetica, Polemica, Rubristica, Historica,* ed. novissima, 9 vols., Romae, 1885-1899.

Ford, John C., *The Validity of Virginal Marriage,* Worcester, Mass.: Harrigan Press, 1938.

Ford, John, C.-Kelly, Gerald, *Contemporary Moral Theology, Volume One, Questions in Fundamental Moral Theology,* Westminster: Newman Press, 1959.

Frattin, Peter L., *The Matrimonial Impediment of Impotence: Occlusion of Spermatic Ducts and Vaginismus,* The Catholic University of America Canon Law Studies, n. 381, Washington, D.C.: The Catholic University of America Press, 1958.

Freisen, Joseph, *Geschichte des canonischen Eherechts bis zum Verfall der Glossenliteratur,* 2. ed., Paderborn, 1893.

Freshfield, H., *A Manual of Roman Law, The Ecloga, published by Leo III and Constantine V,* Cambridge, 1926.

Garrigou-Lagrange, Reginald, *Reality, A Synthesis of Thomistic Thought,* translated by Patrick Cummins, St. Louis: Herder Book Co., 1953.

Gasparri, Petrus, *De Matrimonio,* 3. ed., 2 vols., Paris, 1904.

———, *Tractatus De Matrimonio,* ed. nova, 2 vols., Romae: Typis Vaticanis, 1932.

Girard, Paul Frederic, *Manuel Elementaire de Droit Romain,* 7. ed., Paris, 1924.

Gredt, Josephus, *Elementa Philosophiae Aristotelico—Thomisticae,* 10. ed., 2 vols., Friburgi Brisg.: Herder, 1953.

Grenier, Henrico, *Cursus Philosophiae,* 3 vols., editio altera, Quebec: Le Seminaire de Quebec, 1944.

Gonzalez-Tellez, Emmanuel, *Commentaria Perpetua in singulos textus Quinque Librorum Decretalium Gregorii IX,* 5 tomes, Lugduni, 1673.

Hilling, Nicholas, *Procedure at the Roman Curia,* a translation published by J. F. Wagner, New York, 1907.

Holböck, Carolus, *Tractatus de Jurisprudentia Sacrae Romanae Rotae,* Graetiae, Vindobonae, Coloniae: In Officina Libraria "Styria," 1957.

Hostiensis (Henricus de Segusio), *Commentaria in Quinque Libros Decretalium,* 5 vols., in 3, Venetiis, 1581.

Joyce, George Hayward, *Christian Marriage,* 2. ed., London: Sheed and Ward, 1948.

Jolowicz, Herbert F., *Historical Introduction to the Study of Roman Law,* 2. ed., Cambridge: University Press, 1952.

Kearney, Francis P., *The Principles of Canon 1127,* The Catholic University of America Canon Law Studies, n. 163, Washington, D.C.: The Catholic University of America Press, 1942.

Kienitz, Erwin Roderich von, *Christliche Ehe,* Frankfurt, 1938.

Kuttner, Stephan, *Kanonistische Schuldlehre von Gratian bis auf die Dekretalen Gregors IX,* Studi et Testi, n. 64, Citta del Vaticano: Biblioteca Apostoloca Vaticana, 1935.

Leage, R. W., *Roman Private Law,* 2. ed., by C. H. Ziegler, London: Macmillan and Co., Ltd., Reprint, 1948.

Lega, M. (ed. V. Bartocetti), *Commentarius in Iudicia Ecclesiastica iuxta Codicem Iuris Canonici,* 2. ed., 2 vols., Romae: Azienda Libraria Cattolica Italiana, 1950.

Lehmkuhl, Augustinus, *Theologia Moralis,* 12. ed., 2 vols., Friburgi Brisgoviae, 1914.

Lombardus, Petrus, *Libri IV Sententiarum,* 2. ed., 2 tomes, ad Claras Aquas prope Florentiam, 1916.

Manning, John J., *Presumptions of Law in Marriage Cases,* The Catholic University of America Canon Law Studies, n. 94, Washington, D.C.: The Catholic University of America Press, 1935.

Maritain, Jacques, *Les Degrés du Savoir,* Paris: Desclée de Brouwer, 1946.

McCloskey, Joseph A., *The Subject of Ecclesiastical Law According to Canon 12,* The Catholic University of America Canon Law Studies, n. 165, Washington, D.C.: The Catholic University of America Press, 1946.

McGrath, John J., *Comparative Study of Crime and its Imputability in Ecclesiastical Criminal Law, and in American Criminal Law,* The Catholic University of America Canon Law Studies, n. 385, Washington, D.C.: The Catholic University of America Press, 1957.

Merkelbach, B. H., *Summa Theologiae Moralis,* 3 vols., Parisiis: Desclée, De Brouwer et Soc., 1931-1933.

Michiels, Gommarus, *Normae Generales Juris Canonici,* editio altera, 2 vols., Tournai: Desclée and Co., 1949.

———, *Principia Generalia De Personis in Ecclesia,* Lublin: Universitas Catholica, 1932.

Migne, J. P., *Patrologiae Cursus Completus, Series Graeca,* 161 vols., Parisiis, 1857-1866.

———, *Patrologiae Cursus Completus, Series Latina,* 221 vols., Parisiis, 1844-1855.

Moore, Dom Thomas Verner, *The Nature and Treatment of Mental Disorders,* New York: Grune and Stratton, 1944.

Naber, A., *Theoria Cognitionis Critica,* Rome. Gregorian University Press, 1932.

Noldin, H.-Schmitt, A., *Summa Theologiae Moralis,* 23. ed., 3 vols., Oeniponte: Rauch, 1935.

Noyes, Arthur P., *Modern Clinical Psychiatry,* 4. ed., Philadelphia & London: W. B. Saunders Co., 1954.

O'Brien, Joseph P., *The Right of the State to make Disease an Impediment to Marriage*, The Catholic University of America, Studies in Sacred Theology, 2nd. ser., n. 73, Washington, D.C.: The Catholic University of America Press, 1952.

O'Dea, John C., *The Matrimonial Impediment of Nonage*, The Catholic University of America Canon Law Studies, n. 205, Washington, D.C.: The Catholic University of America Press, 1944.

O'Donnell, Cletus F., *The Marriage of Minors*, The Catholic University of America Canon Law Studies, n. 221, Washington, D.C.: The Catholic University of America Press, 1945.

Panormitanus (Niccolo de'Tudeschi), *Commentaria in Quinque Libros Decretalium*, 5 vols. in 7, Venetiis, 1588.

Payen, G., *De Matrimonio in Missionibus ac potissimum in Sinis Tractatus Practicus et Casus*, 2. ed., 3 vols., Zi-ka-wei: Typographia T'OU-SE-WE, 1935-1936.

Pickard, William M., *Judicial Experts: A Source of Evidence in Ecclesiastical Trials*, The Catholic University of America Canon Law Studies, n. 389, Washington, D.C.: The Catholic University of America Press, 1958.

Pickett, R. Colin, *Roman Law and the Insane*, Ottawa: University of Ottawa Press, 1949.

———, *Mental Affliction and Church Law*, Universitas Catholica Ottaviensis, series canonica, tom. 25, Ottawa, Ontario: The University of Ottawa Press, 1952.

Pirhing, Enricus, *Ius Canonicum in Textus Quinque Librorum Decretalium Gregorii IX*, 5 vols. in 4, Dillingae, 1674-1678.

Plöchl, Willibald, *Das Eherecht des Magisters Gratianus*, Leipzig und Wien: F. Deuticke, 1935.

Pontius, Basilius, *De Sacramento Matrimonii Tractatus*, Venetiis, 1766.

Raymundus de Pennafort, *Summa*, Veronae, 1774, juxta editionem 1720.

Regatillo, Eduardus F., *Ius Sacramentarium*, 2 vols., Santander: Sal Terrae, 1945-1946.

Reiffenstuel, Anacletus, *Ius Canonicum Universum*, 7 vols., Parisiis, 1864-1870.

Renard, Henri, *The Philosophy of Man.*, 2. ed. revised and enlarged by Martin O. Vaske, Milwaukee: The Bruce Publishing Company, 1955.

Reynés, Lorenzo Quintana, *La Prueba en el Procédimiento Canónico*, Barcelona: Bosch, 1942.

Rivier, A., *Precis du Droit de Famille Romain*, Paris, 1891.

Roberti, Franciscus, *De Processibus*, 2 vols., Romae: Vol. I, 4. ed., 1956; Vol. II, 1926.

Roby, Henry J., *Roman Private Law*, 2 vols., Cambridge, 1902.

Rufinus, *Summa Decretorum*, ed. H. Singer, Paderborn, 1902.

Sanchez, Thomas, *De Sancto Matrimonii Sacramento,* 3 vols., Antwerpiae, 1626.

Schmalzgrueber, Franciscus, *Ius Ecclesiasticum Universum,* 5 vols. in 12, Romae, 1843-1845.

Schönsteiner, Ferd., *Grundriss des Kirchlichen Eherechts,* Wien, 1937.

Sesto, Gennaro J., *Guardians of the Mentally Ill in Ecclesiastical Trials,* The Catholic University of America Canon Law Studies, n. 358, Washington, D.C.: The Catholic University of America Press, 1956.

Sherman, Charles, *Roman Law in the Modern World,* 3 vols., New York, 1924.

Smith, Vincent M., *Ignorance Affecting Matrimonial Consent.* The Catholic University of America Canon Law Studies, n. 245, Washington, D.C.: The Catholic University of America Press, 1950.

Strecker, Edward A., *Fundamentals of Psychiatry,* 4. ed., Philadelphia: Lippincott, 1947.

Sohm, Rudolph, *The Institutes,* trans. by James C. Ledlie, 3. ed., Oxford, 1926.

Terruwe, A. A. A., *Wat is Psychisch Gezond Leven?,* Roermond—Maaseik: Romen en Zonen, 1957.

Tongiori, Salvatore, *Institutiones Philosophiae,* 4. ed., Brussels: H. Goemaere, 1868-1869.

Torre, Joannes, *Processus Matrimonialis,* 3. ed., Neapoli: M. D'Auria, Pontificius Editor, 1956.

Triebs, Franz, *Praktisches Handbuch des geltenden kanonischen Eherechts in Vergleichung mit dem deutschen staatlichen Eherecht für Theologen und Juristen,* 3 vols., Breslau, 1929.

Tyrrell, Francis M., *The Role of Assent in Judgment A Thomistic Study,* The Catholic University of America, n. 100, Washington, D.C.: The Catholic University of America Press, 1948.

Upianus, Didymus, *De Matrimonio Ius tum Naturae tum Canonicum,* Venetiis, 1760.

Vanderveldt, James H., and Odenwald, Robert P., *Psychiatry and Catholicism,* 2. ed., New York: McGraw-Hill Book Company, Inc., 1957.

Van Hove, A., *Commentarium Lovaniense in Codicem Iuris Canonici,* Vol. I, Tom. I, *Prolegomena ad Codicem Iuris Canonici,* 2. ed., Mechlinae-Romae, 1904.

Van Welie, F. A. M., *Canoniek Huwelijksrecht,* Nymegen-Utrecht: Dekker en van de Vegt N.V., 1954.

Vecchiotti, Septimius, *Institutiones Canonicae,* 19. ed., 3 vols., Augustae Taurinorum, 1886.

Vlaming, Th. M., *Praelectiones Iuris Matrimonii ad Normam Codicis Iuris Canonici,* 4. ed. by L. Bender, Bussum in Hollandia, 1950.

Wanenmacher, Francis, *Canonical Evidence in Marriage Cases*, Philadelphia: Dolphin Press, 1935.

Wechsler, David, *The Measurement and Appraisal of Adult Intelligence*, 4. ed., Baltimore: The Williams & Wilkins Company, 1958.

Wernz, Franciscus, *Ius Decretalium*, 6 vols., Vol. IV, *Ius Matrimoniale*, Romae, 1904.

Wigmore, John H., *The Principles of Judicial Proof as Given by Logic, Psychology and General Experience and Illustrated in Judicial Trials*, Boston: Little, Brown & Co., 1913.

Willett, Robert A., *The Probative Value of Documents in Ecclesiastical Trials*, The Catholic University of America Canon Law Studies, n. 171, Washington, D.C.: The Catholic University of America Press, 1942.

Zacchia, Paulus, *Quaestiones Medico-Legales*, ed. nova, 3 tomes in 1, Lugduni, 1701.

Articles

Allers, Rudolph, "Annulment of Marriage by Lack of Consent because of Insanity," *The Ecclesiastical Review*, CI (1939), 325-343.

———, "Some Medico-Psychological Remarks, on Canons 1068, 1081, and 1087," *The Jurist*, IV (1944), 351-380.

Amanieu, A., "Aliénation mentale en matiére de Nullité de Mariage," *Dictionnaire de Droit Canonique*, Paris: Librairie Letouzey et Ané, 1935, Tome I, coll. 417-440.

Cavanagh, John C., "Criminal Responsibility and Free Will," *Bulletin of the Guild of Catholic Psychiatrists*, III, n. 2 (Dec., 1955), 24-33.

Duhamel, Joseph S., and Hayden, Jerome, "Theological and Psychiatric Aspects of Habitual Sin." I, "Theological Aspects" by Joseph S. Duhamel. II, "Psychiatric Aspects," by Jerome Hayden, *Proceedings of the Eleventh Annual Convention of the Catholic Theological Society of America* (1956), 130-163.

Felici, Pericles, "De Investigatione Psychologica in Causis Definiendis," *Apollinaris*, XXXII (1959), 202-216.

Harrington, Paul V., "The Impediment of Impotency and the Notion of Male Impotency," Part I, "From Gratian to the Council of Trent," *The Jurist*, XIX (1959), 29-66; "The Impediment of Impotency From the Council of Trent to the Present Time," *The Jurist*, XIX (1959), 187-211; Part III, "The Notion of Male Impotency from the Council of Trent to the Present Time," *The Jurist*, XIX (1959), 309-351.

Hayes, John J., "Mental Disease and the Ecclesiastical Courts," *The Jurist*, XVI (1956), 267-284.

Heston, Edward L., "Some Practical Hints on the Preparation of '*Super Rato*' Cases for the Sacred Congregation of the Sacraments," *The Jurist*, XVII, 279-286.

Le Bras, G., "Mariage (La Doctrine du Mariage chez les Théologiens et les Canonistes)," *Dictionnaire de Théologie Catholique*, Paris: Letouzey et Ané, 1903, coll. 2123-2317.

McGowan, John E., "Fundamentals of Psychiatry in Relation to the Ecclesiastical Tribunal," *The Jurist*, XVI (1956), 251-266.

Oesterle, Gerardus, "Amentia," *Ephemerides Iuris Canonici*, XI (1955), 284-293.

———, "Nullitas Matrimonii ex Capite Ignorantiae," *Ephemerides Theologicae Dovarienses*, XV (1938), 647-673.

Periodicals

American Ecclesiastical Review, The, Vols. I-XXXII Philadelphia, 1889-1905; from 1905; *The Ecclesiastical Review*, Vols. XXXIII-CIX, Philadelphia, 1905-1943; *The American Ecclesiastical Review*, Washington, D.C.: Vol. CX, 1944.

Apollinaris, Romae, 1928—.

Bulletin of the Guild of Catholic Psychiatrists, Stamford, Conn., 1953—.

Ephemerides Iuris Canonici, Romae, 1945.

Emphemerides Theologicae Lovanienses, Brugis, 1924.

Jurist, The, Washington, D.C., 1941.

Proceedings of the Eleventh Annual Convention of the Catholic Theological Society of America, Washington, D.C., 1945—.

Dictionaries

Dictionnaire de Droit Canonique, ed. by A. Villien, E. Magnin, A. Amanieu, R. Naz, Paris: Letouzey et Ané, 1924—.

Dictionnaire De Théologie Catholique, ed. by A. Vacant, E. Mangenot, E. Amann, Paris: Letouzey et Ané, 1903—.

Unpublished Thesis

Curran, Nelson J., *Mental Diseases and Disorders as Invalidating Matrimonial Consent, An Historical Synopsis*, Typewritten Licentiate Dissertation, School of Canon Law, (Archives' unique copy is #8147), The Catholic University of America, Washington, D.C., 1952.

Abbrevations

AAS—Acta Apostolicae Sedis.

ASS—Acta Sanctae Sedis.

Bruns—Canones Apostolorum et Conciliorum Saeculorum IV-VII.

Codex—Codex Iustinianus.

Coll. S.C.P.F.—Collectanea Congregationis de Propaganda Fide.

DDC—Dictionnaire de Droit Canonique.

DTC—Dictionnaire de Théologie Catholique.
Dig.—Digesta.
Fontes—Codicis Iuris Canonici Fontes . . . Gasparri editi.
Inst.—Institutiones.
Jaffé—Regesta Pontificum Romanorum . . . ad annum post Christum natum MCXCVIII.
MGH—Monumenta Germaniae Historica.
MPG—Migne, *Patrologiae Cursus Completus, Series Graeca.*
MPL—Migne, *Patrologiae Cursus Completus, Series Latina.*
Novellae—Novellae Constitutiones.
Potthast—*Regesta Pontificum Romanorum inde ab anno post Christum natum MCXCVIII ad annum MCCCIV.*
S.C.C.—*Sacra Congregatio Concilii.*
S.C.de Prop. Fide—*Sacra Congregatio de Propaganda Fide.*
S.R.R. Decisiones—Sacrae Romanae Rotae Decisiones seu Sententiae (ab anno 1909).
Thesaurus—Thesaurus Resolutionum S.C. Concilii.

ALPHABETICAL INDEX

BIOGRAPHICAL NOTE

William M. Van Ommeren, born November 30, 1926, in Tilburg, The Netherlands, received his early education in Tilburg and at St. Louis, Oudenbosch. In 1939 he entered St. Joseph's Studiehuis in Tilburg and continued his studies in Hoorn and at St. Joseph's College in Roosendaal. He arrived in the United States in December of 1948 and made his theological studies at St. Edward's Seminary in Seattle, Washington. He was ordained to the Sacred Priesthood on April 30, 1952, by the Most Reverend Charles D. White, D.D., Bishop of Spokane, Washington, as a priest of that diocese. After having done parochial and high school work, he served on the Diocesan Tribunal in Spokane. In 1957 he was appointed by the Most Reverend Bernard J. Topel, D.D., Ph.D., to pursue graduate study at the School of Canon Law of The Catholic University of America, where he received the Degree of the Baccalaureate in Canon Law in June, 1957, and the Degree of the Licentiate in Canon Law in June, 1958.

CANON LAW STUDIES*

410. Dee, Rev. Dacian, O.F.M.Cap., A.B., J.C.L., The manifestation of conscience.
411. De la Cruz, Rev. Eufemio, J.C.L., The leasing of church properties in the Philippines.
412. Nessel, Rev. William, O.S.F.S., M.A., J.C.L., First amendment freedoms, papal pronouncements and concordat practice.
413. Roos, Rev. John R., M.A., S.T.L., J.C.L., The seal of confession.
414. Tierney, Rev. William J., J.C.L., Authorized ecclesiastical acts.
415. Van Ommeren, Rev. William M., J.C.L., Mental illness affecting matrimonial consent.

* For a complete list of the available numbers of this series, apply to The Catholic University of America Press, 620 Michigan Avenue, N.E., Washington (17) , D.C., for a general catalogue.

www.ingramcontent.com/pod-product-compliance
Lightning Source LLC
LaVergne TN
LVHW050251080826
844660LV00012B/621

* 9 7 8 0 8 1 3 2 2 5 7 3 9 *